W9-BND-114

Assault on Paradise

Social Change in a Brazilian Village

Assault on Paradise

Social Change in a Brazilian Village

Second Edition

Conrad Phillip Kottak

University of Michigan

McGraw-Hill, Inc.
New York   St. Louis   San Francisco   Auckland   Bogotá   Caracas
Lisbon   London   Madrid   Mexico   Milan   Montreal   New Delhi
Paris   San Juan   Singapore   Sydney   Tokyo   Toronto

Assault on Paradise
Social Change in a Brazilian Village

Copyright © 1992, 1983 by McGraw-Hill, Inc. All rights reserved.
Printed in the United States of America. Except as permitted under the
United States Copyright Act of 1976, no part of this publication may be
reproduced or distributed in any form or by any means, or stored in a
data base or retrieval system, without the prior written permission of the
publisher.

1 2 3 4 5 6 7 8 9 0   DOH DOH   9 0 9 8 7 6 5 4 3 2 1

ISBN 0-07-035766-8

This book was set in Caledonia by ComCom, Inc.
The editors were Phillip A. Butcher, Lori Pearson Bittker,
and Larry Goldberg;
the production supervisor was Richard A. Ausburn.
The cover was designed by Carol Couch.
R. R. Donnelley & Sons Company was printer and binder.

Cover photo: Rene Burri, Magnum.

Library of Congress Cataloging-in-Publication Data

Kottak, Conrad Phillip.
    Assault on Paradise: social change in a Brazilian village /
Conrad Phillip Kottak.—2nd ed.
        p.   cm.
    Includes bibliographical references and index.
    ISBN 0-07-035766-8
    1. Arembepe (Brazil)—Social conditions.   I. Title.
HN290.A73K67   1992
306'.0981'42—dc20   91-28597

About the Author

Conrad Phillip Kottak (A.B. Columbia College 1963; Ph.D. Columbia, 1966) is professor of anthropology at the University of Michigan, where he has taught since 1968. In 1991 he was recognized by the state and the University of Michigan for excellence in undergraduate teaching.

Kottak is the current chair of the General Anthropology Division of the American Anthropological Association. A cultural anthropologist, he has done fieldwork in Brazil (since 1962), Madagascar (since 1966), and the United States. His general interests are in the processes by which local cultures join larger systems. This interest links his earlier work on ecology and state formation in Africa and Madagascar to his more recent research on global change, economic development, environmentalism, national and international culture, and the mass media.

Kottak's last research project (1983–1987) looked at "Television's Behavioral Effects in Brazil." That research is the basis for his book, *Prime-Time Society: An Anthropological Analysis of Television and Culture* (Wadsworth 1990)—a comparative study of the nature and impact of television in Brazil and the United States.

Conrad Kottak's other books include *The Past in the Present: History, Ecology and Cultural Variation in Highland Madagascar; Researching American Culture: A Guide for Student Anthropologists* (both University of Michigan Press); and *Madagascar: Society and History* (Carolina Academic Press).

Professor Kottak's articles have appeared in academic journals including *American Anthropologist, Journal of Anthropological Research, American Ethnologist, Ethnology,* and *Luso-Brazilian Review*. He has also written for more popular journals including *Transaction/SOCIETY, Natural History,* and *Psychology Today.*

Conrad Kottak's popular texts *Anthropology: The Exploration of Human Diversity* and *Cultural Anthropology* are published by McGraw-Hill.

In summer 1990 Professor Kottak did brief field research on ways to preserve biodiversity in Madagascar. His current fieldwork focuses on ecological issues in Brazil.

To Cecilia and Charles Wagley
and to the Memories of
Atahydes Alves de Souza
and
Vandice Nascimento

Contents in Brief

Contents

Preface

The thirtieth anniversary (1992) of my study of Arembepe, Bahia, Brazil is approaching. My research in this coastal town in the western hemisphere's second largest nation began accidentally, but it continues because of the fascinating transformation I've witnessed. Change in Arembepe illustrates economic development, ecological devastation, and the spread of national and world culture and an international political economy. The first edition of *Assault on Paradise* (published in 1983) proved to be of interest to cultural and applied anthropologists, Latin Americanists, and development specialists.

I also wrote *Assault on Paradise* for the novice. In deciding how the narrative would unfold I kept in mind the introductory students I've taught for twenty-three years. I did this for several reasons. First, I began doing fieldwork myself—in Arembepe—when I was a college student. *Assault on Paradise* describes my grappling with the alien nature of another culture, my fledgling attempts at ethnography, and my development as an anthropologist. I write about ways in which my life and career have been intertwined with Arembepe, its people, and its transformation. As a teacher, I know that students like case studies that blend descriptions of another culture with the anthropologist's recollection of his or her own attitudes, feelings, and reactions. I've tried not to forget this while writing *Assault on Paradise*.

The second reason I decided to write for introductory students also reflects my teaching experience. Usually I supplement a textbook with at least two ethnographic case studies. The first describes a tribal society; the second, a "peasant-type" culture, social change, or the world system. Such books as *Yanomamo: The Fierce People, Return to Laughter, The*

Forest People, and *The Harmless People* are all studies of hunter-gatherers or tribal cultivators. Arembepe, by contrast, is a community in a modern nation state. I'm pleased that *Assault on Paradise* has proved useful as a case study for the second half of the introductory course.

My editors have let me tell this story in a way that seems to interest students as it teaches them. I've tried to write a book that is both academically sound and jargon free. I want *Assault on Paradise* to be an effective teaching book. Thus it covers a range of topics discussed in introductory courses. These include ethnographic methods, kinship, social organization, economy, politics, culture and personality, religion, social stratification, race, and gender. Also prominent are the contemporary forces that impinge on Arembepe. These include industrialization (and its ecological impact), urbanization, tourism, and the mass media.

For this new edition, the book was scanned into a computer. This allowed me to reconsider every word, sentence, paragraph, and caption. Several teachers and students have told me they found the first edition readable, but I still tried to enhance readability.

I've also written a new chapter and epilogue, based on my continuing research. Chapter 12, The Global Village, describes my work (1983–1987) on the impact of television and brings the reader up to date on Arembepe and its people. A new Epilogue (1991) gives a further update and reports on my current work on development, pollution, and ecology.

Conrad Phillip Kottak

Acknowledgments

From the list of "Principal Characters," the reader can see that this book introduces not just villagers, but also anthropologists. Arembepe's first encounter with anthropology was as a "field-team village." Between 1962 and 1964 it was visited by various members of the Columbia University branch of the Columbia-Cornell-Harvard-Illinois Summer Field Studies Program in Anthropology. I thank the members of those field teams who worked with me or shared their findings and impressions about Arembepe. I must single out Peter Gorlin and Niles Eldredge, but David G. Epstein, Erica Bressler, and Shepard Forman also deserve special thanks. Maxine Margolis helped with the 1980 fieldwork, as did Jerald Milanich, who carefully sketched the map of Arembepe in 1980 and then had it prepared by his staff at the Florida State Museum. Jerry also took many of the photos in this book. Thanks to Juliet Maria Kottak, Nara Bales Milanich, and especially Nicholas Charles Kottak, for their help, too. Nick has made a substantial contribution to this second edition, including his written contribution to Chapter 12.

As *Assault on Paradise* makes obvious, Betty Wagley Kottak began studying Arembepe with me in 1962 and has been part of this story ever since. I am profoundly grateful for her companionship, assistance, insights, and analyses.

Marvin Harris encouraged and motivated the teenage anthropologist of 1962 to become a professional, guiding me through the doctorate. Robert Murphy and Lambros Comitas read two drafts of my doctoral dissertation and helped me develop my interpretation of Arembepe during the 1960s.

Among our Brazilian colleagues I am grateful to Dr. Thales de Azevedo, Mariá de Azevedo, Maria and Paulo Brandão, and the Azevedo family for years of friendship, assistance, and hospitality.

Obviously this manuscript couldn't have been written without the friendship, help, and cooperation of hundreds of Arembepeiros. Besides those called Alberto, Fernando, Dora, and Tomé in this book, I wish to thank Athaydes Alves de Souza, Vandice Nascimento, Aurino Alves, and Francisco dos Santos for their special help.

I also thank those who have read and commented on *Assault on Paradise,* either in manuscript form or in its first edition. These include Maxine Margolis, Niles Eldredge, Charles and Cecilia Wagley, Mariana Kottak Roberts, G. Harvey Summ, Charlotte Cerf, George Foster, several Michigan students, and the following reviewers for McGraw-Hill: Michael Chuse, Castleton State College, and Richard Polnac, University of Rhode Island.

My editor for the first edition of *Assault on Paradise* was David Follmer, whom I thank for encouragement and support. Jeffrey Longcope brought trade-publishing experience and a nonanthropologist's perspective to his evaluation of an earlier manuscript, suggesting ways to enliven it. He encouraged me, for example, to let villagers tell their own stories.

At McGraw-Hill, Phil Butcher, Sally Constable, Sylvia Shepard, and especially Lori Pearson lent their enthusiasm and support to this second edition. Thanks also to project editor Larry Goldberg and production supervisor Rich Ausburn.

Several agencies and institutions have contributed to our research in Arembepe between 1962 and 1991. The National Institute of Mental Health awarded me a predoctoral fellowship and, later, a small grant to investigate "Local-Level Effects of Modernization." The Foreign Area Fellowship Program gave partial support for fieldwork in Arembepe in 1973. The Horace H. Rackham School of Graduate Studies and the Office of the Vice President for Research of the University of Michigan have also supported my Brazilian research.

My project investigating the social impact of television in Brazil (1983–1987) was supported by the Wenner-Gren Foundation for Anthropological Research, the National Science Foundation, and the National Institute of Mental Health. My ongoing work on ecological risks and awareness was first supported by the Michigan Memorial-Phoenix Project. This research continues, with support from the National Science Foundation. My 1991 field trip to Arembepe was facilitated by a grant to the University of Michigan from NASA (National Aeronautics and Space Administration), through CIESIN (Consortium for International Earth Science Information Network).

Assault on Paradise is dedicated to Charles and Cecilia Wagley, my parents-in-law. Without them, for various reasons, none of this would have happened. Cecilia Wagley has supported me in many ways; she has shared her family and her friends in Brazil and has given me many insights about her country. Chuck Wagley has provided advice, ideas, and information when I needed them. I can only aspire to be the anthropologist and humanist Chuck is. That humanity, coupled with the analytic and interpretive abilities of a skilled ethnographer, is very obvious in his book *Welcome of Tears*. That study of the Tapirapé Indians of Brazil is a work I admire tremendously. Its style and voice helped guide me as I wrote *Assault on Paradise*. This dedication acknowledges the special place Cecilia and Charles Wagley have occupied in my profession and in my life.

For the second edition, I extend the dedication to the memories of Athaydes Alves de Souza and Vandice Nascimento, special friends, great Brazilians.

Conrad Phillip Kottak

Principal Characters

The Anthropologists

Conrad Phillip Kottak (Conrado)
> Author of this book, began fieldwork in Arembepe in 1962; returned in 1964, 1965, 1973, 1980, annually between 1982 and 1987, and in 1991; professor of anthropology at the University of Michigan.

Isabel Wagley Kottak (Betty)
> Began fieldwork in Arembepe in 1962; returned each time with Conrad; has A.B. degree in anthropology from Barnard College and M.S.W. from the University of Michigan, school social worker in Michigan.

David Epstein
> Member of 1962 field team, holds Ph.D. in anthropology from Columbia University; now a lawyer in Irvine, California, and a 1991 four-time *Jeopardy* champion.

Marvin Harris
> Leader of 1962 Brazil field team, Columbia-Cornell-Harvard-Illinois Summer Field Studies Program in Anthropology; graduate research professor of anthropology at the University of Florida.

Peter Gorlin
> Member of 1964 field team stationed in Jauá, helped complete interview schedule in Arembepe; holds Ph.D. in anthropology from Columbia University and M.D. from Harvard.

Thales de Azevedo
> Leader of 1964 Bahia field team, of which Conrad Kottak was assistant leader; renowned Bahian physician and anthropologist.

Niles Eldredge
Member of 1963 field team in Arembepe; curator of invertebrate paleontology at New York's American Museum of Natural History and coinventor (with S. J. Gould) of the punctuated equilibrium model of evolution.

Shepard Forman
Assistant field leader, stationed in Arembepe in 1963; holds Ph.D. in anthropology from Columbia University; directs human rights program at Ford Foundation.

Raymond Rapaport
Undergraduate field assistant to Conrad Kottak in 1973, now a biochemist.

Maxine Margolis
Helped out with 1980 fieldwork in Arembepe; professor of anthropology at the University of Florida.

Jerald T. Milanich
Did mapping and photography of Arembepe in 1980; archaeologist at Florida State Museum, Gainesville.

Iraní Escolano
Brazilian social science researcher; worked on TV research project in Arembepe in 1985 and 1987.

Pennie Magee
Worked on TV research project in Arembepe in 1985; has Ph.D. in anthropology from the University of Florida.

Juliet Maria Kottak
Daughter of Conrad and Betty; visited Arembepe in 1973, 1980, and annually between 1982 and 1985; currently a medical student.

Nicholas Charles Kottak (Nick)
Son of Conrad and Betty; visited Arembepe in 1973, 1980, and annually between 1982 and 1987; did fieldwork on ecological awareness there in 1991; now majoring in anthropology at Columbia University.

The Villagers

Alberto
Fisherman turned barkeeper, Conrad Kottak's best informant, friend, and field assistant in 1973 and 1980.

Tomé
> Through the 1970s Arembepe's most successful fisherman, captain, and boat owner.

Dora
> Anthropologists' cook on several occasions; unmarried mother formerly classified as a village prostitute.

Fernando
> Moderately successful fishing captain; joined a cult and turned to alcohol in reaction to Arembepe's transformation.

Amy
> Claudia's daughter, inherited her restaurant business.

Aunt Dalia
> Businesswoman whose success rested on sales to hippies, ran juice bar in Street Down There.

Carolina
> Alberto's wife, started successful business in Street Down There in the early 1970s; cult participant.

Claudia
> Opened Arembepe's best restaurant in the early 1970s.

Dinho
> Tomé's younger brother; by 1980 owned five boats, marketed fish, and was Arembepe's richest entrepreneur.

Jaime
> Tibrás worker; was water boy for 1964 and 1965 field teams.

Julia
> Psychotic young villager with penchant for nudism.

Laurentino
> Iconoclastic storekeeper suspected of devil worship.

Maria
> "Saint's daughter" in local *candomblé* cult.

Roberto
> Fish marketer from Salvador, visited Arembepe through 1964.

Prudencio
> Agent of Arembepe's absentee landlords.

Sonia
> Tomé's hippie wife.

The Landlords

Jorge Camões
>First of Arembepe's absentee landlords to obtain university education; masterminded Arembepe's real estate boom.

Francisca Ricardo
>Last landlord to reside in Arembepe; died in 1924.

Assault on Paradise

Social Change in a Brazilian Village

Part One

A Story of Change

1 Before: The Sixties

This book is based on several visits to Arembepe[1] (Bahia state, Brazil): in 1962, 1964, 1965, 1973, 1980, annually from 1982 to 1987, and 1991. The book's structure is built on the contrast between the village of the 1960s and the contemporary community. Chapters 3 through 5 give baseline information about Arembepe through 1965, before it encountered the forces that had altered local life so obviously by the mid-1970s. The main forces of change were motorization of the fishing industry, tourism and the "hippie" invasion, massive industrial pollution, and suburbanization through the opening of a paved road to Salvador, the state capital.

These and other trends associated with economic development had drastically altered local life by 1973, when I returned after an eight-year absence (Chapter 6). My 1973 fieldwork provided a picture of Arembepe in transition. Accordingly, Chapter 6, which describes Arembepe in 1973, provides a transition to Part IV (Chapters 7 through 12), which describes the hugely transformed contemporary community. Arembepe has been drawn ever more firmly into the web of expanding Salvador—a metropolis with more than 2 million people—and through it into the modern world system. This book tells the story of that transformation.

It Began by Accident

This is a story of change, but it didn't start out to be that. It began by accident. I first lived in Arembepe during the (North American) summer of 1962. That was between my junior and senior years at New York City's Columbia College (of Columbia University), where I was majoring in anthropology. I went to Arembepe as a participant in a now defunct program designed to give undergraduates an experience in ethnography—the firsthand study of local culture and social life. The program's cumbersome title, the Columbia-Cornell-Harvard-Illinois Summer Field Studies Program in Anthropology, reflected participation by four universities, each with a different field station. The other field sites were in Peru, Mexico, and Ecuador. The area around Salvador, Brazil, had just been chosen for the Columbia field station, and that is where I was sent.

The field team leader was Professor Marvin Harris, who was later to become my adviser and doctoral dissertation committee chair during my graduate work in anthropology at Columbia University, which began in 1963. Also in Salvador that year was Professor Charles Wagley, another Columbia anthropologist, who had worked with Harris and others to establish the program. Through their links with Bahian social scientists, Harris and Wagley chose two villages that were anthropologically interesting but close enough to Salvador to maintain contact with the undergraduates. The two communities lay along the same road. Abrantes, the agricultural village, nearer to Salvador, was the district seat for Arembepe, the more remote fishing village. Liking the coast, I preferred Arembepe, where I was assigned, with fellow team member David Epstein. Harris arranged for us to rent the dilapidated summer house of a city man who sometimes vacationed in Arembepe.

Meanwhile, Professor Wagley's daughter, Betty, a Barnard College student also majoring in anthropology, arrived to spend the summer with her parents in Salvador. She went with us to visit Abrantes and Arembepe and decided she also wanted to do fieldwork in the latter. Betty arranged lodging with a local woman, but since David and I had hired a cook, she ate with us and shared the cost of food and supplies. Betty's mother is Brazilian, and Betty, herself born in Brazil, is bilingual in Portuguese (her first language). This made her more adept at fieldwork than either David or I were. She was also kind enough to translate for us many times.

Having taught anthropology now for more than twenty years, I realize how unusual my first field experience was.

Most anthropologists begin fieldwork, which is required for the doctorate, after a few years of graduate study and not as undergraduates. They usually choose the part of the world they want to work in and the topic they will investigate there. For example, my own longest ethnographic project came just after graduate school. Having taken courses about several world areas, I became particularly interested in Madagascar, a large island off the southeast coast of Africa. I read as much as I could about the cultures of Madagascar. I focused on a problem—the social implications of an economic change, the expansion of irrigated agriculture—that I could investigate there.

With Arembepe, by contrast, someone else—the directors of the field program, for which I was chosen competitively— selected the area, even the village, for me. I didn't have time to do the extensive background reading that normally precedes fieldwork. Nor did I have much time to study the language I would be using in the field.

Although I didn't control the initial choice of Arembepe, I *did* decide to keep on studying it, particularly when, by 1973, it was evident that Arembepe had changed more rapidly in less than two decades than some places change in centuries. My longitudinal (long-term, ongoing) fieldwork during that transformation is the basis of this book.

Most of my preparation for my 1962 fieldwork was in a prefield seminar that Harris offered at Columbia, and another seminar about ethnographic field methods taught by Professor Lambros Comitas. In Harris's class, students talked about the kinds of research we planned to do when we got to Brazil. Harris urged us to do microprojects, focusing on limited aspects of community life that we could investigate easily in three months. The program's founders didn't intend our work to be traditional holistic ethnography—intensive study of all aspects of local life through long-term residence and participant observation. Comitas's seminar, on the other hand, had introduced me to techniques used in long-term, in-depth ethnography. One of my problems in doing fieldwork in Arembepe in 1962 was the conflict between my wish to do a holistic study and the program's preference for a microproject.

The program's goals were modest. I now realize that this was realistic, because we were novices. Harris and the other

leaders wanted us to get our feet wet—to see if we liked
fieldwork enough to pursue a career in cultural anthropology.
Our experience would also prepare us for later, longer fieldwork. As training for our microprojects, our prefield seminar
assignment was to write a library research paper on the topic
we planned to investigate in Brazil.

Harris suggested I study race relations, which already had
a large literature. Comparisons of race relations in Brazil and
the United States are appropriate because both countries
have a heritage of slavery. In both there has been considerable mixture of Europeans, Africans, and Native Americans.
For the seminar, I read extensively. I learned the main differences between the role of race in Brazil and the United
States and wrote a research paper on my findings. Harris and
I later worked out a specific microproject on Brazilian racial
classification, which I discuss later in this chapter.

Although I prepared myself to investigate Brazilian race
relations, my preparation in Brazilian Portuguese was insufficient. Language was my biggest barrier in the field. The only
Romance language I'd ever studied was Latin, for two years
in high school. In college I had taken German, which was no
help at all. I had never been abroad and had no experience
speaking a foreign language: high school and college had
barely taught me how to read one. As a result, I spent most
of the summer of 1962 asking Brazilians to repeat everything
they said to me. This led Arembepeiros to call me a *papagaio*
(parrot)—because I could only echo words that someone else
had originated. I discovered that it's difficult to gain much
insight into native social life when you can't converse as well
as a five-year-old can.

The Sixties

In June 1962, when I first set eyes on Arembepe, the 60-
kilometer trip from Salvador was neither simple nor sure. It
took three hours in a vehicle with four-wheel drive. I first
arrived, and have usually visited, Arembepe during the aus-
tral (southern hemisphere) winter. Located about 13 degrees
south of the equator and at sea level, Arembepe is never cold,
but June and July are rainy, making travel difficult. The clay-
surfaced road was usually muddy, and we always got stuck at

least once in any round trip. The task of getting our heavy jeep station wagon unstuck usually required a work group of field team members and a dozen helpful onlookers. Friendly local people would do most of the work, we learned to hope, particularly when we headed into Salvador for occasional "rest and recreation." Otherwise we would have to enter the lobby of a city hotel covered with red mud, raising doubts about whether we should be given lodging.

On the road to Arembepe, sand, lagoons, and more sand came after the mud. After heavy rains, crossing the freshwater lagoons that bordered Arembepe on the west made the jeep seem like a motorboat. High water washed onto the cabin floor and sometimes stalled the engine. After the lagoons came the dunes, with closely planted coconut trees—posing another traffic hazard. Making it into the village required finding another vehicle's tracks, flooring the accelerator, and for some, calling on deities for help. Once, as a frustrating drive out seemed over, I pulled up in front of the house I was renting to find that the brakes had failed. Only frantic pumping kept me from crashing through the kitchen wall.

But Arembepe was worth the trip. I can't imagine a more

"*We always got stuck at least once.*" *The road to Arembepe, passing through the district seat, Abrantes, in 1964.* (Conrad P. Kottak)

beautiful field setting. The village was strung along a narrow strip of land (less than a kilometer) between ocean and lagoons. More spectacular than any South Sea island I later visited, Arembepe's houses—brightly painted in tones of blue, pink, peach, purple, and orange—stood under lofty coconut palms. To the east, stretches of smooth white sand and protected swimming areas alternated with jagged rocks and churning Atlantic waves. On a sunny day in August, Arembepe was alive with color: the green-blue hues of ocean and lagoons, orange-red of brick and roof tiles, pinks and blues of houses, greens of palms, and white of sand. Colorful fishing boats anchored evenings and Sundays in the port, just east of the central square and the small, white Roman Catholic chapel. The harbor is formed by a rugged, partially submerged reef. Each morning the boats rowed through its narrow channels, then raised their sun-bleached sails to travel to their destinations for the day.

Arembepe belonged in a movie. (Some French photographers did use the chapel as a backdrop for fashion ads that appeared in *Vogue* in 1966.) This conjunction of natural beauty with the middle-class appeal of a "quaint" village subsisting on a wind-powered, hook-and-line fishing industry had already drawn a handful of tourists and summer residents to Arembepe in 1962. Still, the poor quality of the road made it a hard trip even in summer, the dry season (December to February). Only a few residents of the capital—mainly middle-class and lower-middle-class people—had summer homes in Arembepe. Limited bus service began in 1965, but it brought few visitors until the road was improved in 1970.

Poverty and poor public health were the most evident blights that made Arembepe—despite the title of this book—something less than paradise. In theory, Arembepeiros got their drinking water from Big Well, a tiny settlement 2 kilometers away. An entrepreneur who lived there made money selling barrels of water in Arembepe. When well water wasn't readily available, villagers sometimes drank water from the freshwater lagoon. Some mothers even used lagoon water in the powdered milk they mixed for their children. Considering these traditional uses of water—and that the bushes where villagers relieved themselves were on the edge of the lagoon, which rose in the rainy season—it's easy to

During the 1960s, as we approached Arembepe, the clay road yielded to sand. (Conrad P. Kottak)

understand why children suffered from intestinal disorders and extreme malnutrition (the latter partly caused by parasites in their bodies).

Malinowski and Microprojects

I entered this romantic yet imperfect setting as a fledgling ethnographer with ambitious goals and a huge linguistic impediment. Two dimensions of my work in Arembepe bear discussion here. One involves my scientific and professional aims. The second has to do with my personal reactions to an alien setting. First the scientific goals.

As a conscientious anthropology major, I wanted to put the lessons from my classes into practice. I wanted to do the things that Bronislaw Malinowski describes as the ethnographer's work in the first chapter of his classic *Argonauts of the Western Pacific*, a field study of fishers and traders in Melanesia.

I often compared my experiences with Malinowski's; even our field settings struck me as similar. He had also worked in

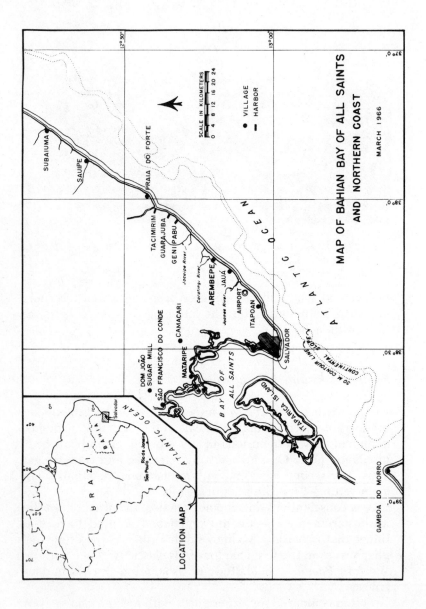

MAP OF BAHIAN BAY OF ALL SAINTS
AND NORTHERN COAST

MARCH 1966

SCALE IN KILOMETERS
0 4 8 12 16 20 24

● VILLAGE
▬ HARBOR

ATLANTIC OCEAN

SUBAIUMA
SAUIPE
PRAIA DO FORTE
TACIMIRIM
GUARAJUBA
GENIPABU
Jacuipe River
Carainga River
AREMBEPE
JAUÁ
Joanes River
AIRPORT
ITAPOAN
SALVADOR
50 M. CONTOUR LINE
CONTINENTAL LINE
CAMACARI
DOM JOÃO
SUGAR MILL
SÃO FRANCISCO DO CONDE
MATARIPE
BAY OF ALL SAINTS
ITAPARICA ISLAND
GAMBOA DO MORRO

LOCATION MAP

BRAZIL
BAHIA
Salvador
Rio de Janeiro
São Paulo
ATLANTIC OCEAN

12° 30'
13° 00'
37° 0'
38° 0'
38° 30'
39° 0'

10

a tropical South Sea setting (the Trobriand Islands). Though Arembepe is on the mainland, the phrase "South Sea island" kept running through my head. Reading Malinowski's description of the moment when the ethnographer "sets foot upon a native beach, and makes his first attempts to get in touch with the natives" (Malinowski, 1961, p. 4), I imagined myself in his sandals. He talked of trying to get to know the natives by observing them making things and by writing down names of tools. Like me, Malinowski initially had trouble communicating with local people. "I was quite unable to enter any more detailed or explicit conversation with them at first. I knew well that the best remedy for this was to collect concrete data, and accordingly I took a village census, wrote down genealogies, drew up plans and collected the terms of kinship" (Malinowski, 1961, p. 5).

I was eager to do those things that Malinowski had done, especially to census the village. But field leader Harris discouraged me, offering another lesson: Before I could gather the detailed and accurate data that ethnography demands, I needed to build rapport; people would have to get to know and trust me. I would have to convince them I wasn't dangerous and that it wouldn't be to their disadvantage to answer my questions. Furthermore, I didn't yet know enough about village life to devise pertinent questions to ask during a census. Accordingly, but regretfully, I put the census on hold and set about "building rapport." David Epstein and Betty Wagley, my companions in the field, were doing the same thing, as did Marvin Harris, when he moved in with David and me to spend August 1962 in Arembepe.

How does one build rapport? "Get to know the men," Marvin told me. To do this I started joining the fishermen for their evening bath in the lagoon. I had my first doubts about the wisdom of this participant observation when I accidentally swatted a floating piece of donkey dung (I like to think I identified the correct mammal) during my third bath. I gave up lagoon bathing when I learned of the lagoon system's infestation by schistosomes—liver flukes. After that, I was careful to avoid the lagoon. I followed the advice of public health officials to rub exposed body parts with alcohol whenever I came into contact with lagoon water. Arembepeiros found these precautions laughable: Not to worry, they said—

small fish in the lagoon ate the liver flukes (and germs in general). There was no health threat to people.

If the lagoon was now off-limits, there was still the chapel stoop, where each evening, after the fleet had returned, baths had been taken, and the day's main meal consumed, men would gather to talk. This was male territory. Only small girls and old women dared approach. David and I would sit and try to talk. My Portuguese was rudimentary; I resented David because he spoke and seemed to understand better than I did. Still, villagers tossed questions my way. They were curious about the United States, but their questions were hardly scintillating: "Were there camels in the United States?" . . . "Elephants?" . . . "Monkeys?" They went through a litany of animals they had seen on the lottery tickets people brought back from Salvador. "Look! Up in the sky. It's a jet from the United States heading for Rio," they observed every other night, reflecting the airline's schedule. Whenever, after arduous mental rehearsal, I found the words to ask a question about Arembepe, I'd get an incomprehensible reply, followed by some such query as "Have you ever seen a bear, Conrado?"

The beautiful, microbe-infested, freshwater lagoon that borders Arembepe to the west, at sundown. (Courtesy Jerald T. Milanich)

"Bear, bear," I parroted.

"Parrot, parrot," they guffawed.

"Yes, I have seen a bear. I have seen a bear in a zoo."

Rapport building was fascinating indeed.

Visions of Malinowski danced in my head as I came to resent this kind of activity as a waste of time. I was eager to do something "more scientific." The microproject that Harris and I had planned involved testing a difference between race relations in Brazil and the United States. In the United States a rule of descent determines racial identity. If an American has one black (African-American) parent and one white one, he or she is assigned, automatically at birth and without regard for physical appearance, to "the black race." In Brazil, it seemed that several factors determine racial identity and that no descent rule operates. Since, however, no one had systematically demonstrated that Brazil lacks such a rule, we decided that a genetically and phenotypically (physically) mixed community like Arembepe would be a good place to test it.

When an automatic descent rule operates, full siblings belong to the same descent group. Thus in the United States, full siblings can't belong to different races. In Arembepe, we set out to find full siblings who were physically very different, to see if they were assigned to different races. We found three sisters with widely varying skin shades, hair types, and facial features. After we photographed them, I finally got to do something more challenging than reporting on North American animals. I chose a sample of 100 villagers and showed the photo of the sisters to all, asking them to tell me each girl's race. Sure enough, I found that many different terms were used, that in Brazil full siblings could belong to different races.

New questions about race emerged from that first survey. We devised another set of questions, based on drawings of individuals who contrasted phenotypically. By questioning another sample of villagers, I found that Arembepeiros used many more racial terms (over forty) than had previously been reported for a Brazilian community. They also used them inconsistently, so that the racial term used for another person might vary from day to day, as might even self-identification. By the time my three months in Arembepe were up, I was fluent in Brazilian racial terminology, and Harris and I had the basis for a couple of journal articles. Although I still felt guilty that I hadn't managed to do a Malinowskian census, I did think I'd accomplished something in my first field experience.

To work again in Brazil, I knew I'd have to improve my Portuguese. I could get only so far talking about race relations. I spent the next summer (1963) taking an intensive course in Brazilian Portuguese at Columbia University while another field team lived in Arembepe. Also in the summer of 1963, Betty Wagley and I, whose romance had begun under Arembepe's full moon, got married; and I began graduate school in the fall.

I was delighted, the following spring, to be offered the job of assistant leader of the 1964 field team. I returned to Arembepe in June 1964 determined to do my census. And not just a census. By then I had studied more anthropology, and my Portuguese had improved dramatically. I felt I was ready to do a full-fledged interview schedule (a kind of questionnaire). Peter Gorlin, who now holds a Ph.D. in anthropology and an M.D. degree, was an undergraduate field team member stationed in Jauá, the next village south of Arembepe. Peter had read Malinowski, too; he was also eager to use Malinowski's "method of concrete, statistical documentation" (1961, p. 24), to satisfy the ethnographer's "fundamental obligation of giving a complete survey of the phenomena, and not of picking out the sensational [and] the singular" (1961, p. 11).

I was ready to do a survey of all the households in Arembepe, and Peter wanted to do the same thing in Jauá. But we needed "an instrument." Our team leader, the renowned Bahian physician and anthropologist Thales de Azevedo, supplied us with one—an interview schedule that had been used in southern Bahia. We revised the schedule for the fishing villages and had it printed.

An *interview schedule* differs from a standard questionnaire in that the ethnographer talks directly, face to face, with informants, asks the questions, and writes down the answers. Questionnaire procedures, which sociologists routinely use, tend to be more indirect and impersonal; often the respondent fills in the form. Sociologists normally work with literate people, who can fill out the answer sheets or questionnaire forms themselves. Anthropologists, by contrast, haven't usu-

1964 field team members Peter Gorlin (second from left) and Erica Bressler with their host family in Jauá, the fishing village just south of Arembepe. Note the range of physical variation among the local people. (Conrad P. Kottak)

ally worked in places where most people are literate, so we have to record the answers ourselves.

Because we are in charge of pacing, we can choose to digress temporarily from the scheduled questions to follow up intriguing bits of information that emerge in the interview. Thus the ethnographer can keep interviews open-ended and exploratory while asking a basic set of questions, to gather comparable, quantifiable information. I learned as much about Arembepe from the open-ended questioning as I did from the formal queries.

Our interviews in Arembepe illustrate still another difference between the research techniques of anthropologists and sociologists. Because sociologists normally deal with large populations, such as the United States, they must use *sampling techniques,* which enable them to make inferences about a larger group from a detailed study of a smaller one. We didn't need to do sampling in Arembepe, because it was small enough for us to do a total sample—that is, to complete the schedule with all the households there—159 of them.

A final contrast between cultural anthropology and sociol-
ogy is worth mentioning. Sociologists often distribute their
questionnaires by mail or hire research assistants to adminis-
ter, code, and analyze them. Ethnographers, by contrast,
work right in the community, where they encounter a series
of real-world obstacles. My main problem as I interviewed in
Arembepe wasn't the few villagers who slammed doors in my
face, or even the droopy-nosed kids who used my pants as a
handkerchief. My problem was fleas. I recall my third or
fourth interview, in a sand-floored hut. Asking my questions
to a dozen smiling members of an extended family, I began to
itch in places I was embarrassed to scratch. I made it to the
end of the form, but I didn't tarry for open-ended inquiry.
Instead I ran home, through the house, out the back door,
right into the harbor at high tide. I let the salt water burn into
my flea wounds. Fleas bothered most of us, especially Betty,
that summer. The remedy for the men was to wear pants and
sprinkle our cuffs with flea powder. We managed to interview
in almost all Arembepe's households, despite the predatory
sand fleas with their seemingly special thirst for North American blood.

Our interview schedule was eight pages long. We asked
questions (for each household member) about age, gender,
racial identity, diet, job, religious beliefs and practices, education, political preferences, possessions, consumption patterns,
and ownership of livestock, boats, coconut trees, land, and
farms. I encouraged Peter not to do a microproject but to
follow the Malinowskian path I'd wanted to tread. He did it
with gusto; in two months he'd finished the schedule with all
the households in Jauá. He hiked up the beach to spend
August helping Betty and me finish the interviewing in Arembepe.

There are advantages, I now realize, in both models for
brief fieldwork. A microproject is easily manageable and
holds out the promise of a modest research paper. The holistic
Malinowskian approach is also valuable. I'm convinced my
Portuguese would have improved much more if I'd done the
interview schedule the first summer, rather than limiting my
talk to rapport building and race relations. I later found this
to be true, when I used a simple interview schedule soon after
beginning fieldwork among the Betsileo people in Madagas-

car in 1966. The first interview schedule doesn't have to be as detailed as the one we used in Arembepe. In Madagascar I used a succession of schedules, about different subjects and of increasing complexity. All gave me comparable information about a group of people, and all increased my ability to discuss a range of topics significant to the Betsileo. Similarly, Peter Gorlin's work with the schedule in Jauá and Arembepe in 1964 helped him improve his Portuguese much more quickly than I had done in 1962.

Doing the schedule had an added benefit I didn't fully realize in 1964: it got at least one member of the field team into every home in Arembepe. Years later I was to hear from many villagers that they remembered those visits warmly. Our questions, asked in their homes, had communicated our personal interest and showed we didn't look down on Arembepeiros.

I found the people of Arembepe to be open, warm, and hospitable, much less wary of outsiders than the Betsileo I studied for fourteen months in 1966–1967. Most Arembepeiros welcomed us to their homes and gladly answered our questions. Only a handful played hard to get, slamming windows and doors as we approached, telling neighbors they wouldn't answer our questions. I had to settle for sketchier information about them and could only make estimates of their incomes and consumption patterns, using public information and behavior. Fortunately (since the 1964 data are the basis for much of the detailed comparison between Arembepe in the 1960s and later), fewer than a dozen households, scattered throughout the village, refused to let us do the schedule.

The interview schedule wasn't the only thing I did in Arembepe in 1964. Soon after my arrival, I met an excellent informant, Alberto, whose name figures prominently in the story that follows. Then a forty-year-old fisherman, Alberto was the eldest brother of our cook. He felt free to visit our house almost every night, and he was eager to teach me about the fishing industry. I also got information about fishing by talking to fishermen and fish marketers on the beach, and by going out in several boats, including that of Tomé, Arembepe's most successful boat captain and owner. Tomé's name, too, is a prominent one in Arembepe's recent history.

In 1965 I had my third chance to study Arembepe. The

results of analyzing the interview schedules and my information on fishing had been so promising that both Marvin Harris and I felt that I might, with another summer of fieldwork, amass sufficient data to write my doctoral dissertation about Arembepe, which I did. This time Betty and I weren't part of a field team but on our own. A graduate fellowship and grant supported my work, and living was still cheap in cash-poor Arembepe. In summer 1965 I again followed the Malinowskian plan, but I already had much of the statistical and observational data needed for the "firm, clear outline" of my community's organization and the "anatomy of its culture" (Malinowski, 1961, p. 24).

What I needed now was flesh for the skeleton. So I spent the summer of 1965 gathering data on the "imponderabilia of actual life . . . collected through minute, detailed observations . . . made possible by close contact with native life" (Malinowski, 1961, p. 24). By this time, I didn't really have to harken back to Malinowski to know that although I had the bare bones, I still needed to find out more about local opinions, values, and feelings; to listen to stories, examine cases, and gather intimate, basic details about everyday life. Like Napoleon Chagnon, the principal ethnographer of the Yanomamo Indians of Venezuela, I knew "how much I enjoyed reading monographs that were sprinkled with real people, that described real events, and that had some sweat and tears, some smells and sentiments mingled with the words" (Chagnon, 1977, p. xi). I wanted to add such dimensions—feeling tones—to my ethnography of Arembepe.

It Was an Alien Place

Those were some of my professional goals and research methods. Another part of ethnography is more personal. No matter how objective and scientific they fancy themselves, anthropologists are not mechanical measuring instruments. We are inevitably *participant* observers, taking part in—and by so doing modifying, no matter how slightly—the phenomena we are investigating and trying to understand. Not recording machines but people, anthropologists grow up in particular cultural traditions, possess idiosyncratic personality traits and experiences, have their own motivations, impressions, values, and reactions. Nor are our informants alike; we come to appreciate them differently. Some we never appreciate; an occasional one we detest.

Raised in one culture, curious about others, anthropologists still experience culture shock, especially on the first field trip. *Culture shock* refers to the whole set of feelings about being in an alien setting, and the resulting reactions. It is a chilly, creepy feeling of alienation, of being without some of the most ordinary, trivial—and therefore basic—cues of one's culture of origin.

As I planned to set off for Brazil in 1962, I couldn't know how naked I would feel without the cloak of my language and culture. My sojourn in Arembepe would be my first trip outside the United States. I was an urban boy who had grown up in Atlanta, Georgia, and New York City. I had little experience with rural life in my country, none with Latin America, and I had received only minimal training in the Portuguese language.

New York City direct to Salvador, Bahia, Brazil. Just a brief stopover in Rio de Janeiro; a longer visit would be a reward at the end of fieldwork. As our plane approached tropical Salvador, I couldn't believe the whiteness of the sand. "That's not snow, is it?" I remarked to a fellow field team member. Marvin Harris had arranged our food and lodging at the Paradise Hotel, overlooking Bahia's magnificent, endlessly blue, All Saints' Bay. My first impressions of Bahia were of smells—alien odors of ripe and decaying mangoes, bananas, and passion fruit—and of swatting ubiquitous fruit flies I had never seen before, although I had read about their reproductive behavior in genetics classes. There were strange concoctions of rice, black beans, and gelatinous gobs of unidentified meats and floating pieces of skin. Coffee was strong and sugar crude. Every table top had containers for toothpicks and manioc (cassava) flour, to sprinkle, like parmesan cheese, on anything one might eat. I remember oatmeal soup and a slimy stew of beef tongue in tomatoes. At one meal a disintegrating fish head, eyes still attached, but barely, stared up at me as its body floated in a bowl of bright orange palm oil. Bearing my culture's don't-drink-the-water complex, it took me a few days to discover that plain mineral water quenched thirst better than the gaseous variety. Downstairs from the hotel was the Boite Clock, a nightclub whose rhythmic bossa nova music often kept us from sleeping.

I only vaguely remember my first day in Arembepe. Unlike ethnographers who have studied remote tribes in the tropical forests of South America or the highlands of New Guinea, I didn't hike or ride a canoe for days to arrive at my field site. Arembepe wasn't isolated compared with those places—only compared with every place I'd ever been. My first contact with Arembepe was just a visit, to arrange lodging. We found the crumbling summer house of a man who lived in Salvador, and arranged to rent it and have it cleaned. We hired Dora, a twenty-five-year-old unmarried mother of two, to cook for us, and another woman to clean house and do our laundry. My first visit to Arembepe didn't leave much of an impression. I knew I'd still have a few more days at the Paradise Hotel, with a real toilet and shower, before having to rough it "in the field."

Back in the city, using her fluency in Brazilian language and culture, Betty Wagley bargained for our cots, pots, pans, flashlights, and other supplies. I don't remember our actual move to Arembepe or who accompanied us. Harris had employed a chauffeur; we stopped to deposit some field team members in Abrantes. I do recall what happened when we got to Arembepe. There was no formal road into the village. Entering from the south, cars threaded their way around coconut trees, following tracks left by vehicles that had passed previously. A crowd of children had heard us coming. They pursued our car through the streets until we parked in front of our house, near the central square. We spent our first few days with children following us everywhere. For weeks we had little daytime privacy. Kids watched our every move through our living room window. Sometimes one made an incomprehensible remark. Usually they just stood there. Occasionally they would groom one another's hair, chewing on the lice they found.

Outcasts from an urban culture, David and I locked our doors. Once he went into Salvador while I stayed the night alone.

"Conrado's scared," said Dora, our cook. "He's afraid of the *bichos* [beasts, real and imaginary] outside." There was

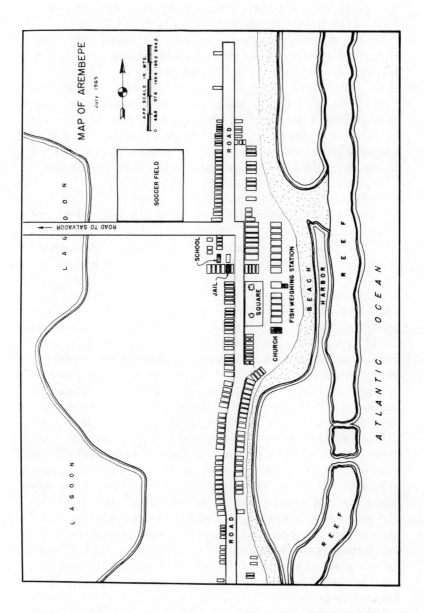

MAP OF AREMBEPE

July 1965

APP. SCALE IN MTS.

0   488   976   1464 1952 2442

LAGOON

ROAD TO SALVADOR →

SOCCER FIELD

ROAD

SCHOOL

JAIL

SQUARE

CHURCH

FISH WEIGHING STATION

BEACH

HARBOR

REEF

LAGOON

ROAD

REEF

REEF

ATLANTIC OCEAN

21

really nothing to be afraid of, she assured me. A dangerous *bicho* had never bothered anyone in Arembepe; most people didn't even have locks on their doors.

Our most annoying intruders were a few drunks who occasionally paid us nighttime visits, seeking alcohol or money to buy it. Fairly late one night (around nine or ten o'clock, after most villagers were in bed), two men pounded on our door. From their slurred speech and loudness it was obvious that both had been drinking. One was a young villager, who said he wanted to introduce us to the other man, a visitor from Camaçari, the county seat. "Some Americans in Camaçari taught my friend how to speak English," said the villager.

"Oh, yeah," we said. "Let's hear him."

"John Wayne," said the visitor.

"Very good," observed David. "Do you know anything else?"

"Yes," the man responded. "Fucky, fucky." (My subsequent travels throughout the world have revealed several such permutations of this four-letter English word.)

The sounds, sensations, sights, smells, and tastes of life in northeastern Brazil, and in Arembepe, slowly grew familiar. I gradually accepted the fact that the only toilet tissue available at a reasonable price had almost the texture of sandpaper. I grew accustomed to this world without Kleenex, where globs of mucus drooped from the noses of village children whenever a cold passed through. A world where, seemingly without effort, women with gracefully swaying hips carried 18-liter kerosene cans of water on their heads, where boys sailed kites and sported at catching houseflies in their bare hands, where old women smoked pipes, storekeepers offered *cachaça* (common rum) at nine in the morning, and men played dominoes on lazy afternoons when there was no fishing. I was in a world where life was oriented toward water— the sea, where men fished, and the lagoon, where women communally washed clothing, dishes, and their bodies.

Arembepe was a compact village, where the walls of most houses touched those of their neighbors, where, through gossip, the peccadillos of individuals and families instantaneously became community property. Privacy was a scarce commodity. No wonder villagers didn't lock their doors—who could steal anything and have it stay a secret? Young lovers found what privacy they could at night.

Even more dramatically than in other places without electricity, Arembepe's night life was transformed when the moon was full. Reflected everywhere by the sand and water, moonlight turned the village by night into almost day. Young people strolled in the streets and courted on the beach. Fishermen sought octopus and "lobster" (Atlantic crayfish) on the reef. Accustomed to the electrified, artificial pace of city life, I was enchanted by the moonlight and its effect on this remote village. Moonless nights impressed me, too. For the first time I could understand how the Milky Way got its name. Only in a planetarium had I seen a sky so crammed with stars. Looking south, distant Salvador's electric lights just barely dimmed the white stars against the coal-black sky, and for the first time I could view the Southern Cross in its magnificence.

Even a devout astrologer would have been impressed with the extent to which activities were governed by the phases of the moon. This was a slower and more natural epoch in Arembepe's history than the years that were to follow. People awakened near sunrise and went to bed early. Moonlight and a calm sea permitted occasional nighttime fishing, but the pattern was for the fleet to leave in the early morning and return in the late afternoon. Boats usually went out five or six days a week; as Christians, Arembepeiros took Sunday as a day of rest. But generally, life in Arembepe followed the availability of natural light and the passing of day and night.

Another force of nature, the weather, influenced the rhythm of life. My visits to Arembepe were during the season of rain and rough seas. Sailboats were vulnerable to high winds and stormy weather, and it was dangerous to negotiate the narrow channels in the rocky reef when racing home to escape a sudden squall. Storms usually lasted no more than a week, but I remember one three-week lull, in 1964. People speculated incessantly about when the weather would improve; they had no access to weather reports. Villagers lamented that they couldn't work. Eventually they began to complain of hunger. Cattle were brought in from farms to be butchered and sold, but many households were too poor to buy beef. Villagers said they were hungry for fish, for something with flesh to complement a diet of coffee, sugar, and manioc flour. The weather even forced us to let up on our interviewing. Our schedule had a whole section on diet—the quantities of various foods that people bought or ate per day, week, or month. We felt embarrassed asking people what they ate in normal or good times when they were starving for protein and, indeed, for all items whose purchase required cash.

The tropical rainy season meant constant high humidity, a perfect climate for molds. My black leather dress shoes turned white with mildew. Peter Gorlin had bought a navy blue drip-dry suit before his trip to Bahia in 1964. Since we attended few formal affairs in Salvador, Peter let his suit hang in a wardrobe in Jauá until he finally needed it. Discovering, a few hours before a party, that it was covered with mildew, Peter checked into a Salvador hotel, took a shower with his suit on, lathered and rinsed it, wore it to the party, and dripped dry for the next few hours.

The tile roofs of the houses we rented in Arembepe were never very effective in keeping the moisture (and bats) out. Whenever it rained, we had to avoid the large leaks, but there was no place we could be completely dry. One rainy day during the three-week fishing lull, Dora told us that lately, smelling the moist walls of her wattle-and-daub (stick-and-mud) hut, she had remembered her craving as a child to lick, even eat, dirt from the mud walls. Arembepeiros sometimes did eat earth, she told us. This geophagy may have been a symptom of iron deficiency in lean times.

Besides the everyday sensations and experiences of a foreign land and culture, there were the special occasions. A few women held prayer sessions in their homes to honor their household saints and pray for deceased relatives. July's big event was the *Chegança*. In the building in the main square that served as the seat of the Fishermen's Society, the fishermen reenacted the Portuguese discovery of Brazil with a few hours of formal song and dance. Saint John's night, June 24, was the lesser of Arembepe's two main annual festive events. (The ceremony for Saint Francis took place in February, the time of Arembepe's most productive fishing, and because of this was much more elaborate.) Following Iberian traditions for Saint John's night, villagers lit bonfires and drank special *cachaça* (rum) concoctions. They cooked delicious confections, such as *cocada* (sweetened coconut candy), and less universally pleasing ones, such as *canjica* (a mushy corn pudding, whose flavor approximates that of pencil

eraser). Childbirth brought forth other barely tolerable mix-
tures, most notably a drink combining *cachaça,* onion, garlic,
and various exotic berries and herbs.

I can summarize my feelings about living in Arembepe in
the 1960s by saying that I had a profound sense of being away.
In those days, almost no one except a fish buyer from Salvador
ever drove a car into Arembepe. I felt cut off from the world.
Only a few villagers owned radios, which rarely brought news
of the rest of the world anyway. I pored over every word of
Time's Latin American edition on each visit to Salvador. We
sometimes planned our trips into Salvador to coincide with
the day the new *Time* came out.

Even for Betty Wagley Kottak, a Brazilian (of dual national-
ity), Arembepe was unfamiliar. It was far removed from the
sophistication, stratification, and style consciousness of Rio de
Janeiro and São Paulo, which she knew well. Betty had been
exposed to much of Brazil's "Great Tradition" (to use Robert
Redfield's term for the culture of literate, mainly urban,
elites) but not the "little traditions" of its peasants and rural
poor. For both of us, then, as for the other field team members, Arembepe provided a strong contrast with all previous
settings in our lives.

I think that our work in Arembepe also gave us a better
understanding of rural America as recently as the 1930s and
1940s. Then, in many isolated pockets, especially among the
poor, night life still went on by candle and lantern. This was
before business, government, and media had fully introduced
rural folk to the industrial world's vast inventory of benefits
and costs.

We learned firsthand about the habits and values of Arembepeiros, how they tried to make ends meet, how they dealt
with fortune and adversity. We got to know many people as
individuals and as friends. Characters like Alberto, Dora, and
Tomé, whose words, stories, and experiences are laced
through this chronicle of a changing Arembepe, are much
more to me than informants. They are people I value as I do
my friends and special colleagues in the United States. Yet
they are the kind of people that few outsiders will ever have
a chance to meet. The anthropologist's special obligation is to
tell their story for them.

2 After: The Road to 1980

When I rode into Arembepe in June 1973—eleven years after my first visit—the setting was noticeably different, as was the trip out from Salvador. Although letters from Brazil and reports of colleagues who had visited Arembepe since 1965 had prepared me for the hippie invasion and for the community's development as a tourist attraction, my first bit of direct evidence for the change was still a shock. Our jet from Rio de Janeiro landed at Salvador's remodeled airport, which lies just off the road that links Arembepe to Salvador. As our taxi headed for the city, where we were to spend a few days making arrangements, I noticed that the road toward Arembepe was now paved, and the turnoff marked with a *road sign*. Perhaps no one but a fellow anthropologist can appreciate my complex feelings on seeing the name of "my" community so publicly displayed. Anthropology, after all, grew up in small-scale, nonindustrial societies, and anthropologists retain at least a vestige of the profession's traditional fascination with the remote, the unusual, and the exotic. That night, as I rode along the familiar beach road to Salvador, I grew increasingly uneasy about my coming encounter with other manifestations of the end of my community's isolation that this road sign portended.

That encounter began the next day—not in Arembepe but watching television in Salvador and reading local newspapers. I learned that a recently opened chemical factory was polluting the freshwater lagoon system that forms the western boundary of Arembepe and other coastal communities. Television camera crews made regular forays to Arembepe to interview its residents about the effects of pollution. Since Arembepe was settled around 1900, its people had used lagoon water to wash clothes and dishes and had taken daily baths in the lagoon itself. All this had changed by 1973. Once so blue-green and deceptively clear, Arembepe's lagoon was now the dead brown of water in a vase of rotting flowers. If liver flukes and other lagoon "germs" were dead, so were the fish that had "eaten them" and that had helped sustain the villagers on days when rough seas prevented ocean fishing. This effect of factory pollution was visible throughout the lagoon system, but it was particularly marked in the inland waters nearest the factory, which stands between Arembepe and Jauá, the next fishing village to the south.

The reporters who visited Arembepe in June 1973 heard complaints by villagers that the lagoon waters now ruined their clothing and burned their eyes and nasal passages. One fisherman said he had abandoned the lagoon after experiencing intense burning of eyes and skin during an evening bath. He had rushed home to wash his face and body in well water. Women complained that waters where they had done their laundry for years now produced huge yellow spots in their clothes. As we had done ever since learning about the schistosomiasis threat, many Arembepeiros were now getting their bathing water from Big Well. The Big Well resident who used to ship barrels of water to Arembepe by mule had bought a truck to transport water (and for other business activities). Another businessman in Arembepe itself imported water from Big Well and sold showers in a ramshackle rooming house he had opened to cater to the tourist trade. Although chemical analysis of a few local wells showed no pollutants in 1973, eventual contamination seemed likely.

Those first few days introduced me to still another dimension of the changes that had swept Arembepe. This was the greatly increased urban middle-class and upper-middle-class ownership of summer homes and beach houses. Because our two small children had accompanied us, Betty and I decided that for a three-month stay we needed better accommodations than we had rented in the past. We learned that several comfortable vacation homes had been built on ocean-front lots south of Arembepe. A friend in Salvador had arranged for us to rent one of those houses—for a rent that, in dollars, was about five times what we had paid on our last visit. Part of this increase reflected inflation of the U.S. dollar and our larger and more comfortable quarters. However, much of the high rental price was a measure of Arembepe's new popularity as a tourist resort for the nearby city—even though it was the off-season.

Our lodging proved to be further south of the fishing village than I had anticipated when agreeing to rent. This was unfortunate, because living half a kilometer away partially removed me from village life and discouraged the nighttime visits that had figured prominently in previous fieldwork.

Once house and car rentals had been arranged in Salvador, I was ready to revisit Arembepe. I set out for "the field" in one of the two very temperamental Brazilian-made Volkswagen beetles I rented successively that summer. This was to be a leisurely drive. I wanted to observe changes along the route. A more daring driver could have made the trip in little more than an hour. After a few miles of *autoestrada* ("superhighway") under construction, I rejoined the familiar two-lane coastal road that had been the starting stretch of all my previous trips to Arembepe. Signs of Salvador's expansion and of its growth as a major tourist attraction within Brazil were obvious. (It is Brazil's oldest and one of its most beautiful, colorful, and interesting cities.) I passed several new beach-front hotels and restaurants, and a growing beach-focused neighborhood, Pituba, which Arembepeiros could now easily reach by bus to buy supplies that used to require a trip into midtown Salvador.

At Itapoan, a fishing village that once had been as isolated as Arembepe was in 1962, now virtually a neighborhood of Salvador, the road leaves the coast and heads inland. Previously the paved road had yielded to clay on entering Santo Amaro, seat of the municipality just south of Camaçari, Arembepe's own municipal seat. Much more distressing than the dirt road, however, just on the other side of Portão, the next village, had stood a decaying and very hazardous bridge over the Joanes River. The paved highway of 1973 simply skirted the periphery of Santo Amaro, Portão, Abrantes, and the other towns along the route. I whizzed over the Joanes River barely recalling that its crossing had once meant that everyone but the driver got out and walked across. This was to reduce the number of fatalities when the remaining bridge planks finally went. The good condition of the road made the next part of the trip, formerly one of the muddiest, rapid and uneventful.

Before I expected it, I saw a road sign marking the turnoff to the farming village and district seat of Abrantes, where several field team members had done fieldwork in 1962 and 1963. Next came the turnoff to Jauá, about 3 kilometers from the paved road, the tiny, charming coastal community studied by Elizabeth Thompson in 1963 and Peter Gorlin and Erica Bressler in 1964. I was surprised to see, at the turnoff, a brightly colored sign (my first hippie artifact) informing me that Jauá was a center of "indigenous" arts and crafts. Since I knew that the only native craft practiced in either Arembepe or Jauá was straw hat making by local women, I correctly concluded that Arembepe's southern neighbor had also experienced a flower-child invasion (on a much smaller scale than Arembepe, it turned out).

I was really not prepared for the Dunes of Mordor—to invoke imagery from J. R. R. Tolkien's *Lord of the Rings*. Sand was already replacing red clay as the dominant soil, and I began to see the huge dunes that, from the air, give the Bahian coast the look of a North Pole with palm trees. However, unnaturally large piles of sand—apparently excavated during the chemical factory's construction—stood on either side of the highway at the top of a steep hill. Passing through this man-made topography, I saw the titanium dioxide factory just to the east—the rust belt in Bahia: a smokestack and grey-green slime. The nearby dunes were covered with sulfurous wastes produced in the manufacture of titanium dioxide (an ingredient used in paints and dyes, which, as one American TV commercial had it, "whitens up our lives"). Here, on the boundaries of my "South Sea paradise," Tibrás (Titanium of Brazil), a multinational corporation, had deposited giant scoops of ersatz mashed potatoes topped by generous portions of Hollywood-vomit gravy.

Then—as testimony to the primacy of business—the road ended. The paved road simply stopped at the entrance to the factory's parking lot. Next came a hardened clay-surfaced road that entered the northern part of Arembepe 5 kilometers farther on. Although this road was better than anything that had existed in 1965, some areas did get messy. Still, I never got stuck during the 1973 rainy season. Soon I

The Tibrás factory in 1980. (Courtesy Jerald T. Milanich)

passed Big Well with its new gasoline pump. Then came the brown lagoon on either side of the road. To the right was something totally new: a squalid little settlement—Caraú-nas—which turned out to be Arembepe's first ghetto, spawned by the subdivision and sale of local real estate. Straight ahead lay Arembepe, which the road entered just north of the central square.

Previously, variation in house placement and building materials had provided evidence for slight differences in wealth, although all Arembepeiros had been members of the national lower class. Brick houses with tile roofs had been concentrated in the main square and just to the north, in an area that had begun as a secondary square but was lengthening into an open rectangle. Moving north, on either side of the two parallel rows, brick houses had gradually given way to wattle and daub, and tiles to palm-frond roofs. The same change had taken place south of the central square, which opened into the narrow Street Down There, whose seaside houses were much nearer the surf than those in the north. Crude huts with palm-frond roofs had reappeared at the southern end of this street, inhabited by the poorest Arembepeiros. These included recent immigrants who had not yet found regular places in fishing crews and odd jobbers at various menial tasks. However, most of the southern household heads had been women with no stable, coresident husband to act as father to their children, or alcoholic males who had trouble working regularly.

Numerous changes were obvious in 1973. For example, many of the people who used to live in the wattle-and-daub huts had moved to Caraúnas, the new satellite village across the lagoon. The huts they had once inhabited at the end of Street Down There were now brightly painted. Their residents were a few hippies who had stayed on after most had left Arembepe in 1971 and 1972. The hut interiors were tidier and more attractive now. For example, in one hut, layers of clean straw mats protected a French woman and her seven-year-old Franco-Italian son from the earth floor.

Change was even more evident further south, where there had previously been just one house. Now, half a kilometer away stood several vacation homes of middle-class and upper-middle-class "summer people" *(veranistas)*. They had bought

Wattle-and-daub huts like these were common in Arembepe during the 1960s. Houses began to thin out near the village's fringes. Shown here, the northern fringe. (Conrad P. Kottak)

One of the substantial summer houses south of Arembepe, the area where we stayed in 1973. (Courtesy Jerald T. Milanich)

the most attractive lots created by the subdivision of the estate that until recently had been held jointly by a family of absentee landowners. Four of these houses overlooked the ocean. The one we rented was desirably located nearest "Old Arembepe," a harbored area where the fishing settlement had been located until around 1900. (The fishermen moved to Arembepe's current location as part of a shift from raft to sailboat fishing, which demanded a calmer harbor and more channels in the reef.) Since the cove that our house overlooked was one of Arembepe's best swimming areas, visitors came on weekends to enjoy the beach, even during the rainy season. The house to the south of us was vacant, as ours otherwise would have been until late August, when its owner, a businessman from an interior city, planned to start his vacation. Beyond was the home of the only year-round residents of this neighborhood, a European-born businessman and his West Indian wife. He commuted to a job in Camaçari, the municipal seat, still a more time-consuming journey in 1973 than the trip to Salvador. The next beach-front lot, a huge one, belonged to a man who had once held high political office—a friend of the landowner responsible for Arembepe's development. The politician and his relatives had bought much of the seafront land further south, but they were not yet building there. New houses were also going up west of the clay road that passed these houses and continued south. These were much more modest but were close enough to the beach to give their absentee owners ready access when they vacationed in Arembepe.

This new neighborhood was reputedly alive with activity during vacations, but it was very quiet during our stay, and we often felt cut off. Our living arrangement required me to go up to Arembepe to do fieldwork, and villagers had to visit me far from their homes. Our old village friends did little to make our isolation easier to bear, since they continually expressed concern about our safety. This was one expression of a noticeably greater local atmosphere of fear and insecurity. "Get a gun," several villagers told us; robbers would surely come to rob and kill "rich Americans." One evening Betty and I managed to get away from Arembepe for our wedding anniversary. Just before we left, we were warned that police from Salvador had been there that day searching for two armed bandits: we'd better be careful on the road and shouldn't pick up hitchhikers (our previous practice). When we got back around midnight, having met no villains, we found our children sleeping soundly despite the noise of exploding firecrackers. Worried about an imminent attack, the villagers we had left in charge were tossing lighted firecrackers out of the second-story window into the back yard, to convince potential aggressors that we had guns.

A summer area was also developing at the northern end of Arembepe, where the main landlord, a resident of Salvador, had built a weekend and vacation domicile befitting the role of community patron he had played ever since my first visit. Unlike the southern summer houses, this vacation house and a few others nearby joined up with Arembepe.

Arembepe's better housing wasn't limited to the outsiders' homes. Throughout the village there were more brick-and-tile structures. Many villagers now had such "modern" conveniences as bottled gas-fueled lamps and stoves, toilets, showers, and refrigerators. Arembepe in 1973 still lacked electricity, that sine qua non of nighttime *movimento* ("urban excitement," which it now has). And it still lacked telephones.

Although there was a new, larger, school, the qualifications of the teachers hadn't improved much since 1965, when neither teacher had more than a third-grade education. Illiteracy was still common, with a third of the adult population totally unable to read or write, and another third barely able to sign their names. Arembepe's school system was the local manifestation of the limited educational opportunities that prevailed throughout rural Brazil. Although about half of Brazil's school-age children (seven to fourteen years old) lived in rural areas in 1970, only 47 percent attended school, compared with 88 percent in the cities (Hausmann and Haar, 1978). In the state of Bahia, one of the nation's poorest, things were even worse. Only 6 percent of students who entered first grade completed eighth. Like most rural schoolchildren in the Brazilian northeast, Arembepeiros "studied" in a one-room school, taught by barely literate women.

Health care, too, remained inadequate. The nearest pharmacies were in Itapoan and Pituba, an hour's bus trip away. Drugs were dispensed without a prescription. Few villagers had ever consulted a physician. They got whatever "expert" medical advice they obtained from pharmacists. Arembepe's health situation was another local manifestation of a more general barrier between lower-class Brazilians and adequate health care. Shamanistic cures were sometimes used instead. Brazil's highest infant mortality rate was in the northeast— 180 per thousand versus 112 nationally in 1964 (Robock, 1975). Although there was one physician for every 2,000 Brazilians in 1970, most doctors worked in cities, mainly in the industrial south (Robock, 1975).

The cold statistics of poverty hit home in Arembepe. Carolina, the wife of Alberto, my best informant, had lost ten of her thirteen children to such diseases as infectious diarrhea, influenza, pneumonia, tuberculosis, measles, and tetanus— all made more deadly by severe malnutrition. Despite the exotic tropical facade, Arembepe's poor public health and short life expectancy had always been obvious warps in paradise.

Although local education and health care had barely improved between 1965 and 1973, evidence of Arembepe's physical growth and differentiation was everywhere. What had once been a single, fairly homogeneous community had broken up along socioeconomic lines into a central village (Arembepe proper) and class-affiliated neighborhoods. The middle- and upper-middle-class people who lived south and north of Arembepe had not been there previously, and the abjectly poor inhabitants of Caraúnas had once been housed in Arembepe itself. A third satellite community had developed 2 kilometers further north, near the Caratingi River. International hippies had joined the few river fishermen who had previously maintained makeshift huts there. By 1973 this had become a small hamlet of sixteen huts.

Arembepe had grown through births and immigration. Outsiders had bought some of the brick houses, mainly in the central square. These vacation homes, though more modest than those in the area where we rented, brought urban visitors into the midst of community life at certain times of year. Three houses now sold rooms and meals to visitors, and several small stores had opened to cater to the tourist industry. Arembepe had expanded not just north and south but in the only other direction possible—west (since the houses on the eastern side are very near the sea). New rows of houses had been built between Arembepe and the lagoon. Several streets perpendicular to the sea led down to the lagoon.

The local population had grown substantially in less than a decade. Compared with 159 houses and 730 people in 1964, Arembepe proper now had about 280 houses and more than 1,000 permanent residents. Add the 44 inhabited houses and 180 people of Caraúnas and the 16 houses and 55 people of Caratingi, for totals of 340 houses and over 1,200 residents in 1973. The population was also much harder to census accurately, since it swelled on weekends, during the dry season and school vacations, and since the immigration rate had increased. Still, Arembepe's 1973 population may have stood *below* its size between 1969 and 1972, when "hundreds of hippies" reportedly rented houses and huts, or camped out on the beach and in the coconut groves north and south of Arembepe, as in neighboring Jauá.

Only a dozen hippies remained in 1973. Arembepeiros distinguished male hippies *(ippis)* from females *(ippas)*. I first met one of them late one morning in a local store. Clad in cut-off shorts, with long hair, he was clearly not a native. I was reminded of the appearance, demeanor, and attire of summer school students I had taught at the University of Michigan. "Hey man," I heard. Lo and behold, he could speak my native language. This *ippi*, Richie from Rhode Island, was a friendly young man who lived a simple life on funds occasionally cabled from home. Like the other hippies, he bathed in the surf, smoked marijuana, and bothered no one.

Besides Richie, Arembepe's 1973 hippies included a young Englishwoman, a few southern Brazilians, and an Argentine couple. The most cosmopolitan of the bunch was the Frenchwoman who had lived with her first husband in Zaire and Madagascar, then in Italy with the father of her son, just before moving to Arembepe. These remnants of the "hippie invasion," villagers assured me, gave no hint of what things had been like at its height, when Janis Joplin, Mick Jagger, and Roman Polanski had visited Arembepe; when people had lain nude, had sex, and smoked marijuana on the beach. (When villagers presented this stereotypical picture of hippie life, they did so with much more amusement and less disapproval than that typically expressed by "mainstream Americans" in the late 1960s and early 1970s.) By 1973, one hippie couple was working at artisanry and seemed integrated into local life. By 1980, a few others had joined them as permanent residents.

Obstacles to Anthropological Objectivity

My eight-year absence had not shut me off totally from Arembepe's notoriety. Friends in Rio and São Paulo had read magazine stories about Arembepe and the hippies, and Bahians had written me about plans to build the factory. However, seeing the changes firsthand was still a shock, and I resented them. I was infuriated by the factory—by its destruction of natural beauty and its threat to Arembepe's existence. I was irritated by the summer people and tourists who, having spent a few months, weeks, or even days in Arembepe, habitually described it to me as if *they* were the experts on local life. I also resented the hippies, although they at least appreciated Arembepe for its beauty, its simplicity, and its isolation—

attributes that had previously made it so special to me. Yet because the hippies were so unlike the old-time Arembepeiros, and so similar to the people I met regularly in my North American university environment, I could view them only as intruders in the tropical paradise I had staked out years earlier. To Arembepe's invasion by outsiders I attributed the villagers' new fears and insecurities, their uncertainty about their future, their experimentation with alien life styles. I was distressed to discover that some of my best friends were being possessed by spirits, joining cults, drinking too much, suffering from poor health, and carrying revolvers.

Anthropologists are trained to be reasonably objective and nonjudgmental in their studies of foreign cultures, but objectivity is difficult. In this case, my own biases against change, my romantic wish to recapture the unaltered past, affected my research in 1973. I did a new village census and map, which allowed me to estimate changes in Arembepe's size, job structure, consumption patterns, and social organization. But I found myself focusing on *familiar features* of local life and avoiding (though not totally ignoring) the new. For example, I examined the kinship composition of households, as I had in the past, to note the main changes. I put Raymond Rapaport, a Michigan undergraduate who had accompanied me as a research assistant, to work studying the fishing industry. Ray kept track of crew composition, catches, marketing, and the newly established fishermen's cooperative. I worked closely with Alberto, whom I hired as my local field assistant, to record births, deaths, and shifts in residence and jobs. I did several interviews with my old informants, usually in my rented summer house. I *drove* to the village, less than a kilometer away, protected by my car from unwanted encounters. I found myself avoiding the central areas where I had spent so much time before. Unlike previous visits, when we had tried to enter every house at least once, I now preferred having informants come to my house instead of going to theirs.

Ray Rapaport suggested that I might want to get to know the hippies better, as he was doing. I should have followed his advice, but in 1973 I never even visited the main hippie settlement on the Caratingi River—"the Aldeia," a fifteen-minute walk north of Arembepe. I let Ray and Alberto do the census there, and I relied mainly on Ray's reports about the hippies.

I now realize that I saw the hippies as rivals. Their youth reminded me of our 1960s field teams. Their quest for the "natural" and the "primitive" was disquietingly familiar to an anthropologist. I felt my own youth and opportunities for adventure slipping away because of my new parental responsibilities and obligations to act like a professor.

Anthropologists are widely thought of as unorthodox investigators of strange places and mysterious people, willing to forgo the comforts of "civilization" for the romance of distant simplicity. Ethnographers are like professional hippies; the hippies were like amateur anthropologists. I wanted the amateur anthropologists to leave Arembepe. I wanted "my village" preserved for the real anthropologists—myself and my field team colleagues. However, realizing that I couldn't have my wish, I avoided the hippies and tried to discount their impact on village life.

I also stayed away from the tourists. It made no difference whether they were urban elite summer-house owners or rude incipient alcoholics spending Sundays in local bars. I concentrated on how the old was changing, and I looked away from what was totally new. The bright spots were the successes of a few of my old friends, such as Tomé, who were making the most of Arembepe's opening to the outside world. It seemed to me that new opportunities might allow a few Arembepeiros to escape from the lower class. On the whole, however, the bad seemed to outweigh the good.

The kinds of people who go into anthropology include many who feel uncomfortable in, or dissatisfied with, their own society, and who therefore seek the alien or the past. The nostalgia for the old Arembepe that I experienced in 1973 grew out of my own impossible wish to rediscover my first "anthropological reality." Arembepe when I first studied it had seemed as different from modern industrial America as any setting I could imagine. It became my ethnographic paradise. My wife and I had met there, had returned many times; it had been "our village." Now we had to share it with many other outsiders. I acted as if, by ignoring them, I might magically get rid of them.

These reactions became apparent to me in 1979 when I

started the first edition of this book. Telling Arembepe's story would require another field trip. Six years had elapsed since 1973, and I wanted to see what had become of the issues that were unsettled before, particularly the pollution problem. My second reason for revisiting Arembepe was just as compelling. I needed to get additional information on areas of village life I had avoided in 1973; hippies, tourism, and the factory. I was ready to deal with those external forces of change more objectively than I had been in 1973.

Chapters 7 through 11 are based mainly on my 1980 trip to Arembepe. (Chapter 12, newly written for the second edition, describes Arembepe in the 1980s, and the new epilogue gives a 1991 update.) Chapters 7 through 11 present an ambivalent, but somewhat more cheerful, portrait of local life than Chapter 6—based on my 1973 stay. By 1980 not only had Arembepe's living standards improved somewhat, there had also been a change in me, the ethnographer. I was less resentful, less personally involved, and able to be less judgmental about a fascinating process of change, which, I realized, could be studied but not stopped.

1980: "The Whole World Is Open to Arembepe"

I suppose that after my depressing 1973 stay, any revisit would have been an improvement. When I returned to Arembepe for about three weeks in August 1980, I was accompanied by an informal field team. Included were two other anthropologists—Dr. Maxine Margolis and Dr. Jerald Milanich—their daughter, Nara; Betty Wagley Kottak, now a practicing social worker; and our two children, Juliet and Nicholas, aged twelve and nine. Although Maxine, Jerry, and Nara stayed only about ten days, it was pleasant and efficient to have several people involved in common inquiry. This reminded me a bit of my early research in Arembepe in 1962 and 1964. Maxine and Betty, both of whom had worked in Brazil previously, helped out with interviewing and other research. Jerry Milanich used his expertise as an archaeologist to map the village, and he used his skills with a camera to take many of the photos included in this book. Juliet, Nicholas, and Nara reported their observations and counted things—including over 300 cars one Sunday afternoon.

My family had spent almost two weeks in Rio before flying up to Bahia. This gave us a chance to get acquainted with national trends before revisiting Arembepe, providing a useful introduction to general changes in Brazil between 1973 and 1980. National forces now affected Arembepe much more than before. Because of the spread of electricity, radio, and television, villagers were much more knowledgeable about national and international events. I could contrast Arembepe's information explosion with 1962, when I had spent evenings—a stranger from a distant land—on the chapel stoop facing endless interrogation about the animals to be found in the United States.

In 1980, as one fisherman remarked, "The whole world is open to Arembepe." Instead of being asked, "Are there elephants in America?" I was told about a fishermen's strike in France and labor unions in Poland. I was asked about the chances and merits of President Carter and Senator Kennedy, who were competing for the 1980 Democratic presidential nomination. Arembepe's participation in the world system was well advanced.

Our stay in Rio had been pleasant, but I had found Brazil less different from the United States than I remembered. Traffic noise and air pollution were horrendous. Consumer products similar to those sold in American stores were everywhere; supermarkets had replaced small stores in many neighborhoods. There were joggers along the beach. Tom and Jerry spoke dubbed Portuguese on Saturday TV. I could even order a *quarterão* (Quarter Pounder) at the Copacabana McDonald's. The impression of a world system eroding cultural differences followed me to Salvador and then to Arembepe, where many roofs now had "fish spines"—television antennas. Arembepe had become part of Marshall McLuhan's world village.

This time, however, I wasn't surprised by the changes I saw on my way out to Arembepe. This was because friends had kept me reasonably up to date, and also because the changes simply continued trends that had been obvious in 1973. The road was better, and there was now a gas station in Portão, just 18 kilometers from Arembepe. I fueled my rented car there on Fridays—since, in the midst of the global energy crisis of 1980, all Brazilian gas stations closed for the weekend. When we reached the Tibrás factory, I was pleased to find that the dunes were now spic and span; there was a neat pile of chartreuse sand inside the factory's fences. Though the factory smokestack still fumed, there was no more Holly-wood-vomit gravy to destroy the beauty of the dunes.

The factory stands on a rise, from which the Atlantic can be glimpsed. On that sunny Wednesday in August 1980, the tropical blue of the ocean was impressive. Still, I wondered about the value of the luxury homes in the new beach-front development due east of the factory. Although lagoon pollu-tion had been stopped, sulfuric acid still poured into the At-lantic, less than 3 kilometers out from those villas.

Pavement now continued on to Arembepe, and beyond. Through joint state-federal financing, an asphalt highway, known as Coconut Road, had been completed as far as 20 kilometers north of Arembepe. Planned as a coastal highway, it was eventually to link Bahia with its northern neighbor, Sergipe.

On the northeastern corner of the asphalted turnoff to Arembepe, on a ridge overlooking the lagoons, stood a new satellite, Volta do Robalo. Volta's growth was the latest mani-festation of the landowning family's lotting scheme; several Arembepeiros had purchased land and built houses there. Volta looked more prosperous than Caraúnas had in 1973; it was attracting wealthier Arembepeiros. Caraúnas, too, which we soon passed on the right, was more attractive. It had doubled in size, to 100 houses—no longer the wattle-and-daub shacks of 1973 but brick structures with tile roofs. Of the four parallel streets in Caraúnas, only the one nearest the lagoon, where the first houses had been built, still had shacks. The most agreeable sight was the lagoon, which had regained its aqua color. Women were washing clothes, as their children bathed, cavorted, and learned to swim.

Just before entering Arembepe, a road sign proclaimed an "urban zone." We had to slow down for raised pavement designed to reduce speeds—as hundreds of automobiles now entered the town each weekend. The road's point of entrance was the same, but there was more pavement. At the entry

The asphalt road, plus electricity, went right into Arembepe by 1980.
(Courtesy Jerald T. Milanich)

point stood a newsstand where nudie and sex magazines were
sold—a local manifestation of Brazil's new *abertura* ("opening"), relaxation of years of censorship by a hard-line military
government.

Arriving around noon, our first need was lunch. We parked
in front of Claudia's Restaurant, where Ray Rapaport, my
research assistant, had boarded in 1973. Our first encounter
with a villager, Claudia's daughter Amy, would have been
more agreeable had we not learned that Claudia and her
husband had both died during the past year. This surprised
us, since Claudia had always been one of Arembepe's most
vigorous people, but neither she nor her husband had lived
past sixty. Inheriting her mother's successful business, Amy
was one of several local women whose status had risen as the
value of local property increased because of greater contact
with the outside world. Women were almost as influential as
men in the store and restaurant business. Some women were
now creating large estates to leave to their children.

There were signs of Arembepe's new sophistication, its
participation in national culture patterns, in Amy's menu. We
had noticed in Rio and Salvador that Brazilian common rum

(cachaça) was enjoying a new popularity as the basis for a series of aperitifs. Arembepe's bartenders knew how to make those drinks, along with others using Bacardi rum, whisky, vodka, and gin. In a village where liquor had once been reserved for alcoholics and festive occasions, bars now stocked Old Eight whisky, Dreher's cognac, and especially cold beer, the favorite drink of weekend visitors. The cost of eating and drinking in Arembepe was now within the range of city prices.

Arembepe in 1980 looked larger and cleaner than my memory of it in 1973. But my overall impression of Arembepe, and of the Salvador area generally, was that change was less noticeable than before. Perhaps this reflects the erosion of cultural differences mentioned previously. However, I believe that the outline of change had already been set in 1973; in 1980 (and continuing through the 1980s), it was simply being filled in. A profusion of bars, restaurants, and rooming houses gave testimony to tourism's growing role in the local economy. The factory managers lunching at Claudia's Restaurant suggested Tibrás's new concern with its image and with the welfare of its neighbors. From Claudia's seaview window I could see the new, larger motorboats that now typified Arembepe's fishing fleet. During August 1980 I noted many other signs of a new, diversified economy and of related social changes. These included the emergence of socioeconomic classes, new religious phenomena, and previously unknown forms of social deviance.

Although the world system has a growing influence on villages in all nations, few communities (in or out of Brazil) have experienced as many changes, occurring as quickly, as Arembepe has. This is what makes Arembepe so special and so worthy of anthropological study. Without even planning it at first, I have been able to observe a process of sociocultural microevolution that parallels changes that, from the archaeological record, took thousands of years to unfold for the first time. In barely twenty years Arembepe moved from a relatively isolated, egalitarian, and homogeneous community to one with occupational diversity, religious differences, high- and low-status neighborhoods, and social classes. In the ancient Middle East, once the economy shifted from hunting and gathering to plant cultivation and stockbreeding, it took 4,000 years for social stratification to develop. Major economic change and an analogous social transformation took place in Arembepe in less than two decades. Arembepe's experience also offers a speeded-up picture of the local-level effects of the "modernization" that is affecting thousands of small communities now being drawn into the world system.

However, before Arembepe's transformation can be described and understood, we must go back to a beginning. We start by considering the customary patterns of Arembepeiro thought and behavior that had managed to survive into the 1960s, for me to witness as the "before" picture in this chronicle of change.

Part Two
Paradise

3 The Structure of Equality

Because of its relatively simple economy and social structure, Arembepe of the 1960s had differed from other Brazilian communities that ethnographers had studied. With a few exceptions (e.g., Johnson, 1971), anthropologists had studied Brazilian communities (usually county seats) with social class divisions. Arembepe, by contrast, had lacked class-based contrasts in wealth, occupation, education, and political power. It had been a lower-class community, with few insurmountable obstacles to achieving success locally, but with many barriers to rising out of the national lower class.

A villager's lower-class identity became particularly obvious when he or she left the community and met, most often in Salvador, members of the middle or upper class. Manners, dress, and speech provided cues that the urban elites use to identify lower-class people. Arembepeiros in the city faced discrimination as poor, powerless, "uneducated" people, and as "country bumpkins."

Within Arembepe the differences in income, inherited wealth, and life style were minuscule compared with the contrasts existing in Brazil as a whole. The local ladder of success had closely spaced rungs, and anyone could climb it. Arembepe contrasted with class-stratified towns, in which inherited wealth gives some people a headstart in economic opportunities and social status. The wealth differences that did exist in Arembepe placed its residents in a graded hierarchy, not a stratified one. That is, there were no sharp differences between a poor and a rich group.

Thus, the data on 1964 household budgets (roughly equal to annual income—see Appendix 1) show a gradual increase from poorest to wealthiest household, with no large gaps. The largest budget reflects an income worth about $1,000 in

1964—far less than Brazilian middle-class households earned. In other words, Arembepe of the 1960s had a social hierarchy but no social classes. In anthropological parlance, its social system was ranked, not stratified.

The village lacked greater socioeconomic contrasts than these because, ever since its founding, it had been cut off from external resources that might have brought greater wealth and power to (some of) its people. The people of Arembepe were poor because of their circumstances, not because they lacked ambition. Many villagers were very ambitious, contradicting the assumptions of those "experts" on Third World economic development who attribute poverty and "backwardness" to such factors as "low achievement motivation" or "inappropriate values."

All successful Arembepeiros were self-made entrepreneurs. Achievement in this small fishing village required exactly those personality traits that the sociologist Max Weber, in his famous book, *The Protestant Ethic and the Spirit of Capitalism* (1958), attributed to the first capitalists. Weber argued that the rise of Protestantism in Europe fostered capitalism by teaching such values as profit making, hard work, rational planning, willingness to take calculated risks, simple tastes, an ascetic life style, stability, trustworthiness, and sobriety. In Weber's view, early Protestantism, by seeing business success as a sign of divine favor, also promoted individualism—since the individual, not the household or family, would be eternally graced or damned.

Appropriate values existed in Arembepe, but economic advance by its people was limited by a combination of meager resources and social factors, known as leveling mechanisms, which kept ambitious villagers "in their place." *Leveling mechanisms* are devices that discourage people from surpassing their peers—punishing those who do, pushing them back to the common level.

Such mechanisms, according to Weber, also existed in European peasant communities before the rise of capitalism. Weber argued that peasant values (shared, he said, with the Catholic church) resisted the rise of capitalism and Protestantism. Peasants, said Weber, worked just hard enough to satisfy their immediate needs. Then they quit, mistrusting people who needlessly worked more than others. The individualism associated with Protestantism and capitalism had to surmount the collectivism of the peasant community, in which gossip and other social pressures brought deviants (including overachievers) back in line.

Anthropologist George Foster's (1965) discussion of peasants recalls Weber's description of Europe before the rise of Protestantism and capitalism. Foster notes the importance of leveling mechanisms in "classic" peasant societies throughout the world. Both Weber's and Foster's analyses apply to Arembepe, though its people were fishermen, not peasant farmers. Foster argues that peasants throughout the world share an "image of limited good," according to which all valued things are finite. Peasants regard the total amount of health, wealth, honor, or success available to community members as limited. One person can excel only at the expense of others. Unless good fortune clearly comes from outside (for example, external wage work or a lottery) and unless the fruits of success are shared with others, successful people face ostracizing techniques (leveling mechanisms). These include gossip, avoidance, insults, and physical attack.

Although it had neither peasants nor Protestants, Arembepe did have a unique mix of community collectivism, the image of limited good, and Protestant-capitalist-individualist values. This value set had emerged without religious support. Although, through baptism, all villagers were nominal Catholics, organized religion played a small role in local life. The people of Arembepe were not the devout Catholics of Mediterranean or east European peasant communities. A priest visited the village twice a year, but only women and children attended the services. "The church is a place for women," said one fisherman. "They're the ones who hold the prayer meetings and cut flowers for the saints." (The "saints" are household figurines.) Men had their doubts about priestly sanctity, particularly the ability of priests to stick to their vow of celibacy.

Arembepe's values were influenced by contacts with nearby farming villages, but they were especially molded by the attitudes and character traits evoked by the fishing economy. Like the hunting-gathering economies that existed everywhere until about 10,000 years ago, fishing is a form of foraging, rather than food production. Like other hunter-gatherers, fishermen live off nature's bounty, rather than planting, tending, and harvesting crops, or stockbreeding animals. Food production is usually more certain than foraging is. Crop yields are more predictable and more subject to human control than is a fish supply. Farmers follow a calendar of cultivation and can usually count on a harvest. Similarly, herders lead their animals through a well-trodden annual trek, as they follow seasonally available pasture.

Fishing is chancier. Seasonal fish runs are larger some years than others. Some days, fishing at a given spot at sea is productive; others, it isn't. "Sometimes the fish get smart and move away. Or they hide in the rocks. Fishing isn't a profession you can count on; everything depends on your luck," remarked Alberto, the fisherman who became my best informant, as we rocked up and down on the Atlantic one day in July 1964, waiting for the first bite.

Fishing calls for less routine and more innovation than food production does. If all fishermen have access to the same technology and territory, as was true in Arembepe, larger catches depend most clearly on harder work. Over time, the crew that works more hours can be expected to catch more fish. Arembepe's captains also pursued varied strategies, some with more payoff than others. Most successful were those who innovated. Such captains tried out new technology, looked for new fishing grounds, and sailed to familiar fishing spots out of season. They carefully evaluated costs and benefits and took calculated risks.

I had trouble getting Tomé, the most successful captain, to agree on a day to take me out fishing. "There's always the chance I'll decide to sail up to Guarajuba [15 kilometers away] to look for guaraçaim [Caranx latus], and I may fish there through the night." Tomé was afraid I might not tolerate a trip lasting longer than the usual eight to ten hours. His practice was to see where the other boats were going, then to try his luck in less-fished, usually more distant, areas, and to fish longer hours. His reward was Arembepe's largest income based on fishing.

Entrepreneurial activity (experimentation, risk taking, and innovation) was the key to productive fishing and to general economic success in Arembepe in the 1960s. The inflation that has continued to plague Brazil was severe during the early 1960s[1]; to have hoarded profits then would have been a recipe for economic disaster. Local entrepreneurs were willing to experiment with many options for reinvesting profits. They put their money in land, coconut trees, boats, new fishing equipment, and consumer goods. Because of inflation, the entrepreneurial behavior and values that were favored on the open sea found reinforcement on the land.

During the 1960s people with intelligence, ambition, and business sense could move from the very bottom to the very top of the local economic hierarchy. To rise further, to succeed in the outside world, was exceedingly difficult. The wealth generated in Arembepe was too meager to propel any native son or daughter into the national middle class. Limited educational opportunities formed another barrier. Only by studying outside could local kids hope to qualify for the greater incomes offered, for example, by Petrobrás, the national oil monopoly. Only a few natives managed to obtain such schooling and such jobs.

The other prominent dimension of Arembepe's value system (community collectivism and leveling mechanisms) acted as a brake on individual economic advance. As wealth grew, so did the obligation to share it. Villagers respected their obligations because no one could be sure that, given old age or infirmity, he or she might not have to depend on others. No pensions or social security benefits were available to lower-class rural fishermen in Brazil in the 1960s. Kinship and community formed Arembepe's only social security system.

An Open, Noncorporate Community

Although the scale of Arembepe's confrontation with the outside world has increased dramatically since 1965, the village had never been truly isolated from external forces. Despite its egalitarian values and unstratified social structure, Arembepe has always been an "open, noncorporate community." This is one of two basic types of Latin American peasant communities identified by Eric Wolf (1955). Arembepe had all the defining features of the open community. These include production for both cash and subsistence, reliance on external supplies, and participation in national culture through the national language. For decades the people of Arembepe have sold some of their fish to outsiders. At first the buyers were small-scale mule drivers who bought fish to resell, mainly in towns nearer Salvador. By the early 1960s buyers were arriving by jeep from Salvador and its suburbs. Coconuts, Arembepe's only other important export item, also went to market in Salvador.

Arembepeiros have long depended on items produced outside the village. Most of the boats in the fishing fleet in the 1960s had been made elsewhere; only one local man still knew how to make a sailboat from scratch. Still, fishing did not yet rely on motors and fossil fuels. The fishermen of Arembepe therefore lacked the concern with costs, supplies, and repairs that accompany such dependence. Villagers bought kerosene, rice, sugar, beans, coffee, lard, matches, soft drinks, beer, rum, and soap from local storekeepers. Arembepe had twelve small stores in 1964, one for every 60 of the village's 730 inhabitants. Three of these did much more business than the others did.

The ties with the external world were mainly economic. Some people had left to study or work outside. A few men were fishing on commercial trawlers out of Salvador, Rio de Janeiro, and other major ports. Some native women worked as domestics in Salvador. A few others had studied *candomblé*, an Afro-Brazilian spirit-possession cult, at a temple in the capital. The family that owned the land on which Arembepe stands all lived outside. Except for one well-educated landowner, who was planning the subdivision of his family's estate, the sale of lots, and Arembepe's development as a resort, the landlords rarely visited the village. They had little to do with life there. Their local representative was Prudencio, an elderly man who collected the nominal rents that villagers paid for their house sites. These rents, worth between $.50 and $1.00 per year in 1964, had been legally set at a higher amount, then eroded by inflation. Prudencio also granted requests to build new houses, and he oversaw the marketing of the produce of the landowners' 5,600 coconut trees.

One fishing captain summed up the role of the landlords and their agent in local life: "Prudencio's the closest thing we have to a chief *(chefe)* here. But that's because he stands in for the landlords. They don't bother us much. They're mainly interested in their coconuts."

Despite Arembepe's economic orientation to the outside world, its people had been shielded from the power relationships that are routinely experienced by most lower-class Brazilians. The poor, seasonally impassable, road limited contacts with Salvador. People had to walk 19 kilometers to catch a bus to the city; the round trip took two days. There had been little in Arembepe's economy or placement to attract powerful outsiders. The estate of land and coconut trees on which the village is located couldn't even support the middle-class life style of the landowners, and the last one had left Arembepe in 1925. All her heirs had urban careers; they rarely visited Arembepe. During the 1960s, one of them, Jorge Camões, the first member of his family with a university education, planned Arembepe's development for tourism. Jorge's knowledge, business skills, political clout, and position in the state division of the national highway agency combined to promote Arembepe's coming encounter with economic development and the world system.

Previously, Arembepe's location—its shielding by sand, lagoons, and ocean—and its limited resources had kept it from being a center of anything. The land's productivity is low. "Nothing grows here. Not even watermelon and peanuts." People got their produce from small farms to the west, but sandy soils reduced the farming potential there, too. Throughout the municipality (county) of Camaçari during the 1960s the main economic activities were charcoal extraction, small-scale cultivation, and coconut production. Arembepe's land is suited only for the last. Its export products were fish, coconuts, and straw hats made by local women. Coconuts brought villagers, including the landowners, a total income of just $5,000 annually. The cash receipts from the entire straw hat industry didn't exceed $50 per year. Fish catches were limited by simple technology—sailboats with small crews doing day-long hook-and-line fishing. Until tourism became practicable in 1970, Arembepe had little to offer outside investors.

Like its economy, Arembepe's political structure was also simple. The village has never been the seat of a municipality, or even of a rural "district." Arembepe's official classification

was "hamlet," within one of the six districts of its municipality, with Abrantes, on the road to Salvador, as its district seat.
Arembepe lacked the roster of tax collector, justice of the
peace, statistical agent, postal official, and other government
workers who are present in even district seats. Government
jobs would have brought greater wealth contrasts into Arembepe and might have threatened the graded hierarchy.
"Abrantes has a few people who are well-off because they
managed to get jobs as civil servants, but there's no one like
that here. All we've got is fishermen and storekeepers." Civil
service positions also would have brought "the government"—with its contrasts in power and authority—right into
Arembepe. But this had never happened.

Arembepe had surprisingly few political figures for a community in a large and populous country. Besides the landlords' caretaker, there was a municipally appointed policeman (subdelegado). He drew a small salary and was afraid to
use the revolver the county had provided. No arrests were
ever made; the jail stood empty, except occasional visitors
who were allowed to sleep there. The policeman's father was
the only villager with a federal position. Long a successful
captain, this old man had become port captain, in theory
overseeing fishing operations between Itapoan, to the south,
and Praia do Forte, to the north. He was supposed to grant
fishing permits to fishermen in this area, but few of them had
such licenses.

The port captain explained: "It's hard for Arembepeiros to
get to Salvador for the papers they need for fishing licenses.
Most fishermen can't even read. Anyway, why do they need
licenses when no one ever comes here to check." No one
replaced this man when he retired, and he continued his
duties informally until his death in 1973, while receiving the
only federal pension in Arembepe.

The roster of local leadership ended with the officers of the
Fishermen's Society and of the Saint Francis Soccer Club. The
soccer club included fishermen, plus native sons employed
outside who came on weekends to play against other communities. Tomé, the most successful fisherman, was the soccer
captain. The Fishermen's Society organized the annual festivals held for Arembepe's patron saint, Saint Francis (Febru-

ary 20), and for Saint John (June 24). The top officer was the treasurer. Normally, the captain-owner with the year's largest catch was elected treasurer, as Tomé was in 1965.

Very little that was collective, communal, governmental, or even political could be detected in Arembepe. The village also differed from the typical rural Brazilian community as described by Charles Wagley (1963, p. 148), in that it was not an urban nucleus for surrounding rural neighborhoods. Arembepe had only one satellite, Big Well, with eight houses. Residents of two agricultural estates a few kilometers to the west, Açu and Coqueiros, came to Arembepe to buy fish and to sell produce. Many of the coconut trees owned in 1964 by 42 percent of Arembepe's adults were in Açu and Coqueiros, and twenty Arembepeiros rented small farms there. Their crops supplemented their incomes and diets from fishing or business.

Many villagers had been born on the western estates. After gaining their freedom in 1889, the slaves whose descendants made up most of Arembepe's 1960s population initially took up subsistence farming on these estates. Their children and grandchildren gradually left farming for seasonal, and then year-round, fishing in Arembepe.

"I remember one of my grandmothers who had been a slave," recounted Alberto. "Once she was freed she moved to Açu and took up with my grandfather. They farmed for a while; then he started fishing. Eventually they moved to Arembepe, and he became a full-time fisherman."

Arembepe's insulation from power wielders was also a result of the split between its economic orientation (toward Salvador) and its political orientation (toward Camaçari). Salvador has traditionally drained Camaçari, like Arembepe, of landowners, rural elites, and local people with middle-class aspirations (Gross, 1964). Camaçari's orientation toward the capital, instead of its own hinterland, was another reason for Arembepe's insulation from power. Because the village got its cash from one place and its political orders from another, economic and political influence did not reinforce one another. Officials in Camaçari lacked control over the marketing of fish and coconuts and could do Arembepeiros no economic harm.

The Costs and Benefits of Kinship

Several factors thus combined to shield Arembepe from the Brazilian power structure. This is why—despite the village's economic dependence on the outside and its inclusion in a nation-state—its social relations were similar to the egalitarian, kin-based societies that anthropologists have studied in many parts of the world. With no major economic gaps or marked contrasts in power dividing the people of Arembepe, they kept up the fiction that they were all relatives. The twin assertions "We're all equal here" and "We're all relatives here" were offered repeatedly as Arembepeiros' own summaries of the nature and basis of local life. Like members of a clan (who claim to share common ancestry, but who can't say exactly how they are related), most villagers couldn't trace precise genealogical links to their distant kin. "What difference does it make—as long as we know we're relatives?"

As in most nonindustrial societies, close personal relations were either based or modeled on kinship and marriage. A degree of community solidarity was promoted, for example, by the myth that everyone was kin. It's important to point out, however, that social solidarity was actually much *less* developed in Arembepe than in societies with clans and lineages— which use genealogy to include some people, and *exclude* others, from membership in a given descent group. Intense social solidarity demands that some people be excluded. By asserting that they all were related—that is, by excluding no one—Arembepeiros were actually weakening kinship's potential strength in creating and maintaining group solidarity.

Villagers were only half-serious when they claimed that everyone was related. This was clear from their other statements about kinship. Like lower-class Brazilians generally, the people of Arembepe calculated kinship more narrowly than do members of the middle or upper class, who, according to Wagley (1963, pp. 196–198), recognize kinship with hundreds of people. Despite this, kinship reckoning in Arembepe was more inclusive than that of typical middle-class Americans. For example, Arembepeiros normally called the first cousins of their parents "uncle" and "aunt," and the children of their own first cousins "nephew" and "niece."

Kinship calculation broke down with more remote relatives. Distant cousins were called either "third cousin" or "distant cousin"; this wasn't a close relationship. Villagers didn't share the anthropologist's delight in tracing genealogies and kin links. I exasperated Alberto with my questions about specific kin links among fishermen. "It doesn't mean anything if people in the same crews happen to be third cousins. Only closer relatives fish together because they're related."

Nor did villagers trace kinship very far back. Rarely did they recall the names of their great-grandparents, and then only of the ones they had known. Last names were used infrequently. Most people were known (sometimes only) by nicknames derived from, say, a physical attribute ("Little Black José"), a characteristic ability ("Breaks Coconuts with His Feet," "Farts When He Sneezes"), or place of origin ("Sergipe," a nearby state). Few villagers knew the full names of even their close kin. This was another sign of insulation from the national power structure. Full names are used in legal contexts that the people of Arembepe generally avoided.

Besides the rights and obligations based on kinship, Arembepeiros acquired others through marriage. Couples could be "married" formally or informally. The most common union (40 percent of the couples in 1964) was a stable common-law marriage. Less common (28 percent), but with more prestige, was legal (civil) marriage, performed by a justice of the peace and conferring inheritance rights. Half the estate went to the surviving spouse, the other half to the children. The union with the most prestige (10 percent of the marriages) combined legal validity with a church ceremony. A few people (8 percent) had been married in a religious service only. A civil marriage was for life, and Arembepeiros used the multiple marriage types to cope with the difficulty of getting divorced in Brazil.

"I lived with one woman for a few years," recounted a retired fisherman. "I got tired of her and left her for another one I liked better. But I still wasn't ready for a legal marriage, so we just had a church ceremony. Later, after leaving her and taking up with my wife, I finally decided I was ready for the civil."

A surplus of women (54 percent) between the ages of sixteen and forty-nine was one reason some women lacked coresident mates. There were eight visiting unions, in which the "husband" simultaneously had another, principal wife. For the men, the visiting union was secondary, but some of those unions lasted several years. The women involved in them were severely stigmatized—labeled *rapariga* (village prostitute). "Those are the good-for-nothing females who live off other women's husbands" was one elderly woman's summary of a common local opinion.

There was a quantum leap in the rights and obligations that went with legal, compared with common-law, unions, even stable ones. Common-law spouses had no right to inherit. Neither did children, unless they had been registered in the parent's name. Only legal marriage created an in-law relationship. A man who married in a civil ceremony agreed to share not just with his wife and kids but also with his wife's parents and siblings if necessary. By contrast, men in common-law unions denied that they had "parents-in-law" or "siblings-in-law."

The rights and obligations associated with kinship and marriage comprised the local social security system, but people had to weigh the benefits of the system against its costs. The most obvious cost was this: Villagers had to share in proportion to their success. As ambitious men climbed the local ladder of success, they got more dependents. To maintain their standing in public opinion, and to guarantee that they could depend on others in old age, they had to share. However, sharing was a powerful leveling mechanism. It drained surplus wealth and restricted upward mobility. The correlation between wealth and obligations was one of the main reasons why Arembepe remained an unstratified, lower-class community.

How, specifically, did this leveling work? As is often true in stratified nations, Brazilian national cultural norms are set by the upper classes. Middle- and upper-class Brazilians usually marry legally and in the church. Even Arembepeiros knew that this was the only "proper" way to marry. The most ambitious local men—usually also the most successful—copied the behavior of elite Brazilians. By doing so, they hoped to acquire some of their prestige (see Kottak, 1966, p. 101).

However, legal marriage drained individual wealth, for example, by creating a responsibility to support in-laws. Such obligations could be regular and costly. Obligations to kids also increased with income, because successful people tended to have more living children. During the 1960s—and even in 1973—villagers used no birth control. Only a few women induced abortions. These were dangerous, and, besides, children were valued as companions, and as an eventual economic benefit to their parents. Boys especially were prized because their economic prospects were so much brighter than those of girls.

The average married woman in 1964 had given birth to 5.6 live children, of whom only 3.2 survived—just 57 percent. Infant and child mortality was the main check on population growth. Children's chances of survival surged dramatically in wealthier households with better diets. The normal household diet included fish—usually in a stew with tomatoes, onions, palm oil, vinegar, and lemon. Dried beef replaced fish once a week. Sawdust-like roasted manioc flour (*farinha*) was the main source of calories and was eaten at all meals. Other daily staples included coffee, sugar, and salt. Bananas, mangoes, and other fruits and vegetables were eaten in season. Diet was one of the main contrasts between households. The poorest people didn't eat fish regularly; often they subsisted on manioc flour, coffee, and sugar. Only the wealthiest people could afford the rice and beans that middle- and upper-class Brazilians view as the basis of "the Brazilian diet." Better-off households supplemented the staples with milk, butter, eggs, rice, beans, and more ample portions of fresh fish, fruits, and vegetables.

Children's distended bellies and reddish hair were among the clinical signs of malnutrition and intestinal parasites. The poorer kids were especially prone to infectious diseases, the main cause of death among them. Malnutrition also affected fetuses; most women had suffered a miscarriage or stillbirth. Like other fishermen, Alberto and his wife Carolina had lost children to malnutrition and disease, but their losses (10 out of 13) were extreme.

I witnessed an especially painful one. In June 1964 Alberto asked me to drive him and his severely ill two-and-a-half-year-old son to a doctor in Itapoan. The boy was vomiting, after several days of diarrhea. He was running a fever and had been unable to sleep. The child's nonstop screams unnerved me during our long drive over the muddy road to Itapoan. We arrived to find that the doctor hadn't been seen that day. The pharmacist prescribed medication, telling Alberto that the doctor always used those pills for the boy's symptoms. I tried to persuade Alberto that we should drive on to a clinic in Salvador, but he refused. I still regret not pushing harder. The boy slept most of the way back to Arembepe, but he died that night, and Alberto, whose surplus cash had gone for the medicine, accepted my offer of a few dollars to help pay for a bare cardboard coffin.

Adequate incomes bought improved diets and provided the means and confidence to seek out better medical attention than was locally available. Most of the kids born in the wealthier households survived. But this meant more mouths to feed, and (since the heads of such households usually wanted a better education for their children) it meant increased expenditures on outside schooling. The correlation between economic success and large families (without birth control) was another siphoner of wealth that braked individual economic advance. Tomé, a fishing entrepreneur, envisioned a life of constant hard work if he was to feed, clothe, and educate his growing family. With an income three times that of Alberto, Tomé and his wife had never lost a child. But he recognized that his growing family would, in the short run, be a drain on his resources. "But in the end, I'll have successful sons to help their mother and me, if we need it, in our old age."

Arembepeiros knew who could afford to share with others; success can't be concealed in a small community. Villagers based their expectations of others on this knowledge. Successful people had to share with more kin and in-laws, and with more distant kin, than did poorer people. Successful captains and boat owners were expected to buy beer for ordinary fishermen; storeowners had to sell on credit. Any well-off person was expected to exhibit a corresponding generosity. With increasing wealth, people were also more frequently asked to enter ritual kin relationships. Through baptism— which took place twice a year when a priest visited, or which could be done outside—a child acquired two godparents.

These became the coparents *(compadres)* of the baby's parents.

Unlike other parts of Latin America, where the coparent relationship is more important than godparenthood per se (Mintz and Wolf, 1950), the two relationships were equally important in Arembepe. Children asked their godparents for a blessing the first time they saw them each day. Godparents occasionally gave cookies, candy, and money, and larger presents on special occasions. Later in life one could acquire another godparent (just one) by being confirmed by a bishop. Through formal marriage, a couple could acquire four more godparents, couples chosen respectively by the bride and groom.

For ritual kinship we reach the same conclusion as for kinship and marriage: ritual kinship obligations increased with wealth, and this limited individual economic advance. Thus kinship, marriage, and ritual kinship, as they operated in Arembepe in the 1960s, had costs and benefits. The costs were limits on the economic advance of individuals. The primary benefit was social security—guaranteed help from kin, in-laws, and ritual kin in times of need. Benefits, however, came only after costs had been paid—that is, only to those who had lived "proper" lives, not deviating too noticeably from local norms.

Gender Issues: Machismo and Male-Female Inequality

We have seen that the main requirements for success during the 1960s were ambition, hard work, and good business and investment strategy. Another must be added: being male. It is no exaggeration to say that almost all the wealth held by Arembepeiros in 1965—through inheritance or income—had been created, ultimately, by the entrepreneurial activity of some male. I divided the village population into three groups (primary producers, secondary producers, and dependents), based on their contributions to the household's cash income and food supply. Most of the primary producers were men. The secondary producers included a few men, about half the women, and a few teen-age boys. The dependent population included half the women and most of the children.

The cash-earning options for women were limited. The manufacture of straw hats from palm fibers generated a *total* of about $50 annually. A few women were the sole owners of successful stores. Others ran businesses or did some farming with their husbands, sometimes as equal partners. Ten married women functioned as co–household heads—making major economic decisions and planning their children's lives.

The behavior of these women stood out as unusual only because of the general pattern of male dominance. Of Arembepe's 159 household heads, for example, 83 percent were males. Reflecting men's easier access to wealth were household incomes and budgets. In a sample of 118 household budgets for 1964 (Appendix 1), the female-headed households ranked at the bottom: 118, 116–111, 108, 103, 101, 97, and 67. None of the households headed by women was in the wealthier half. Their average annual expenditures were equivalent to $109, compared to $314 for the male-headed households.

There is more to the story. Only two of the twenty-eight female-headed households were self-sufficient. One was headed by an unmarried storekeeper, the other by a woman who had inherited coconut trees. Four other women depended on partial support from other households, and the remaining twenty-two relied on other households for most of their support. Eight of these twenty-two were the secondary wives of polygynous males, and their economic situation was most precarious.

The prevailing morality viewed polygyny as improper, and secondary wives were often scorned as village prostitutes. (See Dora's case in Chapter 11.) Typically, the main wife and her relatives enlisted community pressure to end the husband's philandering. When a secondary union broke up, the woman had to rely on her kin until she managed to attract another man. Arembepe had a group of such women—seen as deviants, as the lowest of the low—who were forced into a succession of unions and breakups. The woman's need to support her children left her with few options but to continue the pattern, and, without contraception, her responsibilities grew as new children were born.

A pathetic aspect of daily life during the 1960s was the sight of children from female-headed households on the beach, meeting the fishing boats as they returned in the early evening. Dora, our cook in 1962, customarily sent her oldest son each afternoon to wander from boat to boat seeking a piece of fish for their dinner. The four-year-old boy, who suffered from a congenital heart defect that killed him at age thirteen, was often successful with one of his mother's brothers, a captain. If not, he went to other maternal relatives, since his father lived in distant Camaçari, the county seat. When the boy tired, which he did easily because of the heart condition, he would squat until his energy returned for another try at getting a fisherman's attention. One vivid memory from my early years in Arembepe involves this boy's panting and squatting on the beach, and the joy on his face when he was successful in his quest for fish.

Illegitimate boys sometimes got their fathers to recognize them with a fish. Or else they went from boat to boat, relying on other kin connections, a good day's fishing, or a fisherman's pity to cut the monotony of a diet otherwise limited to manioc flour, coffee, and sugar. Although there was no formal enforcement of the restriction, the beach was off-limits to "proper" women; so women had to send their children to beg. The psychological results of asking for food and for recognition of kinship—and of being rejected, particularly by fathers—have been varied. Some children have grown up to be alcoholics. Others, determined never to relive such childhood experiences, have developed tremendous ambition.

"The thing I hated most during my childhood," said Arembepe's most successful businessman, "was having to beg on the beach. My father was married to another woman, and he was stingy with my mother. Then she took up with another man and my brother was born. After that man left her, it was my job to get fish for them both. I'll make sure my sons never have to beg."

Although Arembepeiros asserted their mutual kinship, the village lacked the clans and lineages of many nonindustrial societies. It also lacked the formal patrilineal or matrilineal rules that determine descent-group membership in such societies. In theory, the kinship system stressed neither the father's nor the mother's side but viewed them as equal. In fact, and reflecting another aspect of local male dominance, kin links through males were more important. One reason for this was a long-term pattern of greater female migration to Arembepe. About 60 percent of the migrants to the village in 1964 were females. Most of these were between the ages of sixteen and forty-nine, the only age group in which females outnumbered males (54 percent to 46 percent). The pattern was for immigrant women—mostly from nearby agricultural estates—to seek husbands in Arembepe. As a result, 42 percent of all wives had been born outside the village, compared with 31 percent of the husbands.

The people of Arembepe have always distinguished between natives and outsiders. This was not a very significant contrast in the 1960s, since two-thirds of the population had at least one parent who had been born outside, and since only a third of the marriages involved two natives. Males and females used different strategies to enter local society. Women often came to visit relatives and stayed on. Men, too, might come because of a kin link. They might take up residence near a relative or friend, perhaps someone who farmed near the immigrant's home. Men who wanted to settle tried to find positions in boat crews. Usually they started fishing with the less successful captains, eventually asking to fish temporarily with other crews when their regular captains missed fishing because of drunkenness or laziness. As an immigrant's reputation for reliability grew he could graduate to a good boat. Some immigrants became well-to-do captains and boat owners.

Male immigrants had many more opportunities than women did to join in community life. They could meet other fishermen on the beach, bathe with other men in the lagoon, and congregate in bars and on the chapel stoop, where most of the fishermen gathered for conversation each evening. Following a general Mediterranean and Latin American pattern, men's access to public space was much wider than women's (cf. Harding, 1975; Reiter, 1975). Adult women left home to wash, fetch water, bathe, shop, or visit neighbors and kin, but women usually met in smaller groups and spent more time indoors.

To stay in Arembepe, an immigrant woman needed to find a husband. Even then, such a woman's position was more precarious than that of a native woman. Without local kin, the

Two residents of Arembepe's northern rectangle, 1964. (Conrad P. Kottak)

migrant faced destitution if her husband deserted her. Without her family close by to offer at least moral support, the immigrant wife often had to tolerate more abusive treatment than a wife born in Arembepe did. The children of a migrant weren't as familiar with their outside kin as they were with the native parent's family. This was the main reason that kin links through males showed up more often in local life—for example, among members of a boat crew.

Thus, the contrasting opportunities of men and women showed up in the economy, in access to public space, and in networks of kin-based support. They also showed up in political life. Arembepe had few authority positions, and men held them all. Most household heads and all boat captains were males. These were just some of many manifestations of the lower value that villagers assigned to females. Parents valued boys more than girls; unhappy was the man who hadn't sired a *macho*. Boys got better food and better treatment than girls did. Discrimination against girls showed up in childhood mortality. More often neglected, girls were less likely to survive than boys were. In 1964 there were 113 boys for every 100 girls aged ten and under. No one admitted that this neglect

The chapel and the eastern part of Arembepe's central square, looking north, in 1963. Most village men are out fishing and the women are busy with chores at home or washing in the lagoon. (Courtesy Niles Eldredge)

was really covert female infanticide, one expression of an economic devaluation of females that ramified through the local social system and ideology. Villagers did recognize that boys got better care than girls did. "Boys need to eat more if they're to grow up strong."

From infancy, male freedom was encouraged; girls were fettered. Girls wore dresses from their third month of life, but boys could walk around naked until near adolescence. During a baby boy's first year, mothers commented on, fondled, and kissed his genitals. Fathers publicly grabbed the penises of older boys, stimulating them to erection, laughing at the child's reaction. Boys were encouraged to masturbate, to engage in homosexual play, and to have sexual relations with willing girls and women, and with livestock. Beginning with chickens, they might move their way up the food chain (as it were)—through turkeys and sheep, perhaps even to cows and mares.

The freedom and sexuality of maleness contrasted with the confinement of female sexuality. Arembepeiros saw virginity as a commodity. They believed that girls had to be virgins if they hoped to marry legally. In 1965 two women had pre-served their virginity until their late twenties. One eventually realized her long-term plan to marry a successful man from outside and to move closer to the city. Only as a virgin, villag-ers supposed, could a local woman make such a match. Legal marriage meant proposal, formal engagement, and a long courting period. Common-law couples, by contrast, eloped, usually after sex on the beach or in the bush. Arembepeiros viewed virginity as a commodity that could be exchanged for the inheritance rights that came from legal marriage. Except for women with inherited estates, virginity was just about all that local women thought they had to offer a prospective husband.

Race Relations

Although gender roles were unequal, the general community pattern of egalitarianism did extend to race relations. Despite marked phenotypical (physical) variation in the population, all villagers had some slave ancestry. Most would have been considered "black" (African-American) in the United States. To study "race relations" in Arembepe, I had to work out (for reasons that will become obvious) a (five-part) scale to mea-sure racial variation. By my scale, only 5 percent of the popu-lation was either "white" (3 percent) or "black" (2 percent). Most (45 percent) were intermediate *(mulato)*. The others were either dark *mulato* (24 percent), or light *mulato* (26 percent). This scheme was my simplification, for statistical analysis, of Arembepe's far more varied and detailed treat-ment of racial variation.

Previous studies in Brazil had clarified certain important contrasts between race relations there and in the United States. The main difference is that the United States has a dual system of stratification, in which both "race" and class divide the population. In Brazil there is a single stratified order in which race, or phenotype, is simply one factor in determining a person's class affiliation. Other determinants are education, wealth, job, and family connections.

A second basic contrast is the rule of hypodescent, which has operated in the United States to assign—unambiguously

These teenagers illustrate the range of physical variation in Arembepe's mid-1960s population. (Conrad P. Kottak)

and for life—anyone with any "black" ancestry to membership in that group (the socioeconomically disadvantaged group, or lower category in the stratified order). Brazil has no such rule. My 1962 research (Harris and Kottak, 1963) showed that even full siblings could belong to different races—an impossibility if a descent rule operates.

A third contrast is that Brazilians use many more terms than Americans do to deal with racial differences. The people of Arembepe shared with other Brazilians an extensive vocabulary of terms to describe phenotypical differences among people. In answering my questions about someone's race *(qualidade)*, they paid attention not simply to skin color—which North Americans focus on by using such terms as "black" and "white"—but also to nose length and form, lip thickness, eye color and shape, hair type and color, and other traits. Just by asking 100 villagers the race of drawings of nine phenotypically contrasting individuals, I found that they used more than forty racial terms. My research on racial terminology (Kottak, 1967b) also showed that Arembepeiros were inconsistent in their use of the terms. Presented with the drawings, which varied skin color, facial features, and hair, there was substantial disagreement about the race of the pictured individual. For one drawing, villagers offered nineteen different racial terms, and the least number of terms for any drawing was nine.

Villagers also disagreed when classifying real people, including themselves. I occasionally asked someone to tell me again what his or her race was, saying that I had forgotten the previous answer. Often I got a different term. When I asked about my race, some people made me a *branco* ("white"), some a *mulato claro* ("light *mulato*"), some simply a *mulato*, and some a *sarará* (a term considered funny, used for someone with reddish skin, which I had when sunburned, and light curly hair). (In the United States, I am "white.") Some people called me one thing one day, another the next. There was a similar variation in their use of racial terms for other villagers. How did this behavior compare with that of other Brazilians, and what was its significance?

Unlike stratified Brazilian communities, where light skin correlates with higher economic status, the only significant association between light skin color and wealth in Arembepe involved land ownership. As more recent descendants of slaves, darker people were less likely to own land than lighter villagers were. Remember that land ownership played only a small role in the local economy. Fishing, and reinvestment of fishing profits (in such areas as coconut trees), were the economic mainstays during the 1960s. There was no correlation between skin color and success in these activities—the basis of the local economy.[2]

This is why my informants, although sharing a large racial vocabulary with other Brazilians, used the terms ambiguously and inconsistently: racial differences had minimal significance in local society. Two equally successful boat captains, one a light *mulato*, the other a dark *mulato*, were best friends and *compadres*. They spent most of their leisure time together. Two poor widows, one "white," the other "black," often sat in front of their adjoining houses and made hats together. Officers of the Fishermen's Society and the soccer club had been men of all shades. Nor did differences in skin shade provide obstacles to marriage. None of the "whites" or "blacks" was married to another "white" or "black." All had married people from the intermediate categories. Prudencio, the landlord's agent and a former municipal assemblyman, was a light *mulato*. His wife, the local schoolteacher, was very dark. The two most successful businessmen were medium and dark *mulatos*. The kin network of any villager spanned an array of racial categories.

Social behavior and the fluid use of racial terms illustrated the lack of racial discrimination in egalitarian Arembepe. When people are sensitive to racial differences, and where phenotypical variation correlates with access to wealth and power, there is more concurrence on categories. This seems to be so in stratified Brazilian communities (see Wagley, 1952). When there is no agreement on the definitions of terms or the classification of actual people, the minimal conditions for converting racial awareness into racial discrimination are absent. They certainly were absent in Arembepe in the 1960s, and this was just one more expression of the egalitarian local social structure.

4 The Protestant Ethic and the Spirit of Fishermen

Imprisoned in the lower class for life, Arembepeiros of the 1960s faced miserable public health, malnutrition, and high infant mortality. How can I possibly liken Arembepe to paradise? The reason is that its people were, in my judgment, much luckier than other lower-class Brazilians I have seen and read about—people who must contend with at least as many of the disadvantages of poverty while lacking the benefits of full employment (for men, at least), insulation from state demands, production for subsistence as well as cash, and egalitarian social relations.

We have seen that the people of Arembepe were shielded from outside interference in their lives. Powerful outsiders didn't care much about these remote villagers. There was no one to tell them they should pay taxes, join the army, or fill out government forms. Disputes were settled informally, and no one ever got arrested. Rarely did a priest arrive to tell villagers they were sinners and would burn in hell. Arembepeiros relied only minimally on supplies produced outside their municipality. They caught their own animal protein. Most of the rest of their diet, including their manioc flour, came from nearby farms. One local man still knew how to build a fishing boat. Villagers didn't face the chronic unemployment and still poorer public health conditions of northeast Brazilian cities. Arembepe was free of industrial pollution and crime.

Most striking was local economic freedom. To be sure, villagers couldn't aspire to more than working-class jobs. Still, no one stopped them from fishing as much as they wanted on the open sea. No one set artificially low prices for their fish, and they could sell their produce on an open competitive market. It was in this open economy that the entrepreneurial,

Weberian personality type could flourish and that a graded socioeconomic hierarchy based on individual achievement could take shape. Such an open economy is not universal in fishing societies. Indeed we shall see that closure of fishing opportunities figured prominently in Arembepe's own transformation between 1965 and 1980.

A brief comparative look at technologically simple fishing communities in other parts of the world shows that Arembepeiros were as fortunate compared with other fishermen as they were compared with other lower-class Brazilians. Reviewing the literature on fishing in several societies, Lambros Comitas (1962) generalized that people will rarely select fishing as an occupation when they have the choice of farming or wage work. Finding fishing less attractive and lucrative than these other jobs, people must be forced into fishing by economic need. The people of Coqueiral, a Brazilian fishing community 300 kilometers north of Arembepe, which Shepard Forman (1967, 1970) studied at about the same time I first worked in Arembepe, provide much more support for Comitas's generalization than Arembepe does. Only half the men in Coqueiral were active or retired fishermen, whereas in 1964, 74 percent of Arembepe's male work force (180 men) fished as their main job, and another 8 percent fished as a secondary occupation.

Compared with other fishing communities, then, Arembepe presented a paradox. Because it was *more of* a fishing community, it was a *less typical* fishing community. To understand why, we must consider features of Arembepe's fish production and marketing that gave its fishermen advantages absent in most small-scale fishing industries—and thus made the choice of a fishing career an attractive one. Although the employment options open to Arembepeiros were limited to working-class jobs, villagers did have some choice about how they made their living. Jobs available to men during the 1960s included fishing (primary occupation of 74 percent of the men), business (11 percent), artisanry (5 percent), local wage work (4 percent), outside employment (4 percent), and farming (2 percent). Women made straw hats, ran stores, made nets for casting in the harbor, prepared food for visitors, and washed clothes or fetched water for better-off households.

The most attractive jobs were outside Arembepe. A few young men were well enough educated to find work with

Petrobrás—the federally owned oil monopoly. Some of them made their homes in Arembepe, coming home to parents, wife, and children on weekends. When I filled out a short interview schedule in August 1965 about Arembepeiros' economic aspirations and their evaluation of jobs, most people cited Petrobrás worker as the most desirable. Because my respondents' economic horizons didn't extend beyond working-class employment, none of them even mentioned such middle-class professions as physician, lawyer, or even druggist or bank teller. Although Salvador's proximity and growth provided Arembepeiros with better job prospects than were available to more isolated communities, most native sons eventually worked in the village. For example, only 26 percent of oldest sons were working outside in 1964.

Within the village, fishing and business offered the best chance for success. Although the highest cash income of an ordinary fisherman (noncaptain) was just over $400 in 1964, Tomé, the captain and owner of the most productive boat, made about $1,000 that year. This was almost as much as the three most successful businessmen made. Tomé actually had the largest *effective income*, because his occupation—like that of all fishermen—provided food. The concept of effective income—the cash remaining after food expenses are deducted—is necessary to evaluate relative economic success in Arembepe, since some jobs provide food, and others don't. Tomé's situation was especially good since he also had a small farm plot where he grew vegetables and fruits.

The top rungs of the economic ladder belonged to successful businessmen and captain-owners. Next came less successful business people and captain-owners, and ordinary crew members of the most successful boats. At the bottom were women with no coresident men. Just above them were people who worked at odd jobs and in farming, and the least successful fishermen, including a few unreliable captains. Any ambitious villager chose fishing, business, or outside employment over farming or locally available wage work. Bricklayers and house carpenters earned about a dollar a day. Work as a coconut picker, husker, or collector paid even less and was available only seasonally. Alcoholics made a pittance, generally to buy rum, by running errands.

All the successful people in Arembepe had more than one job. In 1965 Tomé, for example, fished as captain, owned his

Zuca, one of Arembepe's most successful captains. (Jerald T. Milanich)

boat, farmed a small plot, and sold coconuts. (Eventually his
money-making activities expanded to include fish marketing
and long-distance fishing.) Partly compensating for the fact
that fishing provides food while business doesn't, the nonfishermen had more time available to farm and to pursue
various money-making schemes. One land-based entrepreneur, for instance, ran two stores, transported drinking water,
marketed fish and coconuts, farmed, sold his own coconuts,
and owned shares in three boats. Only 38 percent of the
fishermen had multiple jobs, compared with 74 percent of the
businessmen.

I must stress again the openness of Arembepe's economic
hierarchy in the 1960s, the possibility of rising from the very
bottom to the very top, through ambition, hard work, and
good business sense. Arembepe's relative good fortune compared with other fishing communities has to do with Salvador's expansion and its seemingly inexhaustible demand for
fish. During the 1960s Arembepeiros saw the cost of their
fish rise faster than the general inflation rate; and some of
them profited, reinvested, and experimented at a frantic
rate.

Arembepe's fortune stands out sharply in comparison with Forman's (1970) Coqueiral. There, the mayor of the municipality and the president of the local fishing guild conspired to block any increase in the price that fishermen got, and prohibited fishermen from marketing their own fish. Lacking Arembepe's proximity to a city, Coqueiral was economically and politically dependent on its municipality. The Coqueiral situation highlights Arembepe's luck in having its market relations with one place and its political ties with another. In Arembepe, at least through 1973, fishermen were gaining more control over the production and marketing of their product. This pattern can be understood and illustrated through a description of the fishing industry.

The Sailor's Life

During the mid-1960s most fishing was done in small (6 meters long and 2 across at the widest point) plank launches— hull sailboats powered only by wind or rowing. (These boats were all motorized by 1973.) The number of active boats stabilized at thirty-one in 1959, after years of increase. The fleet stopped growing because space was limited in the harbor, formed by a partially submerged reef just east of the beach. Boats entered and left the harbor through five breaks in that reef.

All fishing on the open sea was with hook and handline. Nearer shore a few other techniques were used. One old man owned a canoe and a large dragnet, which he set in the harbor, usually in summer. Villagers began experimenting with trammel nets, which float vertically in the water, in 1965. Trammel nets ultimately proved most useful in lobster fishing. During a short-lived lobster boom, the amount of trammel netting shot up from 250 meters in 1965 to 4,300 meters in 1973. Women and children used dip nets to catch small fish in the lagoon, but industrial pollution had ended this option by 1973. A few men set traps for shrimp in rivers north and south of Arembepe. At low tide, boys fished with poles from the reef, and women and children gathered mollusks and sea urchins on the reef.

The mainstay of the economy has always been hook-and-

Arembepe's small natural harbor, protected by a sandstone reef. Shown here, boats sail out to sea on a day with very low tide—at a time of full moon. (Conrad P. Kottak)

line fishing on the open sea. The most productive fishing took place right above the continental slope, a rapid fall in ocean depth that begins at the end of the continental shelf. The shelf is the gradually sloping submerged coastal plain, which extends only 11 kilometers offshore from Arembepe, compared to a worldwide average of about 50 kilometers. Here was another major factor in Arembepe's favor. Because *the continental slope is near shore,* villagers have ready access to several species of fish that live between 35 and 200 fathoms. In particular, they can fish for the horse-eyed bonito *(olho de boi),* a large migratory species with an annual run.

There were three fishing seasons, as one fisherman explained. "June, July, August, into September, that's the winter. That's when fishing's bad; we have to stick close to shore because of the weather. In the summer, from October to January, the ocean is smooth as glass. It's easy to sail and row, and visit the distant banks. In February we start the harvest of the bonito. We leave early in the morning for The Wall, where we fish all day, sometimes until the boat is full. We fish like that throughout the fall, from February to May."

In summer and fall, villagers sailed three or four hours to the slope, where most fish were caught in rocky cliff areas at depths of 60 fathoms or more. During the winter rainy season, when sudden squalls and rough seas are common, boats did most of their fishing close to shore. They sailed for less than an hour to fish over the rocky parts of the rock and sand bottoms that occur between 8 and 20 fathoms. Fear of bad weather was the main reason most winter fishing took place near shore.

Although there were five seats, and named positions, in a fishing boat, the average crew in the mid-1960s had only four men. This was due to a labor shortage. Most fishermen had regular places in four- or five-man crews. Some had usual second choices, crews they fished in if their main boat stayed in.

The main distinction in the boat was between the captain and the ordinary fishermen. During the mid-1960s captains might own all, half, or no part of their boats. At the end of each day's fishing, "the boat"—that is, the owner(s)—received about 25 percent of the proceeds from marketing the crew's total catch. The four- or five-man crew divided the remaining 75 percent equally. Captains who solely owned their boats got 25 percent as "the boat's" share and another 15 percent as crew members. After deducting maintenance expenses (less than $100 per year), the average captain-owner cleared about $500 annually, plus fish for his table. Successful captains made twice that. Captains who co-owned their boats, usually with a local businessman, split "the boat's" share and expenses.

In 1965 access to the local fishing technology was open to any ambitious man. The cost of a new, fully equipped boat was almost equal to the annual income of an ordinary fisherman. But money to buy a boat could be made in commercial fishing outside Arembepe, or a man could earn a half-share by working as captain for a year or two. He would apply his captain's commission (25 percent of "the boat's share) to pay off half the cost of the boat. The combination of half-ownership and hard work might then produce enough additional money to buy a boat of one's own. Fishermen used all these strategies in the mid-1960s.

The fishermen also benefited from the spiraling price of

fish. In 1965 the selling price of a kilogram of fish was 500 percent of the 1962 figure, while a new, fully equipped boat cost just 250 percent of its 1962 value. From another angle, a boat had cost 800 kilograms of fish in 1962, compared with only 400 kilograms in 1965. As the value of their product increased, fishermen started ordering boats of their own. The owners of the three largest stores had all owned shares of boats in 1964. By 1965 they had lost their captains, sold their shares, or retired their boats. "I've owned a boat ever since I took over my father's business," a middle-aged storekeeper told me in 1965. "But I can't find anyone to be my captain. All the good captains want boats of their own. They forget that people like me helped them get their start by letting them fish for a half-share."

The nonfishing owners in 1965 were people who were somehow active in the fishing economy—one man in naval carpentry and two others in fish marketing. By 1965 twenty-one captains (out of a total of thirty-one) owned all (five) or half (sixteen) of their boats. Three more captains were about to complete payments for half-shares. The value of a boat had fallen by then to $150. The average captain–half-owner, getting 28 percent of his boat's annual marketed catch, cleared about $400. With that money he could easily buy the second half-share, or dissolve the relationship with the nonfishing owner by making a down payment on a new boat.

This emerging pattern gave expression to the resentment by fishermen—especially captains—at having to share the fruits of their labor with nonfishermen. The growing ability of captains to buy their own boats was a powerful check on the profits that nonfishing owners could derive from the fishing industry. "Who wants to share profits with someone who sits onshore and does nothing. Nothing, while I do all the work," said the captain whose former partner was the storekeeper quoted previously. Captains shared ownership with, or worked for, nonfishing owners only because of (1) economic need, (2) kinship, or (3) the captain's lack of ambition or regular work habits.

After most captains had withdrawn from such partnerships, the only captains that nonfishing owners could attract were the least successful. Since unreliable captains tended to attract unreliable crew members, there was a real limit to the profits of the nonfishing owner. Given the shortage of both captains and ordinary fishermen, the nonfishing owner of the 1960s was as dependent on the capricious activities of his captain and crew as the ambitious fisherman had once been on the nonfisherman's willingness to provide capital.

Sailboats weren't particularly valuable or durable, with the average one about ten years old. The boats needed minor repairs annually and major ones after about seven years. "Nowadays," reported a man who in 1965 had just ordered his own boat, "it costs just as much to do a major overhaul as it does to buy a new boat. Even when you add in the cost of equipment for the new boat—sails and masts, water barrels, and a mooring in the harbor—it still would cost half as much to do thorough repairs on an old boat as it does to get a new one. This is why people are selling their old boats [to buyers in fishing villages to the north] and buying new ones. The new ones last longer than a boat that's been repaired."

Inheritance of boats was rare and thus didn't perpetuate wealth contrasts from one generation to the next. A boat's value was not as a commodity but as a means of production for an enthusiastic captain and crew. Without personnel, a boat's value could fall to nothing, as this story about Laurentino, a one-time nonfishing owner, shows.

Laurentino, who ran one store inherited from his father and another that he had started himself, had once owned shares in four boats. Laurentino had more trouble finding captains and crew than most villagers did because he was a very unpopular man. Unlike other storekeepers, Laurentino refused to extend credit. He was also reputed to practice *candomblé*, the Afro-Brazilian cult that barely existed in Arembepe during the mid-1960s. "They say he's got a demon *(cão)*, a devil dog he keeps caged in his shop," said our cook, as she asked me to walk her home one dark night. "I've never seen it, but last night his door was partway open, and there was a strange light coming from inside. I'm not walking by there by myself." Laurentino's antisocial behavior led to his isolation, through gossip, avoidance, and other leveling mechanisms that eventually ended his profits from the fishing industry. By 1965, Laurentino had given up trying to find captains and crews. He had managed to sell just one of his boats. The others he had chopped up and used for firewood—an excellent illustration

of the limitations on nonfishing owners' profits within the
fishing industry.

Even in the early 1970s after motors had been introduced
(financed by government loans to successful captains), there
were limitations to the control of the fishing industry by nonfishermen. Arembepe's simple fishing technology had a low
value and short lifespan, and anyone could gain access to the
means of production through hard work. The nature of the
fishing economy, particularly its technology, is another reason
the socioeconomic hierarchy remained graded, rather than
stratified. (We shall see in Chapter 8 that all of this had
changed dramatically by 1980, when it cost 5,500 kilograms of
fish, rather than the 400 kilograms of 1964, to buy a boat.)

Excelling in an Egalitarian Society

The social and economic checks that kept owners who did not
fish from obtaining substantial profits from fishing didn't operate against captains. Still, the difference between the captain
and the ordinary fisherman was critical. In an egalitarian
community, this was the only significant contrast in the main
unit of daily production—the fishing crew. The captain's duties included fishing and, for most captains, ownership responsibilities, either sole or shared. One ordinary fisherman
described the captain's role.

"When the weather's bad, or looks like it could be, the
captain makes the decision about whether the boat should go
out. The boat leaves when the captain's ready. Once we're on
the other side of the reef, he'll tell us where he thinks we
should start fishing. If we don't catch much, he decides when
we should try a different spot. The captain says when the
fishing day ends and we head home. He's in charge of navigation. He knows where we are by reading the landmarks, and
he gives the orders to raise or lower the masts and anchor."

My observations of several captains confirmed the basics of
this fisherman's summary. The captain's special role ended
when fishing began—after a spot was chosen, a rocky bottom
established by dropping a plumbline, the boat properly posi-
tioned, and the anchor let down. Until the captain issued the
order to set sail for home, or move to another spot, he fished

like everyone else. Although his lines were sometimes nylon rather than the cheaper cord used by ordinary fishermen, the captain's fishing was no more skilled than that of any other crew member. Captain and crew alike sat for hours in the sun—as I did several times—rocked up and down on Atlantic waters, felt the sting of sudden rain, and shared the danger of negotiating the channels during rough weather.

Even churning seas rarely caused seasickness in an experienced sailor. "Are you going to vomit, Conrado?" I was asked at regular intervals each time I went out. A few men told me they had tried fishing but chosen another occupation because they got seasick. Everyone expected me to do the same. I found seasickness hardest to resist one hot afternoon as the stench of rotting *manjuba* (sardinelike bait fish), next to which I had been seated, wafted in my direction. I imagined the tiny, glassy-eyed cadavers turning from silver to brownish green.

There was a distinct fellowship of the sea, a camaraderie born of those hours of shared waiting punctuated by an occasional flurry of activity, as luck brought hooks and fish together over a rocky feeding ground. If fishing at a given spot was good for one, it was usually good for all. Because of this, all boats used the "joint line" system of dividing the day's catch of small fish. Larger fish, which were rarer catches, were also pooled in some boats. In others they were sold independently by the man who caught them.

The captain's special role resumed when he gave the orders to lift anchor and set sail for home. He decided to beach the boat in rough weather, when it seemed likely that fishing would be postponed for a few days, or when there was danger that boats, crowded in the small harbor and jostled by large waves, would collide and be damaged. Beaching the fleet was a rapid, arduous, communal task, undertaken as threatening weather brought boats home earlier than usual on a winter afternoon. Every man on the beach—whether or not his boat had fished that day, whether or not his boat was already beached, even whether or not he was a fisherman—was expected to help. This involved laying out and positioning the massive wooden rollers, pushing and pulling the vessel up to the dunes, to safety beyond the highest waves of inclement weather.

Like any other owner, the captain turned over his boat's contribution to the Fishermen's Society for the February festival. Boat owners were supposed to contribute 5 percent of their annual marketed catch for the patron saint's festival. "Nobody really gives more than 2 percent," one captain-owner confided to me, "and most don't even do that." Owners decided when boats needed to be caulked, painted, or otherwise repaired. Captain-owners faced loss of livelihood if their boat was damaged, but accidents were rare. The worst one I ever heard about happened in 1961. The sole survivor told me how he had clung to the wreckage of his boat. "A fish, a barracuda, stayed with me all those hours, until I washed up on shore. That must have been my guardian angel. I would have drowned if he hadn't been there." Owners paid for repairs and maintenance expenses. Captain–half-owners, of course, shared both risks and benefits with their nonfishing partners; but the duties of captains who fished only for a commission ended with the day's fishing.

The average crew in 1965 marketed about 3,500 kilograms of fish annually. Add to this 1,000 to 1,500 kilograms more that fishermen and their families ate, for a yearly catch of about 5,000 kilograms. This is an average; some crews regularly caught much more fish than others.

How was the *fact* of differential production, which translated into observable life-style differences, explained in an egalitarian community? How did Arembepeiros square their frequent assertion, "We are all equal here," with the obvious fact that they were not? Since much of the differential wealth in Arembepe was based on profits from fishing, villagers' explanations for success at sea are particularly important.

I soon found, however, that Arembepeiros held different opinions about two key questions: (1) What enabled some boats to catch more fish than others? and (2) What distinguished captains from ordinary fishermen? The answers I got to these questions reflected the respondent's reference group. Four such groups were relevant: (1) successful captains, who were men ranging in age from the twenties to the mid-forties, (2) older captains who had once belonged to the first group; (3) the least successful captains, of various ages, who fished less regularly, primarily because of alcoholism; and (4) ordinary fishermen, who included retired captains and captains-to-be.

By 1965 I recognized that the opinions held by some of these groups were misconceptions that interfered with their understanding of what actually determined fishing success. I had also come to realize that such confusion and misunderstanding were essential. Wide public recognition of the fact that people *could*, through concerted effort, raise the level of production would have threatened Arembepe's egalitarian ethos—the insistence that, despite current appearances and temporary contrasts in fortune, all villagers were really equal.

What, then, were the divergent opinions? Ordinary fishermen and unsuccessful captains contended that *luck* enabled some captains to catch more fish than others. "Some captains take luck with them, so that wherever they drop anchor, they catch fish," said an ordinary fisherman. Actually, the men who mentioned luck didn't like to admit that some captains did better than others and to acknowledge the differential success that was visible in catches, life styles, and contributions to the Fishermen's Society. Ordinary fishermen and unsuccessful captains saw few distinctions among captains. They insisted that although some captains seemed to be having better luck than others right now, all were really equal.

By attributing success to luck and by refusing to acknowledge evidence for differential success, these people were thinking very differently from the most successful captains. Among the best captains, those who belonged to group 1, there was a totally different emphasis. They stressed the value of individual achievement, business success, and the rewards of hard work, planning, management, and reinvestment. (They rejected the previous view that there was no need to try harder, since success rested on luck, which was, after all, beyond human control.)

Successful captains, when asked what determined success in fishing, always mentioned attributes that recalled Weber's Protestant ethic. Although they didn't boast about their own success, they readily admitted that some captains were better than others. One explained, "The boats that catch the most fish are simply the ones that fish most regularly. Those captains stay out longest, and their crews work hardest." He divided captains into three groups, as I have done. The "first-class captains" were the young, hard-working captain-owners or co-owners who made the largest contributions to the Fishermen's Society. This captain's opinions about what determined success also revealed another theme, the importance of good vision (see next section) for landmarking, which contributed to confusion about the skills needed in fishing.

The element of confusion was in his discussion of the "second-class captains," those with "failing vision," who made lower contributions to the Fishermen's Society than the first group. In this category he placed formerly successful captains who could "no longer see the landmarks of fishing spots." Most of these were respected older men who had belonged in the first group fifteen or twenty years earlier.

As "third-class captains," my informant mentioned men of all ages who never had been and never would be successful, primarily because they drank too much rum. Most were non-owners, men who fished for a commission, who shifted between boats, who commanded weak allegiance from crew members, and who sometimes worked as ordinary fishermen in other boats. They often missed fishing because of drunkenness or illness, and their crews shared their foibles. Except for this man's contention about the "failing vision" of the captains in group 2, his beliefs about determinants of success and his classification of his colleagues agreed with my own.

Francisco, a fairly successful captain in 1964. (Conrad P. Kottak)

enio/etic

The opinions of the unsuccessful captains and ordinary fishermen did not. The luck, or chance, to which they attributed fishing success could explain only *short-term* variations. In the long run luck should even out for crews that spend the same amount of time fishing. Objective analysis supports the opinions of the successful captains. The factors that actually determined long-run differences in production were several physical and personality traits that made certain captains good fishermen.

What were those keys to success? Because they were in their twenties and thirties, the best captains had good health, which allowed them to take their boats out regularly. Because they were dependable, they attracted hard-working crews. Their physical strength permitted them to tolerate longer hours at sea, to work harder, and to have less fear of unpleasant weather. Like Weber's Protestant-capitalists, they took calculated risks. They tried to maximize yields by straying from the dominant pattern in a given fishing season. Even during the winter, for example, they went to the continental slope, where several fish species are concentrated in a rocky cliff area. Sometimes they traveled north to fish in grounds that Arembepeiros normally didn't use. Often their risks paid off in larger catches.

Also like Weber's Protestant-capitalists, although to a lesser degree, they valued sobriety. Successful captains drank less, preferred beer to rum, and imbibed only on festive occasions. More expensive in relation to alcohol content than crude rum, beer was a status symbol, and it was less intoxicating than rum. Successful captains could drink more without getting drunk. They never missed fishing because of insobriety. Like Weber's entrepreneur, who commanded the confidence of customers and workers, Arembepe's best captains enjoyed greater crew allegiance and attracted better crew members, people who were willing and able to work longer and harder at fishing.

As rewards for their traits and activities, successful captains had better homes and diets, more possessions, and a more comfortable life style than other villagers. On weekends they walked around the village, and visited bars, with short-wave radios they had purchased with their profits. This conspicuous consumption partly violated both the worldviews that have been attributed to people like Arembepeiros (as discussed in Chapter 3): Weber's Protestant-capitalist ethic and Foster's image of limited good. By valuing consumer goods and "the good life," Arembepeiros differed from early Protestants, who hid their success in the simplicity and asceticism of the middle-class home. In tolerating some life-style contrasts, Arembepeiros presented a partial contrast to the image of limited good. That worldview, according to Foster, leads peasants to regard life-style differences as evidence that certain villagers are profiting at the expense of others, and to use leveling mechanisms to reduce the "upstarts" to the common level.

Its fishing economy was the main reason Arembepe stood between the image of limited good that Foster attributed to peasant societies and the Protestant ethic that Weber linked to early capitalism. Under favorable conditions—like those prevailing in Arembepe in the 1960s—successful fishing calls for certain personality traits. Surveying data on personality structure from several societies, Barry, Bacon, and Child (1959) found that foragers[1] emphasized achievement, competition, self-reliance, and independence. These traits are particularly important for open-sea fishermen—because it's hard to demarcate property at sea, to control marine resources, to supervise production, and to store the product. Within the constraints of the technology, labor, and marketing available to them, Arembepeiros could increase fish production without endangering the species they relied on.[2]

To Arembepe's fishermen the ocean was an almost limitless frontier. The main barriers to a larger fishing territory were technological, such as the reliance on wind power. By contrast, as Foster has noted, *peasants'* resources are limited and their payoffs often come all at once, at harvest time. For Arembepeiros, like other open-sea fishermen, chance and hard work governed the level of production, given existing technology and marketing possibilities. Good wasn't limited but could be increased without harming others.

Given the values and behavior that led to success in an open fishing economy with favorable marketing opportunities, the most successful Arembepeiros were independent and achievement-oriented. Still, Arembepe shared traits with nearby peasant villages, including its general poverty and aspects of the image of limited good—the ideology of equality, obligations to share, and leveling mechanisms. Now consider one of the most curious arenas in which aspects of these worldviews met.

The Riddle of the Spots

Most Arembepeiros *erroneously* believed that a particular physical attribute—good eyesight—explained why some people were captains and others were not, and why—aside from luck—some captains were more successful than others. Specifically, this attribute was said to permit a captain to locate and remember discrete fishing spots through a visual triangulation system of landmarking.

Fishermen recognized and named both broad zones of the ocean floor and smaller spots within them. Both were called *pesqueiros*. The fishermen correctly believed that most fish were caught in rocky areas, where smaller fish fed on vegetation, and larger fish species ate smaller ones. The fishermen of Arembepe thought that some rocky areas had more fish than others, and they used landmarks to identify them. Most winter fishing (using landmarks) was done within 4 kilometers of the shore in four zones of rock and sand bottoms. Most summer and fall fishing (without landmarks) was done over the continental slope, where boats lined up and fished within sight of each other. Plumbing was always used to locate these slope fishing grounds.

Although I question neither the existence nor the usefulness of landmarking in Arembepe, I believe that Arembepeiros had an exaggerated belief in the precision, scale, and significance of the landmarking system. It isn't unusual for ethnographers to find, after careful investigation, striking contrasts between their own conclusions and the beliefs of some, or even most, informants. What might account for such a difference between the native's account (the *emic* explanation) and the anthropologist's (the *etic* account)? One possibility, of course, is that the anthropologist is wrong. Another is that informants are consciously lying. Or it may be that natives consider the matter in question too trivial for careful thought or lack the scientific knowledge needed for an accurate explanation. Often, however, an exaggerated or inaccurate belief that is widely shared turns out to have a definite function, which the anthropologist discovers is of critical importance to the social system.

Sometimes that function is to block full understanding of, or to *mystify*, native recognition of what is going on, since full understanding might pose a threat to the system's smooth functioning. Some examples of mystification in our own society include politicians' contentions that weapons are "peacemakers" or that "laziness" is the reason for joblessness. These American mystifications have the function or effect of diverting our attention away from true causes—the lobbying and clout of giant military-industrial institutions, and an insufficiency of jobs and opportunities, which makes unemployment inevitable. By interfering with people's understanding of the status quo, mystification helps discourage actions that might change it. This was exactly the case with Arembepeiros' beliefs about the role of landmarking and the spots in determining differential fishing success.

Arembepeiros' beliefs stood in the way of their complete recognition of much more important determinants of fishing success (i.e., entrepreneurial behavior and values). However, this mystification was fully compatible with, and indeed was expectable within, a classless, achievement-oriented community, which like Morton Fried's (1960) "egalitarian society," attributed all differences in accomplishment by people of roughly the same age and gender to personal characteristics over which individuals have little conscious control. In Arembepe as in the egalitarian society, people thought that some individuals excelled because they happened to have certain talents, abilities, or personal traits—physical, spiritual, or psychological. The egalitarian society poses a sharp contrast to the stratified society, in which people's class background always affects their status and opportunities as adults.

Most Arembepeiros viewed luck and good vision as the criteria for fishing success. These were appropriate ideas for an egalitarian community. Luck, after all, is impersonal and beyond human control. Sharpness of vision is a personal physical characteristic over which individuals (lacking eyeglasses) also lack control. Making these the criteria of success helped resolve the contradiction to egalitarian structure and ethos posed by the *fact* that individuals *could,* by hard work—over which they obviously did have control—raise the level of production.

As noted, the only significant contrast in the crew was between captain and ordinary crew member. Accordingly, villagers had to view the captain as endowed with certain special skills that justified his larger share of the catch. The ability to locate and remember fishing spots became the primary test of what it took to be a captain. Ordinary fishermen then had a ready excuse for not being captains. It wasn't that they were lazy, stupid, or unreliable. It was just that their eyesight was too poor to permit them to see and to line up landmarks.

The exaggeration of landmarking's significance becomes clear when we focus on what really happened when a boat reached a fishing spot. When returning to a spot that had previously been marked, the boat sailed until the captain lined up one set of markers, then sailed on line with the first set until he saw the second set come into line. Before lowering anchor and dropping sail, someone always dropped a plumbline, to see if the bottom was rocky—and thus to see if the crew had reached their destination. Sometimes plumbing went on for more than half an hour. When many plumbings were needed, the markers were usually forgotten and positioning done solely by plumbline results.

I discovered that the exaggerated impression of the precision of the location system was being created mainly by older captains. Some of them claimed to know how to find very small spots—for example, the size of a boat. The younger captains denied that spots could be so small. So did an expert on fishing and navigation I consulted in Salvador, who told me that landmarking techniques used by Brazilian coastal fishermen could differentiate no spots smaller than 8 by 8 meters—about five times the figure offered by the older captains.

I interpret the older captains' statements about the landmarking system as comparable to the privileged information (often of a supernatural sort) that older men claim, and are believed to have, in many egalitarian foraging societies. In Arembepe, too, old men were perpetuating, and many young men accepting, a myth about what led to success. In a community where male supremacy and masculine vitality were highly valued, captains could not offer their failing overall strength as a reason for their declining catches. But they *could* gracefully mention one definite and uncontrollable physical attribute—good eyesight—believed to fail inexorably. This gave them a culturally acceptable way of explaining their impending or actual retirement as captain. Failing vision was a convenient excuse for the older captain's declining productivity, the real cause of which lay in a general loss of vitality that the community's emphasis on *machismo* made it necessary to disguise.

The physical infirmities of old age, which limited regular fishing and exertion in general, could include failing vision; but they weren't confined to it. (In fact, by 1965 several former captains had obtained prescription glasses, but they hadn't reclaimed the captain's role.) By citing failing vision as the reason for their retirement, older captains could maintain the respect of younger men for a physical attribute that supposedly had once granted them large catches. By insisting that loss of accurate vision was the inevitable outcome of a life at sea, older captains held out to their younger colleagues the prospect of a similar fate. Ordinary fishermen, too, believed that success was fleeting and fickle, and that the life-style differences that existed at one moment, founded on luck and eyesight, might be leveled out the next.

The older captains' mystification concerned not just the landmarking system's precision but also its scale. Captains claimed to have marked and memorized between 5 and 200 spots. Older captains always claimed to know the most. "I could mark about 100 spots," remarked one fifty-five-year-old captain. "But that's nothing. There are captains who know between 200 and 300." Still, Tomé, the most successful captain, claimed to have marked just 20 spots, and another young entrepreneur gave a similar number. "Twenty's the average," said the latter. "No one could remember 100 spots; even 50 would be remarkable."

Despite Arembepeiros' contention that captains needed the ability to locate spots, I must stress now that most fishing did not entail marking spots at all. Only the zones fished during the winter, the ones nearest shore, had spot landmarks. Plumbing rather than landmarks was used to identify rocky bottoms in the more distant summer and fall fishing zones.

"There are landmarks for The Wall [the slope], but even captains with a hawk's eyes have trouble seeing them from way out there," said one fisherman. "That's why plumbing is always done."

If the spots were fewer, less precise, and less significant than most Arembepeiros believed, did they have *any* economic utility? Niles Eldredge (1963, p. 27), a 1963 field team member who also studied Arembepe's fishing industry, has argued reasonably that spots were marked and memorized because a landmarking system eliminated much of the time-consuming plumbing activity. This utilitarian reason, along with the function of locating *general* areas of the ocean floor (zones and large rocky areas), may adequately explain the widespread use of landmarking through visual triangulation among coastal fishermen throughout the world.

We should also remember, in assessing the relevance of spots to the captain's role, that the valued attributes of the captain were defined by technological and economic constraints. As Alberto, an ordinary fisherman who said that his poor eyesight and memory had always kept him from being a captain, put it, "If I had enough money to buy a small motor-boat, I could go out to The Wall any time I wanted. That way I could easily catch more fish than even the best captain fishing close to shore. Even with a small boat and a motor, I could become the most successful fisherman in Arembepe." Confirming some of Alberto's points are changes that took place between 1965 and 1973. With motorization in the early 1970s came year-round fishing in summer and fall zones as well as entry into the captain's role by former noncaptains— and even former nonfishermen. I examine these changes in Chapter 6.

A combination of local and regional factors granted Arembepe rare good fortune. I have discussed the local factors here and in Chapter 3. Chapter 5 is about the regional ones. The combination of circumstances made the personalities of many Arembepeiros similar to the Weberian Protestant-capitalist type. This is why—despite erroneous opinions held by many villagers about what determined success—the real determinants were neither the "luck" nor the "good eyesight" that were compatible with an egalitarian, male-supremacist ideology but the individualistic, achievement-oriented personality traits of the Weberian entrepreneur. A major point of Chapters 4 and 5 should not be missed: The entrepreneurial personality types of Arembepeiros *did not cause* the community's fortune. Just the reverse: Arembepe's favorable local and regional conditions created and nourished these personality traits—despite a simultaneous and countervailing ideology of equality, sharing, and leveling. The "riddle of the spots" bridged the opposition between these ideologies. That is, the riddle helped make it possible to maintain both doctrines in the same community. We shall see later on, however, that these traditional beliefs in efficacious spots, once so critical in the fishing economy, are now almost defunct because of technological changes.

entrepreneurial ethic &
ideology of equality
maintained by
mystification of bases
for success differentials

5 The Bigger Pond

Along with productive fishing, marketing opportunities that rewarded increased productivity nourished the entrepreneurial personality type in Arembepe during the 1960s. In marketing, the fishermen of Arembepe were again fortunate, posing an exception to Forman's (1970) generalization that most of the world's fishermen have limited access to marketing and limited control over the prices they get. Some of the reasons for Arembepe's good fortune have been mentioned previously. Fish marketing deserves more attention here, since it was Arembepe's main link with the outside world, generating about two-thirds of local cash income in 1965.

Arembepe's marketing opportunities have steadily improved throughout its history, particularly since the 1950s, when jeeps with four-wheel drive first came to buy fish. Previously, several middlemen had used mules, donkeys, and burros to take fish to Portão, 18 kilometers away, to be trucked to Salvador. This pattern did not end suddenly. When I first studied Arembepe in 1962, rainy season access remained difficult, and many fishermen still sold to mule drivers. Only about half the boats sold to a motorized agent, Roberto, who despite his vehicle's four-wheel drive, sometimes didn't make it to Arembepe during the winter. Many people maintained their long-term arrangements with the mule drivers, who could be counted on to reach the village and collect their perishable fish in good weather and bad.

The days of the old marketing system were clearly numbered. By 1964 improvements in the road had brought two new motorized buyers to Arembepe. The owner of a wholesale fish store in Itapoan, who sold fish to a nearby air force base and to restaurants on the road to Salvador, sent his godson. A second wholesaler took his share of the catch all the way into Salvador. By 1965 both these men had agreements with the owners of several boats. They had weaned customers away from former buyers by offering more money.

Villagers' links with the mule drivers had been both social and economic. Ties of coparenthood (compadresco) often added social cement to the economic bond. Even Roberto, the motorized agent who bought half of Arembepe's fish in 1962, had kept up good social relations with his customers. He had two village godchildren, and he took his obligations to them seriously, eventually providing food and lodging while they attended school in Salvador. Roberto had arranged with a captain-owner and his wife for room and board on nights when there were no fish to take to Salvador. During the rainy season it was often hard for Roberto to know, in Salvador, if weather in Arembepe had permitted fishing. Still, since a dozen boats relied on his being there to get their fish to market before they spoiled, he had to err in the fishermen's favor. So close did Roberto's social relationship with Arembepe become that in August 1962 he brought his bride there for a second wedding party and a brief honeymoon.

By 1965 Roberto had severed his economic relationship with Arembepe and was spending his time on business interests in Salvador. His withdrawal had been gradual. In 1964 he still maintained buying rights in seven boats. He had arranged for their fish to be transported and sold to the fish store in Itapoan, whose owner paid Roberto a commission.[1]

Although steady improvements in access to Salvador were decreasing the dependence of fishermen on particular buyers and raising the price of their fish, Arembepeiros had always had a degree of choice about who got their catch. The old pattern—before motorized marketing—was for each boat to have its own mule driver, to take the fish to Portão. The number of these middlemen swelled as catches increased during the summer and the bonito harvest. Villagers never had to rely on a single buyer for their fish; there were always several middlemen. These men, like Arembepeiros themselves, were lower-class people who had found a small niche in, and eked a meager living out of, the technologically simple distribution system that linked town and country.

One of these mule drivers was instrumental in the original

decision of our field team to study Arembepe in 1962 and in arranging lodging there. His home was in Abrantes, the district seat, where he had become acquainted with Maria Brandão, a sociologist at the University of Bahia. He told Maria about Arembepe, then a remote village scarcely known in Salvador. She suggested to field leader Marvin Harris that it would be an interesting place for some of the student anthropologists to live. Maria's mule driver friend also arranged lodging for Betty Wagley with his common-law consort, an Arembepe businesswoman. By 1965 the driver had abandoned both his business and his lover in Arembepe, illustrating the pattern of change in the fish marketing system.

Arembepe's marketing advantages are well illustrated in events between 1962 and 1965, the period during which the role of the external middleman was replaced by direct sale to wholesalers. Like that of the mule drivers, even Roberto's withdrawal from fish marketing expressed this shift. Despite his jeep, Roberto had been a middleman like all the rest. He had always resold to wholesalers in the city. Roberto is by far

Betty chats with a boat owner as the fleet returns one afternoon in 1964. The men on the beach are owners, marketers, and middlemen. (Conrad P. Kottak)

the most popular fish buyer ever to work in Arembepe, but he too was forced out because he couldn't offer as high a price as the wholesalers did. While Roberto was phasing out his involvement in Arembepe's economy, a series of new agents arrived. The particular wholesalers from Itapoan and Salvador mentioned earlier were the most successful of five motorized fish buyers between 1962 and 1965.

The entry of these two into local life warrants discussion, since it provides an excellent illustration of how Arembepe's ideology of equality influenced the way villagers acted with outsiders. The motorized agents were members of the lower middle class, from an urban environment in which class contrasts were evident in daily life. They brought to Arembepe their own set of expectations about how they should treat, and be treated by, lower-class people. However, the outsiders soon learned not only that those expectations contrasted sharply with those of villagers but that business success in Arembepe demanded that outsiders adopt its values and expectations.

When in Arembepe Roberto had become an Arembepeiro. Subsequent outsiders never immersed themselves as deeply in its social system. They didn't have to, because as wholesalers they could offer better prices and service. Still, their behavior did evolve noticeably as they worked their way into the economy. The wholesaler from Salvador attracted his first customers with higher prices, but he began to lose them because of his aloofness. Unlike previous buyers, he refused to give villagers emergency rides in his jeep, and he never engaged in repartee with locals. Most damaging to his reputation were two accidents. One killed an old-time middleman from Portão. In the other, the buyer's son ran over a local child. Trying to correct his damaged image, the wholesaler hired a driver-agent who felt more comfortable dealing with villagers, and he tried to curb his own aloofness. Nevertheless, his role in Arembepe was already being eyed by a local businessman, who knew exactly how Arembepeiros expected marketers to behave. The local man had replaced the man from Salvador by 1973.

The Itapoan fish store owner was a wealthy man who didn't come to Arembepe himself but sent a godson. Both these men had roots in Itapoan's lower class, but the godson lacked his godfather's wealth (land, coconut trees, eight boats in Itapoan, and a very successful fish store) and his middle-class aspirations. They offered a good price for Arembepe's fish, and the godson knew more about getting along with fishermen than did the wholesaler from Salvador. But here again, different expectations led to the external buyer's eventual failure. In February 1965, during the Saint Francis celebration, the visiting Itapoan fish shop owner got drunk and, trying to teach his wife to drive, plowed through a fence into a back yard, injuring a fisherman. He offered to pay the victim's medical expenses. Later, when asked for compensation for four months' lost work time, he refused to pay. Someone claimed to have overheard his wife remark, "How dare he ask you for that. The fishermen here rely on you. You don't have to depend on them." This comment, retold often in winter 1965, stirred resentment among the fishermen, who had a very different opinion about who depended on whom. Villagers considered the Itapoan businessman and his wife "uppity." They acted like *grafinos* (elegant people), though their roots lay in the lower class. Here again, ambitious villagers were planning to take over the outsider's role. Arembepeiros' own fish marketing had displaced the buyer from Itapoan by 1973.

The Patron's Shadow

These encounters between Arembepeiros and outsiders, along with those considered later, contrasted with the relations between social classes and between patrons and clients that have been described for most of Brazil. For example, most Arembepeiros would have been unfamiliar and uncomfortable with the following stereotype.

> When addressing a member of the upper class, a Brazilian peasant will invariably lower his gaze, hat in hand, and shuffle his feet in an embarrassed mockery of his own humility. He will defer to the landowner, the shopkeeper, and the tax collector in countless ways, accepting that it is right and proper for him to do so, as long as proper behavior is reciprocated in turn. (Forman, 1975, p. 76)

Arembepeiros have been involved in unequal social relations with outsiders, but these have exemplified what Forman calls "patron-clientship" as opposed to "patron-dependency." With patron-dependency the rural Brazilian is *forced* to continue a set of exchanges with a social superior. With patron-clientship, by contrast, the lower-class person has some choice among potential "benefactors" who offer rewards for his services and loyalty (Forman, 1975, p. 69). Forman (1975) calls the shift toward patron-clientship a major change in the Brazilian rural social system, as competition increased among the rural masses for patrons, and among patrons for clients. Forman attributes this breakdown of patron-dependency to growing commercialism. The rural population, instead of staying put on the land, was in flux. Patrons were losing followings once fixed on their land.

Arembepe's weak patronage system and its similarity to patron-clientship aren't surprising. The local economy, after all, has never been based on land or permanent agriculture. The nearness of the state capital has also meant that Arembepe has experienced earlier than most rural areas the commercialism that radiates from the cities. To be sure, the people of Arembepe have needed to enhance their access to capital, income, credit, information, and other benefits available from outsiders (see Gross, 1973, p. 134). But there is a critical difference: Arembepeiros have never had their movements restricted, nor have they ever been stopped from making a living by more powerful people. The patronage relationships that *have* affected Arembepe, despite its long-term shielding from the national power structure, will now be examined.

Historically, the most likely candidates for the role of patron (and oppressor) were the owners of the land on which Arembepe is located. However, as noted in Chapter 3, the landlords had sought their fortunes in Salvador and had little to do with the village. The estate's last unitary landlord was Francisca Ricardo, who lived in Arembepe between 1875 and 1924, when she died. Francisca was a slaveowner and a member of a landed rural aristocracy. In the 1880s, just before abolition, she had her slaves plant more than 5,000 coconut trees, whose fruits provided her heirs with more than $1,000 annually in the 1960s. Francisca was the last landlord to get her livelihood from this estate, which ran for 6 kilometers along the coast and extended 2 kilometers inland.

On her death, the estate and trees were divided into three

equal shares, for her three daughters or their heirs. All three daughters had already joined the trek of Camaçari's rural gentry to Salvador. Until the late 1960s, when Jorge Camões, Francisca's great-grandson, began to subdivide the estate into lots, the land was held jointly by Francisca's (fourteen) adult heirs. The landlords recognized an informal division into three parts, stemming from Francisca's daughters—one south and one north of Arembepe, and one that included the village.

One daughter, the heir to the estate south of Arembepe, never participated in village life, maintaining only an economic interest in her land and coconuts. The other two daughters died before their mother, but *their* daughters, Emily (Jorge Camões's mother) and Nora—particularly the latter—played larger roles in local history. The orphaned Nora was raised in Arembepe by her grandmother, Francisca. Older villagers, recalling the tricks boys used to play on the crotchety old woman, expressed pity for Nora, who had to put up with Francisca's increasing testiness. Nora became a romantic figure for villagers by marrying a former priest, a German who left the church for love of Nora. The couple and their three children maintained a vacation home in Arembepe. Many villagers felt that they had grown up with Nora's two sons and daughter.

From my first visit I was struck by Arembepeiros' directness in dealing with outsiders, by their lack of the exaggerated deference and politeness I observed elsewhere among lower-class Brazilians. Many villagers did show respect to well-educated outsiders and to people with professional or managerial jobs, or high political office. But they refused to defer to outsiders because of money alone, and they strongly resented an outsider's expectation that they do so. I was particularly interested in seeing if the pattern held up when villagers dealt with the landlords. Sure enough, I discovered that most of the landlords who lived in Arembepe after Francisca's death had been incorporated in the local social system. Except for Jorge Camões, who has been Arembepe's most obvious but most socially distant patron, the landlords were treated in about the same way as were villagers of similar age, gender, and personality type.

Nora's German husband, for example, always got respect—as a well-educated man, a scholar, a university professor, and a speaker of seven languages. Villagers spoke of him with affection. They bragged about his accomplishments, just as they expressed pride in Jorge's university degree (the first one by a member of the landowning family) and in a female landowner's certification as a high school teacher. Villagers also joked that any man who'd leave the priesthood deserved their admiration. In 1964 I accompanied a few villagers to see the former priest and his sons in their suburban Salvador apartment. My companions treated the old man with greater deference than they would have shown toward an old man in Arembepe, but they joked and used familiar language (the informal "you," for example) with his sons, who were their age peers.

Francisca's other granddaughter, Jorge's mother, shared the central third of the estate, which included Arembepe, with her two brothers. The three siblings were interested mainly in their coconuts. They left decisions about their land to Jorge, letting him make all the arrangements for subdivision, from which they eventually profited. Jorge's mother never lived in Arembepe. She was born, grew up, and married in a suburb of Salvador where her father, Francisca's son-in-law Miguel Camões, had a middle-class job.

As a widower, Miguel retired with a comfortable pension and moved to Arembepe around 1920. Following his mother-in-law's death (soon after his arrival), he served as "chief" of Arembepe for two decades, until 1942. Miguel replaced Francisca as landlord-in-residence and became Arembepe's last landowner chief. He supervised the harvest and sale of his coconuts and granted permission to build houses and huts. He co-owned a sailboat and headed a fishermen's cooperative that existed briefly around 1940. Local memory of Miguel's impact on village life doesn't suggest that he limited villagers' freedoms or interfered much in their economic activities. Despite being middle class, Miguel is remembered as a benevolent participant in community life.

His two sons, both retired civil servants like their father, moved to Arembepe after his death. One lived there for almost a decade with his second wife, thirty years his junior. The other son played a larger role in local life. He opened a store, and as part-owner of a boat, contributed to the fishermen's association. Unlike his father, he never played a leadership role. Both brothers eventually moved back to the Salvador suburb in which they had been born and raised, but because the second brother still visited Arembepe during my fieldwork, I was able to observe his interactions with villagers. This landlord was treated like, and acted like, an older Arembepeiro. He had learned how to modify, when in Arembepe, whatever cultural rules he observed in the stratified town where he lived. His "style shift"—to borrow a term from sociolinguistics (see Labov, 1972)—was obvious in what he did and said. For example, he gave certain villagers the warm hug *(abraço)* that men who are socially equal use in Brazilian greeting ritual. He also knew how to use the familiar and formal "you" forms as villagers employed them. He used familiar terms with people his age and younger, and formal terms *(o senhor, a senhora, Seu, Dona)* with much older people. Villagers reciprocated, using either formal or familiar terms with him just as they did with local people. For example, Prudencio, who in this landlord's absence took care of his coconut trees, treated him with the familiarity reserved for friends.

These cases of Arembepeiros' dealings with their landlords and of the landowners' participation in village life illustrate the weakness of the patronage relationships in which villagers have participated. For landlords, just as for wholesalers seeking fish, success in the local economy demanded behavior appropriate to Arembepe, guided by an ideology of equality. The people of Arembepe befriended, respected, or ridiculed landowners for their behavior and accomplishments, not merely because they were landlords. This is part of a lack of class consciousness that was a prominent feature of local ideology, discussed in more detail in the next section of this chapter. The openness and directness of villagers' behavior with landlords also reflected the fact that the landlords had themselves downplayed the patron's role, never seeking to limit their tenants' freedom or mobility.

In 1965 villagers were somewhat uneasy about Jorge Camões's plans for the estate's subdivision. Still, I often heard favorable comparisons of Arembepe's landlords with those of other fishing villages. The people in a fishing village to the north had just won a partial victory in protracted litigation against their landlords. A fisherman told me the story. "Those awful landowners tried to evict people who had lived there all their lives. They wanted to tear down their houses so they could turn the village into a coconut plantation. One of the sons of the family had studied agriculture at the university. He wanted to try new ways of growing coconuts, at the fishermen's expense." The court allowed the villagers to remain but curtailed their freedoms. Marketers couldn't enter the village, which was now surrounded with a barbed-wire fence. Fishermen had to take their fish outside to be sold. Villagers were prohibited from roofing their homes with tile, nor could they even repair their houses. Despite the villagers' nominal victory in court, badgering by the landlords continued. That village's days as a fishing community seemed numbered.

Arembepeiros were well aware of the contrast between other landlords and their own, whom they labeled "the best." Still, they worried about Jorge's plans. Jorge told me that there would be three groups of lots: beachfront property, lots between the village and the lagoon, and lots west of the lagoon system. (This division was evident in Arembepe in 1973; the last group of lots formed the site of Caraúnas, a new, extremely poor satellite.) For the first time villagers would be able to own their house sites. Previously only the dwellings had been owned. Nominal rents had gone to the landlords, via Prudencio, for the land where the houses stood. Most of Arembepe's more valuable houses—those with brick walls, tile roofs, and cement floors—had been assessed by municipal officials, and their owners paid an annual tax. This arrangement helped guarantee their investments. A landlord who wished to evict a householder was required by law to pay the assessed value as recompense. This, of course, was only partial protection, since house values were spiraling with inflation.

Jorge assured me he had no plans to dispossess villagers with substantial investments in homes. He planned to give them their present lots, unless the transfer fee was higher than a small sales price, which he would then accept. Jorge also planned to (and did) encourage poorer villagers, those with wattle-and-daub shacks, to move west of the lagoon, where he gave them lots in what was to become Caraúnas.

In 1980, with much of the subdivision done, only a few villagers felt cheated. Many people had bought their old house sites. Others had traded their beachfront houses for larger homes and lots nearer the lagoon, made from equivalent materials. Here again, an Arembepe landlord did not ride roughshod over his tenants, although he did look out for his own interests. Notice once more the contrast with the general condition of the Brazilian peasantry. In discussing the conditions that led to the formation of the revolution-minded peasant leagues in northeastern Brazil in the 1960s, Forman stresses tenants'

> constant threat of summary eviction. . . . Peasants have little recourse when they are ordered off the land by the hired guns of the rich, who emphasize the immediacy of their demand by destroying crops and sometimes houses. In no case does a landowner allow a tenant to remain on the land for any length of time approximating ten years, when laws of usufruct would give the tenant permanent rights. (Forman, 1975, p. 55)

Arembepeiros had been remarkably well shielded from such threats and actions.

Jorge and Prudencio, his agent, were only shadows of the *coroneis* (colonels or local oligarchs) whose careers in rural Brazilian politics have been described by Daniel Gross (1973). Jorge supported Prudencio's candidates in municipal politics, and Prudencio made sure Arembepeiros voted "along with Jorge" at the state and national levels.

Jorge guided his actions so as to minimize local resentment for several reasons. Even after the 1964 military coup, which reduced national party politics to a government party and a token opposition, Jorge hoped for a role in state politics. No matter how small, Arembepe was his base. A patron's "most important asset is his reputation, and therefore, in some sense the most important task his dependents can perform is to enhance his reputation by spreading the word of his 'goodness' throughout the countryside" (Forman, 1975, p. 77). Since Jorge couldn't predict the future of Brazilian politics, he tried to keep his following, despite the stifling effects of a dictatorship on elective politics.

Jorge also knew that buyers of lots in Arembepe would value a resident lower-class population to supply cheap labor (as servants and menials) and products (e.g., fish and coconuts). He recognized Arembepe's charm and beauty and correctly foretold that city people would extol its quaintness and seeming isolation.

Unfortunately, Jorge could not predict that the heirs of

Francisca's cousins (fallen gentry like his own ancestors, but with more need for money) would agree to sell their land south of Arembepe to a multinational corporation that would devastate the countryside by constructing a chemical factory. Yet this sad event also sheds light on the conditions that have governed Arembepe's relations with outsiders and that have underlain its weak patronage system. The German-based corporation in question had been seeking a factory site up and down the Bahian coast. Repeatedly, however, learning of the factory's potential for pollution, would-be sellers were blocked by neighboring landed interests and their agents in government. Jorge's own political clout proved insufficient to halt a sale by his distant cousins that has devalued his own investment.

Readers who are familiar with sharper class contrasts may now understand more clearly just how narrow the gap has been between Arembepeiros and their landlords. Francisca's heirs have had varying degrees of success in the Bahian middle class, but Jorge holds the family's first university degree. He alone warrants the title "Doctor," which enhances the status of an aspiring patron. Neither Jorge's uncles nor his mother studied beyond primary school. Some Arembepeiros have better educations. No wonder villagers have treated most of their landlords as equals. The people of Arembepe have no conception of landownership's historic role in Brazil as a criterion of high social status. No obvious contrast in education, behavior, or even life style has compelled villagers to defer to such people.

But with Jorge there is a tremendous difference. Here we find Arembepe's closest approximation to classical patronage relationships. Unlike the other landlords and the fish buyers, Jorge has never fully learned the local social system. He never adopted the ideology of equality. He did not shift style, behaving one way to lower-class people outside Arembepe and another way to Arembepeiros. Jorge acted like a patron, and villagers had to shift *their* style. They deferred to Jorge. Although Arembepeiros had little practice acting out patron-clientship, here they were fast learners.

Some villagers have tried to make Jorge a more active participant in their lives, without much success. By 1965 he had five local godchildren, but he couldn't remember their names. When I asked him for this information, he turned to Prudencio, who supplied it. Unlike the relationship between Jorge's uncle and Prudencio, in which both used familiar terms and treated each other as equals, Jorge used familiar terms with Prudencio—a man twenty-five years his senior— and got formal terms in return. Jorge treated villagers in that oblivious manner that high-status Brazilians sometimes adopt when dealing with social "inferiors"—although he did this unconsciously and without malice. Jorge simply lacked interest in learning to act like a local. He had no plans to participate in village life as an Arembepeiro.

Although Jorge had mastered his role as patron, he was unaware that villagers needed coaching as supporting actors. As Jorge's agent, Prudencio took over the job of teaching, through the example of his own behavior, how one acted toward a patron. Prudencio could also illustrate the rewards of patronage. Jorge let Prudencio market the fish from the two boats he bought in 1964 and 1965. Although Prudencio never admitted to receiving a salary, he may have extracted a portion of the land rents he collected. He certainly made money supervising the marketing of the landlords' coconuts. Prudencio's wife, though hardly more qualified than certain other village women, had been the municipally appointed and salaried schoolteacher since 1946. Even more significantly, their sons had used the patronage of Jorge and his uncles to find good outside jobs. Villagers knew that they got to Jorge through Prudencio and that to do so they needed to act like Prudencio.

Prudencio was a critical link in Arembepe's relationship with the outside world. Besides the economic benefits, Jorge's backing permitted Prudencio to pursue his ambitions in county politics. Still, Prudencio's wealth, income, and life style never raised him beyond the lower class. Like successful fishermen, he merely stood at the top of a local success ladder. His ambitions were mainly political. His sons, more obviously than Prudencio himself, profited economically. Villagers respected Prudencio for his own accomplishments and his role as landowners' agent. Although local people granted Prudencio special prestige, and although he had a reputation and influence in municipal politics, he was always careful to observe local cultural rules. He took his social obligations seri-

ously. Not surprisingly, in 1965 he had more godchildren than
any other villager. Prudencio was always careful to respect
the ideology of equality. In life style and behavior he remained firmly in the local social system.

Prudencio was one of those talented people whose particular abilities can stand out clearly in an egalitarian community,
where people have a chance to "make it on their own." Prudencio made it in politics and as a mediator between the
villagers and the landed interests that helped shape their
destinies. Prudencio did not simply link Arembepe to the
landowners and to outside politics. He also served as a model
for one of the success paths available to villagers. Other
Arembepeiros have been models for different paths, for example, that of the aspiring captain-owner or the businessman.
Such men have all mediated and promoted change.

Although many villagers sought Jorge's help through Prudencio, they knew they couldn't expect the same benefits that
Prudencio and his family got. Thus, as is generally true of
patron-clientship (as previously distinguished from patron-
dependency), villagers sought their own patrons. Local people tried to establish individual personal links with outsiders.
For example, all the people who own vacation homes in
Arembepe have maintained patronage relationships with particular villagers.

During the 1960s, middle-class outsiders injected small
amounts of cash into the local economy by offering menial jobs
to villagers, either in Arembepe or as domestics in Salvador.
Unmarried women and female household heads usually preferred domestic work in Arembepe to a similar job in Salvador. Although wages were less, women had access to a better
diet for their families. The lower-middle-class owner of the
house we rented in 1964 and 1965 insisted that we hire two
local women as cook and washerwoman. She had employed
our cook's sister as a seamstress and wanted our wages to go
to a local family she knew. The homeowner also wanted
someone she could trust, to ensure that her house and possessions got good care.

Our landlord's request created a problem for me, since I
had previously employed two other local women whose patron was the owner of the house I rented in 1962. From that
stay they had come to regard me as their patron and expected

to be reemployed. My solution was to split various tasks among three of the women and the adolescent son of the fourth. This arrangement provided cash and food for several households.

During our work in Arembepe many villagers befriended me and other team members and acted as our informants. Each anthropologist established especially close relationships with certain villagers. Others, recognizing these bonds, concentrated on different field team members. To varying degrees, these villagers were all seeking the patronage of particular outsiders. Thus on my return in 1973, when (for the first time) my research grant included money for a local field assistant, it was natural for me to hire Alberto, my most reliable informant. Betty was asked by Dora, our 1962 cook, with whom Betty had a close relationship, if she could cook for us again.

Individuals, Not Classes

Keeping this discussion of Arembepe's links to the outside world in mind, comparison with Coqueiral, a coastal village 300 kilometers to the north, which Shepard Forman was studying while I was working in Arembepe in the mid-1960s, will illustrate some additional reasons for variation among rural Brazilians. Again, it will help show why—despite Arembepe's poverty, illiteracy, powerlessness, and poor public health—I have dared to call it paradise. Unlike Arembepe, Coqueiral had the bad (but much more typical) luck of being linked both politically and economically to its municipal seat. Most of its people were at the bottom of the county's stratified hierarchy, which was headed by the owners of the large sugar plantations nearby. Below the plantation owners, but with privileged access to the county elite, was the group that Forman (1970) calls Coqueiral's "local bigwigs"—the top layer of the local stratified hierarchy, the president of the fishermen's guild and the major coconut-tree owners. The fishermen occupied a degraded position, with an income below the (then) minimum wage of $20 a month. Rewards easily available in Arembepe were missing in Coqueiral.

The crucial difference was Coqueiral's much greater poverty, compared with Arembepe's steadily improving fortunes. Reflecting this contrast, Coqueiral had many *fewer* leveling mechanisms. The witchcraft accusations, gossip, social ostracism, and crew desertion that worked against "upstart" Arembepeiros (people who ignored community obligations and violated the ideology of equality) had no parallels in Coqueiral. This was because the external support of Coqueiral's bigwigs was too powerful for such mechanisms to be effective. Moreover, the other villagers were too poor for leveling to be necessary.

Given these contrasts, Coqueiral had class consciousness, which Arembepe lacked. According to Forman the fishermen of Coqueiral are

> well aware of the nature of the bonds which tie them to the dominant segments of society and which clearly limit their mobility. They think in terms of 'We and they' and 'everything for them, nothing for us.' They contrast themselves to the rich and the powerful and fear that they themselves are 'nothing in the world.' When queried as to why they do not try to improve their situation, they correctly cite lack of opportunity. (Forman 1970, pp. 137–138)

Confronted every day with the glaring contrast between their own life styles and the life styles of the local and municipal elites, Coqueiral's fishermen developed a class consciousness. By contrast, Arembepe's economy offered a series of rewards to lower-class people. This hindered the emergence of class consciousness, even of group consciousness. Given a local ladder of success, villagers saw the contrasts in wealth, income, and prestige in terms of individuals instead of classes.

Precisely because Arembepeiros knew that individual villagers could improve their lot, their view of their own place in Brazilian society was an imperfect one. This was yet another socially significant mystification—like the riddle of the spots in Chapter 4. Because Arembepeiros viewed success and mobility purely in local terms, most of them remained unaware of the implications of the local leveling mechanisms (e.g., expected sharing in proportion to success). Nor were they fully conscious of the larger barriers that constrained them: their lower-class background, limited education and job skills, and ultimate powerlessness against external interests—from hippies to multinational corporations—that would eventually intrude on village life.

Arembepeiros were deluded into seeing local success as true success. Local achievement was as satisfying as mobility in the national class structure. Hidden, therefore, behind the local ladder of wealth and social status were larger social and economic forces that blocked mobility and kept all Arembepeiros in the national lower class. The people of Arembepe never developed a consciousness of themselves as belonging to a national class because they were too busy competing with each other in local entrepreneurial activities.

Experiencing the World Outside

Although fully familiar with poverty, someone who never left Arembepe might, therefore, never have discovered that he or she was a member of a national lower class. As we saw previously, a requirement for outsiders' success in Arembepe's economy was that they modify their behavior to fit the ideology of equality. This impeded the introduction of external social patterns, such as those based on class differences.[2] The main way to learn about the national class structure was to live outside. Of course, villagers who left took along their ideology of equality. How long and how firmly they clung to it depended on how often they went outside, where they went, and how long they stayed. People who made occasional trips to Salvador's stores, houses of prostitution, or supermarkets might complain of the rudeness of city folk without realizing they had experienced patterns in a national stratification system. Women who worked as domestics learned about the "politeness" that city people expected. But many of the middle-class families who vacationed in Arembepe complained that Arembepeiros made poor servants and usually quit. During the 1960s most villagers were content to live out most of their lives at home. Although at least one person in half the households had worked outside, most had done so only temporarily in order to bring cash, the means to a more comfortable life, back home.

Because they rarely visited the city, Arembepeiros had trouble finding their way around when they did go. The trip took at least two days and one night. There was the 18-kilometer walk to Portão, followed by a long, crowded bus ride. The city voyager was a resource to be tapped. Arembepeiros asked their relatives and neighbors to run errands for them in the city—to buy, for example, cloth for a dress to be made on one of the few (manual) sewing machines in the village. Once in Salvador, villagers didn't stray far from the stores and vendors near the bus station.

One expression of Arembepe's lack of formality and ignorance of external norms was irritating to us. During our first stay, village children, fascinated with the young strangers who had come to study them, saw no reason why we shouldn't be just as closely scrutinized. During our first month, our privacy was shattered each time we opened our window by a dozen kids leaning in to watch our every move. If we asked them whether they wanted something, they usually said no. The most tenacious girl, we discovered, did have designs on our chocolate bars (they kept disappearing when we left the room). The rest were there simply to observe the domestic behavior of the strange young men with pale skins and typewriters. "Good manners" go along with a well-developed class structure. Poor people are expected to know how to act with members of the privileged classes. Arembepeiros didn't tell their children not to bother the Americans, because in a homogeneous community where everyone had had years to learn about everyone else, what could be wrong with sizing up the newcomers as quickly as possible?

Those who had learned the most about the outside world were the villagers who had fished on commercial trawlers out of Salvador or Rio de Janeiro. Men who had lived in Rio complained about crime, overcrowding, and particularly the cost of food and lodging. They talked of their longing for wife, parents, children, and the small Bahian village of their birth. These men had experienced the plight of the urban poor, the inconvenience, impersonality, and squalor of Rio's *favelas* (shanty towns), the slums of nearby Niterói, the tenements and hovels of Salvador's inner city.

They had seen the huge contrasts between the life styles of unskilled laborers and those of the elites. Some local women had worked in comfortable apartments and homes in Salvador. In Rio, Arembepeiros had walked along the beaches of

Betty strolls past a row of houses in northern Arembepe in 1962, accompanied, as usual, by a horde of children. (Conrad P. Kottak)

Copacabana and Ipanema, past the high-rise luxury apartments—their ornate lobbies replete with jungle plants, marble tables, and abstract paintings—each building heavily guarded against criminal intruders. Tomé, who had fished out of Rio for seven years, told of having his clothes and watch stolen when he left them unguarded on the beach while he took a dip in the ocean. Even those native sons who were doing very well, in villagers' estimation, working for the national oil company on the outskirts of Salvador, were learning what it meant to be a member of the lower class, albeit of its upper segment.

Havinghurst and Moreira (1965, p. 100) divide Brazilian society into five classes: upper, upper middle, lower middle, upper working, and lower working. As rural fishermen, Arembepeiros belonged to the lower working class, which also includes farm laborers, unskilled urban workers, and peasants. The upper working class—to which the oil workers belonged—includes people with skilled and semiskilled jobs in factories, public service, railroads, transportation, and communication. Fifteen native sons were working for the oil company in the mid-1960s, drawing an average annual salary worth about $1,700. Compared with even the most successful local captain-owners and business people, this was a large and regular salary—about ten times the cash income of the ordinary fisherman. Their incomes supported Arembepe's most opulent life styles. One man had a three-year-old jeep, the only locally owned motor vehicle in 1965. Another was planning to buy a car. Both were among the rare villagers with kerosene refrigerators and stoves powered by bottled gas, brought to Arembepe by automobile.

Most villagers agreed that Petrobrás employment was the best job an Arembepeiro could get. Requirements for work in oil weren't stringent. A good word from landlord Jorge and a third-grade education permitted the applicant to take an exam. Natives who passed made between $500 and $2,500 per year. Their work took them to Salvador and its suburbs and to drilling sites in adjacent municipalities. By living in stratified towns, these men learned that despite their success compared with Arembepeiros, they were still members of a national lower class. Although they could afford possessions that most Arembepeiros lacked, their salaries couldn't support middle-class life styles. Nor did their manners, conduct, speech, or education distinguish them noticeably from members of the lower working class. Thus, although a Petrobrás job was an Arembepeiro's greatest ambition, the actual experiences of oil workers outside made it clear that they were small fish in a mammoth pond.

Arembepe's relations with the outside world during the mid-1960s may now be summarized. Villagers' links to wider systems were favorable compared with other rural communities in northeastern Brazil. Improving access to Salvador and favorable marketing opportunities meant that the distribution of Arembepe's fish was never monopolistically controlled. Nor had outsiders ever derived substantial profits from Arembepe or its people. The separation of Arembepe's economic and political affairs, which contrasted strongly with the situation in rural Brazil generally (Gross, 1973, p. 141), was another reason why entrepreneurial activity flourished. The local economy supported more prosperous life styles than those available to other Brazilian peasants and fishermen. Yet a worldview that evaluated success in individual terms, and mainly in a local context, kept Arembepeiros from fully recognizing and confronting the local leveling mechanisms and the wider barriers to social mobility.

This was the relatively egalitarian and insulated village I left in 1965. This chapter's discussion of motorized fish buyers and Jorge's plan to sell real estate gives ample evidence, however, that Arembepe's insulation, which had never been complete, was about to end. The arrival of our field team in 1962 can be seen as part of the first phase of what was soon to become a dramatic process of internationalization. After all, who is more likely than an anthropologist, a missionary, or a trader to make earliest sustained contact with a remote village? These were the professions of most of the strangers who had come to Arembepe through the mid-1960s.

In the late 1960s and early 1970s, as I was busy investigating and writing about cultural diversity in an even more remote part of the world—the island of Madagascar—a wave of new outsiders, many foreign, repeated my discovery of Arembepe. Many of them had moved on by the time I next returned, in 1973. Others, and their creations—most notably the titanium dioxide factory—stayed on. As I saw it, this band of outsiders had managed to devastate my community in less than a decade. Chapter 6, based on my encounter with Arembepe in 1973, sets the stage for the description of today's radically altered community.

Part Three

Assault on Paradise

6 The Browning of Arembepe

This chapter delves beneath the surface changes mentioned in Chapter 2 to examine specific ways in which increased contact with the outside world and changes in the local economy had affected social relations and attitudes in Arembepe between 1965 and 1973. Given its nearness to a big city, it was expectable that Arembepe would experience, sooner than more remote places, the effects of the "Brazilian economic miracle." Centrally planned by a military government that had ousted an elected president in the "Revolution of 1964," the "economic miracle" produced a spectacular average annual real growth rate of 11 percent in Brazil's gross national product between 1968 and 1974.

The prime movers in Brazil's economic development have been the government and the multinational corporation. Both have influenced life in Arembepe. Brazilian development strategy has emphasized highways, and the road that since 1970 has linked Tibrás, the factory near Arembepe, to Salvador was the local expression of the doubling of Brazil's paved highway network between 1965 and 1973. Brazilian automobile production (controlled mainly by multinationals) grew even more dramatically. It had grown fivefold, to almost 1 million cars a year by 1975.

The most basic changes in Arembepe were that its population was swelling, particularly from immigration, and its economy was becoming more diverse. There were signs of growth everywhere. The stage had been set for all the major changes that were obvious in the 1980s.

Middle-class summer people had built houses north and south of the village. A new settlement, Caraúnas, with fifty houses and 200 people, lay just west of the brown lagoon. Construction was booming in Arembepe itself. Since there was little space to the east, the seaward side, most houses were being built between Arembepe and the lagoon, extending the village westward. Even lower-middle-class people from the capital were well enough off to buy many of the houses in Arembepe's central square and northern rectangle. Usually they tore down the old dwellings to build more durable, comfortable, and ostentatious quarters. As access to the city improved, a flood of newly prosperous city people sought beach property to use during weekends, holidays, and summer vacations. Arembepe, just an hour away on a mostly asphalted road, seemed a good place to build.

Villagers also felt that they were benefiting from a booming economy. Many now put their extra cash in rental property, rather than farmland or coconut trees. Several villagers were converting their homes into duplexes, extending them backward, on lots they had bought from Jorge as his lotting scheme proceeded. A new living pattern showed the importance of rentals. Villagers with duplexes would vacate their usual quarters in front, more accessible to the sea breezes, and live in back while summer people rented their homes. Although only 10 percent of the houses were rented during our 1973 stay, a third had been rented—and would be again—in December and January.

Improved bus service and automobiles also brought a weekly influx of nonrenters. City people visited Arembepe for weekend picnics, bathing, and revelry—mainly on Sunday. As it is throughout Brazil, Sunday is the Bahian family's day to eat out. (For Brazilians who can afford maids, Sunday is the usual maid's "day off.") The picnickers who came to Arembepe were mainly *farofeiros*, lower-middle-class and working-class people who brought along plastic containers of *farofa*, refried manioc flour mixed with egg or meat. Among more elite Brazilians, the term *farofeiro* is disparaging. When city folk told me Arembepe had become a haunt of *farofeiros*, they were saying it had become a honky-tonk beach, like New York's Coney Island.

Weekend visitors also came to eat fresh fish, either fried or served as *muqueca* (a fish stew made with tomatoes, onions, coconut, and palm oil). Arembepe now had ice chests and refrigerators (fueled by bottled gas), so that fresh fish could be kept for direct retail sale to tourists. Several villagers had opened restaurants and bars. Refrigeration also meant cold beer, and a pattern of heavy weekend drinking had started by 1973. Stores, bars, and restaurants were springing up all over town—responses to Arembepe's quantum leap from insulated fishing village to internationally known tourist attraction.

The more notorious side of Arembepe's transformation involves industrial pollution and hippies. These two multinational intrusions were linked. As early as the mid-1960s, the German-Brazilian corporation that would eventually build Tibrás (Titanium of Brazil) just 5 kilometers from Arembepe was looking at potential factory sites in Bahia. The original plan was to build Tibrás in southern Bahia, near the city of Ilhéus. However, a combination of political pressure and difficult access to water, roads, and electricity there led Tibrás to choose the Arembepe area instead.

In making titanium dioxide, a basic ingredient in paints and dyes, Tibrás uses no local resources. The main raw materials are a black sand imported from Australia and sulfur from Mexico and Venezuela. Unlike southern Bahia, water, roads, electricity, and politics posed no insurmountable obstacles in the area near Arembepe. The freshwater lagoon system offered abundant water. Preparations for a paved highway were already underway, along with plans to open Arembepe to tourism. Tibrás sped up road construction by paying 80 percent of the paving cost between the factory site and Portão, 13 kilometers away. The factory was electrified by 1970, although electricity from a different source, the state power department, didn't reach Arembepe until 1977.

The local social system was a final factor in the decision to locate the factory near Arembepe. The "fallen gentry" of the municipality of Camaçari could muster neither clout nor coalition to block an industry whose potential for pollution had already been exposed by the national media. Tibrás got its land by buying parcels from small-scale local landowners, most of whom thought themselves lucky to get higher prices than they had ever imagined for their nonbeachfront property. Arembepe's landowners owned none of the land where the factory was constructed.

A curious dialectic between the positive and negative effects of Tibrás on tourism and village life has dominated local history since 1967, when Tibrás began to hasten the completion of the road. On the one hand, tourism in Arembepe would have lagged for years if Tibrás had not intervened to pave the highway. On the other, industrial pollution subsequently threatened Arembepe's reputation as a tourist site. The initial agreement had been that Tibrás and the state road department would share the costs of asphalting the road, which would eventually reach Arembepe. Ultimately, Tibrás paid more, since state funding couldn't keep up with Tibrás's schedule for completion. Thus Tibrás was mainly responsible for the paved road that became Arembepe's main link with the outside world and that made it more accessible to tourists, including the hippies, whose heyday in Arembepe (1970–1971) followed completion of the highway to the factory site.

Yet Tibrás also caused the pollution that attracted so much media attention in 1973. Tibrás wastes (ferrous sulfate and sulfuric acid) hadn't just permeated the lagoons. They were also being dumped offshore, which threatened the fishery that had sustained Arembepe for years. Although Arembepeiros acknowledged that the road was good for business, although a dozen local men had jobs at the factory, and although Tibrás personnel ate meals, rented rooms, bought fish, and brought other business to Arembepe, local opinion had turned against the factory by 1973. Villagers were particularly annoyed at the destruction of the lagoons where they customarily washed and bathed.

The ensuing media coverage gave Arembepeiros a new kind of clout, which eventually halted the most obvious pollution. Throughout Bahia and Brazil, people were hearing about the destruction of a "natural," "simple" fishing village by a multinational corporation. One man joked that Bayer, the German company that owned 38 percent of Tibrás, had deliberately planned the pollution so as to increase suffering—and the demand for Bayer aspirin in Bahia. (In reality, Arembepeiros were complaining more about burns than headaches.) With state and national opinion mustered against the factory, it was evident that something would have to be done. (It had been—through more effective pollution controls—by 1980.)

The pollution scandal was Arembepe's second encounter with the media. Its post-Woodstock invasion by international hippies had already brought it national recognition, through stories in the Brazilian equivalents of *Time* and *Newsweek*. There had been hippies in Arembepe as early as 1966–1967. At first they came in summer and were mainly Brazilians. As the hippie movement itself became international, and as flower children dispersed after the 1969 Woodstock Festival (in Bethel, New York), young people from all over the world, including many Americans, began to trickle into Arembepe.

In 1970–1971 the trickle became a flood. Many hippies lived in Arembepe proper, but the main hippie enclave became "the Aldeia." This was a settlement on the banks of the Caratingi River, whose waters, prevented by sandstone formations from finding an immediate outlet to the Atlantic, back up and wash south to form the area's distinctive freshwater lagoon system. Use of the term *aldeia*, otherwise applied to the villages of Brazil's Native American (Indian) tribes, symbolized the hippies' attempt to rediscover nature and to create a simple, communal, and "primitive" life style.

There were also economic reasons for the hippies to like Arembepe. As the vanguard of the outsiders who would eventually choose Arembepe as a vacation spot, hippies appreciated not just the natural beauty but the cheapness of food and rents. The wattle-and-daub and palm-frond huts on the northern and southern fringes of the village could be rented for next to nothing. Local women could be found to prepare food and do washing. Most of the hippies were urbanites who didn't want to work. They could eke out a pleasant and relaxed existence on the money they had brought along, and occasional contributions from relatives. The hippie migration from Arembepe to the Aldeia wasn't just a search for isolation. It became an economic necessity with the arrival of the lower-middle-class tourists from Salvador, who were willing to pay higher rents than the hippies were. The cost of housing, food, and living rose as tourism increased.

There had always been a small village where the Aldeia grew up, a thirty-minute walk north along beach or lagoons. In summer, when the lagoons dried up, Arembepeiros had always gone to the Caratingi to wash and bathe. The combination of isolation, year-round water, cheap supplies, and spectacular setting was sufficient to attract international hippies and the Brazilian students who joined them during summer vacations. Only twenty hippies lived in Arembepe proper and in the Aldeia in winter 1973, although more came during the summer.

There's no way of knowing just how many hippies had visited Arembepe at the height of the movement. Villagers spoke of "hundreds," even "thousands." There were concerts in the Aldeia by Brazilian rock stars. A visit by Mick Jagger became part of the Aldeia's quasimythical past for the stragglers who stayed on. In 1980 I was shown the ruins of the "House of the Sun," where Jagger and Janis Joplin are said to have slept. The ritualized retelling of the Jagger-Joplin story by hippie after hippie reminded me of the creation myths and mythological charters that anthropologists encounter in other societies. In the fragmented social system that is all that remains of a once-populous Aldeia, Mick and Janis had become the analogues of Adam and Eve.

Although I have overcome the resentment toward the hippies I felt in 1973, I still believe that the media accounts of the hippie invasion overestimated their impact on local life. The hippies should be seen simply as part of Arembepe's general tourist boom. Tourism and industrialization have worked together to transform local life. Joining hundreds of other temporary, seasonal, and more permanent residents, the hippies helped introduce the culture patterns of the outside world to Arembepe, along with new fears, aspirations, and insecurities.

Occupational Diversity

It was evident in 1973 that Arembepe's days as a mainly fishing village were numbered. It was becoming one of those more typical, occupationally diverse fishing villages mentioned in Chapter 4. Fishing remained the most common job, but the percentage (53 percent of the men) was down sharply from 1964, when 74 percent had claimed fishing as a primary occupation. The number of local business establishments had increased. Women had responded more quickly than men had to the new business opportunities (see Appendix 6). Business had always been one of the few areas where local women could do well. Some of Arembepe's most successful ventures in 1973 were run by women such as "Aunt Dalia" (so named by the hippies), who catered to the flower children of southern Arembepe, and Claudia, who ran the best local restaurant. A quarter of the women who worked for cash in 1973 were business people. Almost as many women (sixteen) as men (twenty) ran businesses.

Arembepe was on the verge of a tourism and business boom. Still, many men were reluctant to abandon other jobs because they were worried about pollution and its chilling effect on tourism. Once this problem was solved, and the tourist trade returned, several men could support their families through business. But during the 1970s, the women did most of the innovating aimed at the tourist trade. (Appendixes 2 and 6 give data on local jobs in 1964, 1973, and 1980.)

Jobs in construction swelled between 1964 and 1973—from 5 percent to 15 percent of the men's primary occupations.

"Aunt Dalia," who by 1973 had built up a good business catering to the hippies of southern Arembepe. (Courtesy Jerald T. Milanich)

Masons, carpenters, and bricklayers came in from outside, and several villagers began to learn those trades. Other villagers found jobs as caretakers for summer people. Villagers prosperous enough to expand their homes supplemented their usual cash with rental income. Factory jobs had also expanded by 1973, ranking just below building as the third most common occupation of local men (11 percent). A dozen villagers worked at Tibrás; others still worked for the national oil company.

Investments in rental units were replacing farm plots and coconut trees as means of protecting surplus cash from inflation and supplementing primary income. By 1973 most fishermen had sold the plots that a dozen of them had farmed a decade earlier. They used their gains to improve and expand their homes, to rent to outsiders. The costs of a farm plot on one of the western estates (three hours walking plus manual labor) were no longer worth the benefits (fresh fruits and vegetables). Cash was now available from tourists in Arembepe. When the vacationers left, the rental-unit owners could enjoy the better quarters they had built to suit city tastes. Fresh produce was now as close as a direct bus ride to the supermarket in Pituba. Local business people also continued to sell fruits and vegetables. With more time for land activities than fishermen had, business people had always had an easier time farming. Along with the residents of the western estates, they increased their output of farm produce to meet rising local demand.

Two familiar features of the local economy were disappearing. Previously, most families had raised chickens. Those who farmed occasionally owned cattle, donkeys, and other livestock. By 1973 most of the chickens eaten locally, like most of the meat, came from the supermarket. The second change was in ownership of coconut trees. About 40 percent of Arembepe's households had owned trees in 1964. The number dwindled during the 1970s as Jorge bought up coconut trees to clear house sites and sell along with the land.

Although Arembepe had never had a purely subsistence economy, the decline of livestock and coconut-tree ownership are additional, if minor, illustrations that the village was giving up its ability to supply its own subsistence needs as its reliance on external products and cash increased. The pattern of growing dependence on the outside world was evident in many areas of the economy in 1973. To summarize: I have noted the increasing prominence of tourism, business, construction, and factory employment; and the declining significance of farming, livestock, and tree ownership. The web being spun out of multiple strands of external dependence was also enveloping fishing—still the mainstay of the local economy. Certain changes in fishing patterns and technology ramified throughout community life.

Motorization and the Fishermen's Cooperative

In the 1960s the most expensive item in the fishing industry had been the fully equipped sailboat ($150 in 1965), and there were several ways in which enterprising fishermen could become boat owners. An older pattern by which a boat was co-owned by its captain and a nonfisherman was changing to full ownership by the fishing owner. In part this shift reflected a marketing advantage: in the 1960s the price of fish had been inflating faster than the cost of a new boat. By 1973 it cost $1,700 to buy a fully equipped motorized boat. There were also gas, oil, and maintenance expenses. (Fishermen still used sails for part of their daily voyage.)

Land-based entrepreneurs were the first to buy motors, but barriers to control over fishing by nonfishermen remained. First, the price of fish had continued to rise faster than the general inflation rate. This reflected growing demand for fish by Salvador, a rapidly expanding metropolis and tourist center, and increased competition among buyers as access to Arembepe improved. A second reason for fishermen's continuing control over fishing was the availability of low-interest loans from SUDEPE (Superintendência do Desenvolvimento da Pesca), the agency charged with "developing" Brazilian fishing industries.

In 1970 SUDEPE had begun a series of visits designed to persuade Arembepeiros to form a fishermen's cooperative. Villagers were told about successful cooperatives elsewhere, and they learned of motorization loans and other benefits.

Previous efforts to build such an organization in Arembepe had failed. This one succeeded initially because the cooperative offered several incentives to join: loans, refrigeration, bait, gasoline, oil, and other supplies. Fishermen were encouraged to keep up their membership—and to sell their fish to the cooperative—by competitive prices (until 1973) and by the debts they contracted to buy motors for their boats. Members weren't supposed to withdraw until their loans were repaid.

The cooperative bought daily catches, stored the fish in an ice vault, and arranged either local sale or transport to urban fish markets. The cooperative and ice vault were housed in a shed just south of the chapel, near the beach where the fishermen unloaded their catch. Local men were paid to record catches, dispense cash and supplies, and deduct loan payments. A SUDEPE agent from Salvador monitored operations on a monthly basis and made sure loan payments were prompt. He also compiled daily catch data into monthly statistics, which provided me with useful data (Appendix 3) on the year-round productivity of local fishing.

Several changes accompanying the cooperative had the immediate effect of improving the time- and labor-effectiveness of fishing. For example, the availability of ice, which permitted preservation of fresh fish, stimulated production. The example of the cooperative also spurred local innovation. One entrepreneur built a massive ice vault. Another did the same, serving some of his refrigerated fish to tourists in a small restaurant and hotel he added onto his store. Formerly, in the rainy season, many boats had remained beached or in the harbor for days, or only fished near shore for family meals. There had been no point in doing a full day's work, captains reasoned, when one couldn't be sure that buyers would make the trip out from Salvador in bad weather. With local ice vaults, fish could be sought, caught, and stored any time.

Ice and motors combined to broaden fishing opportunities, in time and space. Motorization reduced the time it took to reach familiar, productive fishing grounds once used only in the calmest months—December through April. A quick return to harbor was now possible in a sudden storm. Motorization also expanded the range of fishing. Tomé—since my first visit Arembepe's most daring, innovative, and enterprising fisherman, and now its most successful by far—had bought a larger, enclosed, motorized vessel. He captained this boat as far away as the coast of Sergipe—150 kilometers north. Tomé took along a load of ice and sometimes stayed away for four days. (This pattern, called "ice fishing," dominated Arembepe's fishing industry by 1980.) Even the traditional boats, once motors were added, began to fish in more distant banks.

The combination of motors and ice therefore meant more distant fishing trips, fresher catches, and effective storage. The ice vaults also provided ready access to bait—one of the cooperative's most popular products. Formerly, each fishing day, local experts in cast-net fishing had caught sardines and other small fish near shore. This bait fishing had been time-consuming and uncertain, so that here again the cooperative and refrigeration removed a fetter on the fishing industry. Now villagers had a ready supply of local and imported bait.

Data gathered in 1973 (Appendix 3) suggest that, because of these and other changes, fishing productivity had increased significantly since 1965, and that the old seasonal constraints were less important. The rainy season no longer limited productive fishing. The average monthly catch for June through August 1972 almost equaled the monthly average for the whole year. The most significant change was that the average annual marketed catch had grown by about 60 percent—from 3,500 to 5,500 kilograms.

To summarize: Motors, ice, and purchased bait extended the fishing range in time and space, and the immediate effect was to increase production. This meant that the most enterprising fishermen wielded more buying power than ever before. Larger catches and incomes that had outpaced inflation were enabling captain-owners to pay off their motorization loans and to decrease any residue of dependence on nonfishermen.

During a long interview with Tomé in 1973, I found out that he not only owned Arembepe's largest boat (plus an ordinary motorboat used by his two youngest brothers) but also had bought a van to transport his fish to a fish store near Salvador. There he received almost half again as much for his fish (5 cruzeiros per kilogram) as the cooperative was paying (3.4 cruzeiros) in March 1973, when he withdrew from it. Once Tomé saw that he could do better marketing his fish himself,

he rapidly repaid his loan and stopped selling to the cooperative. After deducting gasoline and other marketing costs,
Tomé increased his annual income by about $2,000.

Tomé's confidence and success in dealing with the world
outside were increasing dramatically. He had obtained financing for his van from a Salvador bank, where he had also
been assured of help with future enterprises. By August 1973,
his annual income—barely $1,000 in 1964—surpassed my sal-
ary as an associate professor at the University of Michigan.

Tomé merely led the way. With new opportunities to profit
from fishing, other captain-owners were following his example, repaying their loans so as to increase the price they got for
their fish by severing their relationship with the cooperative.
Weberian Protestant-capitalist values could still spell success
in Arembepe in 1973. Tomé and other entrepreneurs were
reaping the advantages of easier access to Salvador. As they
displaced fish buyers from Salvador and Itapoan, these sons of
Arembepe were themselves becoming large-scale suppliers,
taking fish to wholesalers at central delivery points (Salvador's suburbs). They, and other captain-owners, could also
sell their catch retail to the outsiders who had become a
regular feature of the local scene, especially on weekends and
in summer.

From Skills to Property

While the contrast between land-based entrepreneurs and
enterprising captain-owners continued to decrease, *overall*
socioeconomic differentiation was sharpening. Part of this had
to do with the effects of changes in fishing technology on the
relationship between captain and crew. Specifically, the link
between crew member and captain-owner was becoming less
social and more economic. Because of the costs of motorization, the gap between the captain-owner and his crew was
widening. As more captains became full owners of their boats,
more were receiving "the boat's" share of the daily catch.
"The boat" had previously received one-quarter of the crew's
daily catch. By 1973, reflecting the cost of the motor, interest
payments, gas, and oil, this had increased to one-third. (Another of Arembepe's mystifications: Fishermen weren't really

sure about how much of their fish the boat owner got. "The boat's" share had always been called *o quinto,* "the fifth," of the catch, suggesting a lower contribution than fishermen actually gave. By 1973, instead of giving 25 percent when they paid "the boat's fifth," crew members were handing over one fish out of three for the privilege of fishing.) The captain-owner who fished with three other crew members now got one-third of their total catch (for "the boat"), plus his own quarter (on the average) of all fish caught, for a total of about 50 percent of the boat's catch.[1] The crew member's share was only 17 percent, down from 20 percent in the 1960s. To state the change more dramatically, the captain-owner now got 3 times the crew member's share, compared with 2.3 times that share in 1964. The gap widened further between 1973 and 1980.

Consider another aspect of the growing separation between captain and crew. Previously, like the population of Arembepe itself, captains belonged to a graded socioeconomic hierarchy. The enterprising younger captains were at the top. Older, less vital men stood below them, and "slouches" and alcoholics were at the bottom. The best captains had the most stable crews, caught the most fish, and owned all or part of their boats. Ordinary fishermen in the successful crews got a fair share of the prosperity of their boats and had higher incomes and better diets than the poorer captains. In 1973, by contrast, wealth from fishing was going disproportionately to two clearly separate groups: (1) entrepreneurs (captain-owners and nonfishing owners of motor boats) and (2) other fishermen (ordinary crew and captains who worked on a commission basis for nonfishing owners). The hierarchy of gradual contrasts was dividing and congealing into discrete groups. Social ranking was being transformed into social stratification. (And, as is discussed in the next two sections, considerable tension was being generated by these changes.)

Motorization also meant that the personal skills (eyesight and landmark memory) once believed to distinguish among captains, and between captains and crew, were no longer very important. Most fishing now went on in the summer and fall zones where refined landmarking skills had never been used. So unnecessary had the captain's traditional skills

become that even men who had never fished before bought
motorboats and served as their captains. What clearly *did*
distinguish between members of some crews in 1973 was
differential access to the means of production. Many captains
had large investments in motors and boats, whereas ordinary
fishermen did not. These captains were now drawing a higher
income because of their *property* rather than their special
skills.

The Rise of Stratification

Social distinctions that in the past would have been leveled
out had served as the raw material out of which more permanent contrasts were being constructed—given the changes in
technology and marketing. Socioeconomic differentiation
among fishermen increased markedly as access to the means
of production became more restricted. Men who could afford
to motorize or who were considered sufficiently reliable to get
loans were (1) land-based entrepreneurs—who still had trouble keeping good captains and crews; and (2) successful fishing owners—those who had well-maintained boats, good local
reputations, and possessions to back up their loans.

Those who benefited the most from the changes in fishing
were precisely those people who happened to be at the top of
the hierarchy at a time of major economic and social change.
Previously, their differential success would have been sub-
jected to the leveling mechanisms described in earlier chapters. Their wealth would not have survived their deaths in-
tact, and Arembepe would have remained hierarchical but
unstratified. Now, however, it seemed that some villagers
could look forward to rising out of the national lower class.

What was happening in Arembepe in the 1970s has happened many times as communities have been swept from
egalitarian to stratified social relations. That is, contrasts that
would have evened out under the old socioeconomic conditions were being frozen into discrete categories of privileged
and underprivileged people.

As we have seen, the basis of the captain-crew distinction
was shifting from skills to property, and the rewards of fishing
were becoming increasingly unequal. There had always been

distinctions among captains, based mainly on age and personality. Now, however, the contrast between the successful captain and the slouch ramified throughout social life. As had been true in the 1960s, the men who were the most willing to be captains for nonfishing owners weren't very ambitious or dependable. Some of the old alcoholic captains still worked for a commission; but several of the hired captains, like many ordinary fishermen, were part of Arembepe's growing immigrant population. Most immigrants lived not in Arembepe proper but in less-favored Caraúnas. These fishermen lacked the social ties based on kinship, marriage, and ritual kinship that had always provided social support in the community. Lacking such relationships and residentially isolated, immigrants had trouble finding places in the best crews, and thus in forging links with the villagers who could help them the most. Arembepe's graded hierarchy was turning into different social worlds.

The poorest villagers were being physically distanced from community life and deprived of the fellowship of the parent community. Economic contrasts between owners and workers

Caraúnas, photographed from across a restored lagoon in 1980. (Courtesy Jerald T. Milanich)

were growing. Poor immigrants continued to arrive to tap a booming economy, but they faced new obstacles to full integration in local life. Arembepe now had strong contrasts in life style. Tomé and other entrepreneurs could afford good brick houses with such modern conveniences as indoor plumbing, refrigerators, and gas lights. But the emerging underclass of hired captains and ordinary fishermen spent their evenings in Caraúnas, with the fetor and mosquitoes that surrounded the spoiled lagoon—in a facsimile of the first urban ghetto.

Although many ordinary fishermen still held places in successful boats and thus could afford to stay in, and gradually renovate, their houses in Arembepe, even they were noting the growing contrast between captain-owner and ordinary crew member. Fishing people who had always valued their independence from land-based entrepreneurs had grown more dependent on wealthier fishermen—the captain-owners who granted their livelihood. Social relations in the boat were becoming more like employer-employee relationships. "Things aren't the same since the owners started taking every third fish," asserted one fisherman. Another change in the division of the catch—the extension of the "separate line" principle to small fish and not just large ones—further confirmed the decreasingly social nature of fishing. Previously crews had used a joint line system. They pooled their small fish, dividing them up equally in the evening. The fisherman just quoted went on about the changes: "Now each man marks every fish he catches with his own brand. He puts aside one out of three for 'the boat.' The rest are weighed and sold separately."

Compared with clan- and lineage-based societies in Africa or Oceania, Arembepe had never been a very "community-spirited" place. Villages I studied in Madagascar (Kottak, 1980) had a better developed social sense. They conceptualized an ongoing community of past, present, and future members—a social collectivity independent of its individual members. Even the Arembepe of the 1960s would have scored low on any "social solidarity" test. Kin-based obligations had been only to close kin—parents, siblings, and children. By 1973 the tendency toward atomistic individualism and the decline of community were becoming much more marked. Fishermen were accusing captain-owners of being "interested only in money" and—to increase it—of consulting "spirit mothers" (*mães de santo*), figures in the *candomblé* cult that had flowered in Arembepe between 1965 and 1973.

The Magic of Success and the Growth of Religion

Candomblé, an Afro-Brazilian medico-religious system, which previously had been undeveloped locally, was attracting more and more villagers. Its spread to Arembepe was another dimension of the community's suburbanization, as villagers spent more time outside and as outsiders flocked to Arembepe, so that urban culture patterns were being quickly adopted. In the 1960s some Arembepeiros had consulted a curer on a nearby agricultural estate. Most villagers had made the trip to see that curer work his magic through spirit possession. The shaman hedged his bets: Besides intervening with the spirit world, he had some medical knowledge and prescribed commercial medicines.

Access to the spirit world was closer to home in 1973. *Candomblé*, whose "spirit mothers and fathers" (*mães* and *pais de santo*—literally, mothers and fathers of saints) are influential religious figures in Salvador, had become popular in Arembepe. In the 1960s occasional small-scale *candomblé* ceremonies, with lively rhythms and vigorous dancing, leading ideally to the dancer's possession, had been organized by a few native women who had studied at one of the cult houses in Salvador. Not many villagers had attended. When they did, their goal had not been to enlist spiritual support but simply to "enjoy," as on any festive occasion. By 1973 a spirit mother from Salvador had moved to Caraúnas. She was being consulted by Arembepeiros and was organizing much better attended ceremonies. One native son had also moved to Caraúnas to promote *candomblé* locally after spending years in Salvador.

Having heard that Arembepe now had real *candomblés*, I was eager to attend one. Only one was held during my 1973 visit. It was organized by the spirit mother and father in Caraúnas one Saturday night in August. There were many familiar faces among the participants, including a woman who had returned to Arembepe in 1964 after studying *candomblé* in Salvador and her daughter, who had cooked and cleaned house for members of the 1963 field team. Other participants included Laurentino, the storekeeper whose "devil dog" struck fear in local hearts, and his brother, who had a reputation for becoming deranged and running naked through the streets. Many participants I didn't recognize. They were associates of the organizers and included people from Salvador who had come out for the festivities. Local participants wore colorful costumes, another reflection of the new prosperity. In the past the people of Arembepe couldn't have afforded such elaborate dress.

Marvin Harris had taken our 1962 field team to a *candomblé* house in Salvador, where we had witnessed a proper ceremony, so I knew more or less what to expect. The Arembepe event, with its smaller band and fewer dancing "saints' daughters" (acolytes of the spirit mother or father), was a disappointment. Hour after hour the dancers shuffled lackadaisically around the clearing. When, I wondered, would someone get possessed? "Don't believe that anyone's ever possessed," warned Alberto. "I don't know when they'll start pretending." The drums beat on insistently. One woman began moaning quietly, which, someone told me, meant that she had received a saint. This was nothing like the *candomblé* in Salvador, where half a dozen frenzied women had careened across the floor, colliding like amusement park racing cars, and hooting like banshees—leaving no doubt they were with spirit. By two in the morning I had seen nothing new and decided to go home and get some sleep. The next day, people who had stayed on told me there had been a few possessions. My informants shared my impression that the event had been unconvincing, or at least unexciting.

From discussing *candomblé* with Arembepeiros in 1973, I formed the impression of a belief system in flux. The villagers neither fully accepted nor fully rejected the beliefs and behavior associated with *candomblé*. Rumors circulated about which villagers were clients of the spirit mother in Caraúnas. This gossip was symptomatic of a growing insecurity and suspicion among villagers. Alberto's wife, Carolina, was suffering from an illness they attributed to magical causes. Soon after my arrival in June 1973, Carolina had an attack and moved in with her brother, the spirit father in Caraúnas. Alberto's thirteen-year-old daughter proved susceptible to malign possession. One evening a frantic Alberto got me to drive her to the pharmacist in Itapoan. Her uncle, the spirit-father, had been unable to fend off what turned out to be her second possession that year. The pharmacist's treatment proved effective—a glucose injection from a syringe huge enough to scare off the most tenacious spirit.

The modes of thought necessary for *candomblé* to succeed in the 1970s existed, but were dormant, in the Arembepe of the 1960s. The village of my initial encounters had been remarkably ritual-free. All Arembepeiros had been baptized as Catholics. The resultant ritual kinship (godparenthood and coparenthood) and individual worship of favorite saints were the main local expressions of Catholicism. Two large-scale celebrations *(festas)* were held each year. Saint John was honored June 24 and Saint Francis, Arembepe's patron saint, on February 20. The latter event, which took place in the most productive fishing season, was much larger than Saint John and attracted many outsiders. Still, organized religion had little to do with the bacchanalia that accompanied the Saint John and Saint Francis celebrations.

By 1973 local exposure to organized religion had barely increased. Access to churches outside was easier, but a priest visited Arembepe no more often than in 1965 (twice a year). In theory Brazil is the world's largest Roman Catholic nation; 92 percent of its people claim that faith. Still, only women and children went to chapel in Arembepe; men had nothing to do with formal church participation (except for baptisms). On one of the priest's rare visits, I heard him chastise those attending for their lack of interest in religion. Men claimed to pray to their household and individual saints, but there were no rituals prior to fishing—even during the risky season of rain and rough seas.

Although behavior that was obviously religious was uncommon in the 1960s, villagers did express vague beliefs in such Brazilian folklore creatures as mules without heads, balls of fire, and werewolves. More significantly, they shared common peasant beliefs—that local people profited at the expense of others (the image of limited good) and that wealth could come from pacts with the devil. Villagers were particularly fearful and suspicious of the storekeeper who supposedly had caged a demon.

The *candomblé*-related beliefs and activities of 1973 should be seen not as something entirely new but as an extension and generalization of this preexisting belief system, in a community whose socioeconomic structure was changing from graded hierarchy to stratification. Particularly significant was the fact that villagers had extended their accusations of profiting with supernatural help from storeowners to successful fishermen. I think that increasing supernaturalism was a direct reflection of Arembepe's rapid transformation. Economic changes, alien contacts, and new insecurities favored the growth of religion, as some villagers sought supernatural solutions for unfamiliar problems. Increasing belief in *candomblé* was also a cognitive device that villagers used to interpret what to them must have been a mysterious fact—that local wealth was growing much faster than ever before. And of course, increased cash was itself an underpinning of the new ritual activity, which the old Arembepe couldn't have afforded.

The case of Carolina, Alberto's wife, and their possessed daughter illustrates the relation between wealth, psychological insecurity, and supernaturalism. Carolina's spiritual afflictions developed soon after she opened a small store, which sold low-value items, such as soft drinks, lemons, and kerosene, to neighbors and tourists. Carolina's successful small business was one of many that emerged in response to the tourist trade and the cash flowing into a suburbanizing community. After years of poverty, Carolina's new business activities were fast rivaling her husband's earnings as an ordinary fisherman. Their household income had doubled.

Carolina's business kept doing well despite her illness. An intensification of her condition *and* their daughter's attack closely followed *my* return to Arembepe in 1973, which Alberto had interpreted supernaturally. Although he hadn't known that I would be coming back after eight years, Alberto claimed to have had a dream just before my return—that I would bring money to help him finish building his brick house. I doubt that Alberto ever gave up the belief that my return—and my hiring him as an assistant at a good wage—had supernatural causes.

I believe that, unconsciously, Alberto's wife and daughter (spurred on by a closely related spirit father) were punishing themselves psychosomatically for their family's economic success. In the old days Arembepeiros—good captains, for example—had *gradually* acquired a reputation for success. *Rapid* improvement in fortune had been a rarity and was usually explained in supernatural terms. In the 1970s, rapid growth in wealth was a fact of everyday life, a local manifestation of the "Brazilian miracle."

How are miracles explained? Most Arembepeiros were shackled by a value system that mistrusted marked economic improvement and attributed it to devil pacts. People raised with these beliefs and values found it hard to cope with their new success. Some, like Carolina, who came from a supernaturally oriented family, developed psychosomatic illnesses. They attributed these maladies to the same kinds of devilish spirits, working negatively, that they had previously seen as working positively to promote the success of others. In effect they were saying to other villagers, "No, I can't have made a pact with the devil, despite my apparent prosperity. Far from it, since evil spirits are really harming me more than they are hurting other people." Leaving the specifics of Carolina's case aside, more and more villagers *were* being attracted to *candomblé*—almost surely as a means of dealing with stressful aspects of change. We shall see that in 1980 *candomblé* continued to provide a context for expressing contradictions between the old value system—from a more egalitarian and stable past—and forces of rapid change.

Facing changes too sudden and complex to decipher, Arembepeiros used magical thought to make the new order understandable. Previously they had accused only land-based entrepreneurs of trafficking with the devil. Now ordinary fishermen extended this explanation for success to their own coworkers—the captain-owners who were beginning to act like bosses.

Some of the captains were getting nervous. Fernando, previously a successful captain-owner, had acquired a motorboat and was drawing the new profits. He was also straying from the path that had made him successful. He was drinking too much and actually attending *candomblé,* thus reinforcing other villagers' developing explanation for his success. His insecurity had led to a risky habit—carrying a gun, to use against robbers, dangerous strangers, and other threats he imagined to be lurking in the night. (Fernando's case is fully examined in Chapter 11.)

It wasn't just the economy but a variety of changes that had contributed to the atmosphere of unfamiliarity, uncertainty, fear, and insecurity, as Arembepe grew more vulnerable to external forces. Still, I believe that changes in the relations of production were being expressed in the behavior of Fernando and other fishermen. Captains had to deal not only with their crew's hostility but with their own intensifying achievement drives and competitive urges. These psychological manifestations of change showed up in the behavior of Fernando and (with varied expressions) many other villagers (see Chapter 11). By contrast, a few, like Tomé, managed a comfortable aloofness.

"I know others resent my success, but I don't care. I've got four successful brothers, five sons, and many sources of income."

Tomé was secure; but he stood at the top of the heap, and character stability and adaptability had been factors in his rise.

Innovations and the Risk of Overfishing

Although social relations and the psychological adjustment of individuals were suffering in the mid-1970s, Arembepe's economy was thriving. How long could the boom last? Might not the new technology (combined with industrial pollution from the nearby factory) deplete local marine resources?

Fishing productivity in Arembepe has always varied, seasonally and from year to year. In July 1972, for example, the cooperative's records show that the fleet caught 125 percent of their average monthly catch, whereas fishing was generally bad in July (and throughout winter) 1973. The drop in winter catches between 1972 and 1973 may have been due to overfishing. It may also have had something to do with the stream of industrial wastes flowing into the Atlantic only 3 kilometers south of Arembepe's harbor. Bad weather didn't seem responsible; boats went out most days but didn't catch many fish. Still, I suspect that the drop was a normal year-to-year fluctuation. If overfishing were to blame, it should have shown up in the January–March 1973 season, when slightly *more* fish were caught than in those months in 1972.

Whatever its cause, the lean 1973 winter fishing season did bring into sharp relief a new diversity and experimentation in the fishing industry. New technology was opening niches besides those already discussed; and if the old niches were withholding their usual rewards, many Arembepeiros were finding substantial profits in the new ones—night fishing and lobster fishing. Previously, a few boats had fished at night, at certain times of the year, using kerosene lamps to catch fish attracted by light. Bottled gas permitted villagers to own and operate much more powerful lamps, which they took out in their motorboats to use in night fishing.

The total fishing pattern had changed dramatically. In the 1960s the fleet had set sail in the early morning and returned in the evening—sooner if fishing was bad, later if good. In winter 1973, boats left and returned at all hours of the day and night. This less predictable pattern hadn't been practicable before refrigeration—permitting storage of fish until their transport to the city.

The economic shift affected social relations. Previously the boats had left and returned together. After unloading their gear and dividing their catch, men had shared an evening bath in the lagoon and ambled over to the chapel stoop to talk. In 1973 boats left and returned individually, and fishermen's activities on the land were thrown into disarray. Young men still got together for the Sunday soccer game, but lagoon pollution and the new fishing pattern had forced abandonment of the communal bath. The chapel stoop had been turned over to old men and alcoholics. These were additional ways in which local social life was fragmenting.

Like night fishing, lobstering was an innovative adaptation to the lean season in 1973. A dozen villagers now owned more than 4,000 meters of nylon trammel nets. Trammel nets, which hang in the water and were first used locally in 1965, didn't prove much of a boon to traditional fishing, which continued with hook and handline. But five fishermen (including Tomé and two of his brothers, who together owned more than half the nets) had found them effective in lobster fishing. Previously, a few fishermen had been skilled at catching lobsters, on the reef at night, at low tide, when the rocky surface was greatest. The lobster catches of the 1960s were small, and none was exported.

In 1972 net owners expanded the scale of lobster fishing, so that it contributed significantly to their incomes. Between August and November 1972, for example, a monthly average of 150 kilograms of lobster were sold to the fishermen's cooperative, at three times the unit cost of fish. These had been the leanest hook-and-line fishing months in 1972, with catches only half the year's monthly average. The same five fishermen resumed lobster fishing in June 1973, and production rose to over 320 kilograms per month through August. Although the cooperative had held the cost of fish at almost the November 1972 level, the price of lobster had risen to four times that of fish by June 1973. This was a further incentive for increased lobstering. In June 1973, fishermen's receipts from lobster rose to 80 percent of their total fish sales to the cooperative.

The records of the cooperative show that lobster fishing ceased when hook-and-line fishing became productive again. An improvement in regular fishing was evident when the first large catches started appearing on the beach. The news spread quickly, and fishermen headed for the traditional banks and abandoned the rocky areas near home where the lobster nets were set.

The lobster boom was short-lived. Because lobstering proceeded in a more restricted territory (the rocky areas near shore), it was more vulnerable to overproduction than was open-sea fishing, whose territory expanded through new technology. The brief popularity of lobstering was attributable to its cost-effectiveness—high prices for low labor investment. The nets were easily set and collected. These tasks required two quick trips in a motorboat, instead of a hard day in the sun on the open sea.

By 1980 nets that had once yielded several kilograms of lobster were catching just 1 or 2 kilograms per setting. Lobster prices had fallen relative to those of fish, and it was hardly worthwhile to set the trammel nets. There is little chance of a resurgence of lobstering. Catches continue to decline, and Arembepeiros ignore national conservation laws requiring small lobsters to be thrown back. Villagers still eat whatever-sized lobster they manage to catch.

In the remaining chapters, we will see most of the trends perceptible in 1973 intensifying with time. Arembepe's occupational structure has grown more diverse, and social relations between captain-owners and ordinary fishermen have become more distant. Fishermen travel farther and have grown more dependent on external supplies. Population has kept on growing, and stratification has become more pronounced. Immigrants and tourists continue to arrive, and new settlements have grown up through lotting. Pollution of the ocean has continued, although Tibrás took measures to stop the destruction of the freshwater lagoons. In the 1980s people washed and bathed there again as they had done in the 1960s. There has been no halt to Arembepe's opening up. Today it is one turnoff on a paved highway projected to reach Bahia's northern neighbor, Sergipe state. It is time to tell the more recent story.

Part Four
Reality

7 Another Sunrise in the Land of Dreams[1]

Pleasantly, my first encounter with Arembepe in 1980 brought to mind the sleepy, sun-drenched village I had first seen in 1962, and not the sleazy suburb I remembered from 1973. Given the excellent paved road and the quick trip (about fifty minutes) from our seaside hotel in Salvador, I expected to find more cars in the central square on that Wednesday in August. Had I picked a Sunday to return, my first impressions would have been very different. My most trusted informant and former field assistant, Alberto, for example, would have been busy with his thriving bar and store in the lower street. I would have spent the day dodging, and enduring the embraces of, beer-bloated old friends and acquaintances. I would have seen at once exactly the kind of resort that the Arembepe of 1980 had become—a honky-tonk beach town, a weekend haven for Salvador's working class and lower middle class. Among villagers, I would have noticed that heavy weekend drinking, just perceptible in 1973, had intensified because of certain changes in the economy.

The fishing pattern, for example, had changed radically. Most of the old open sailboats (*saveiros*) had been sold or abandoned. The larger ones had been converted into *barcos*, motorized fishing vessels with enclosed cabins. Fishing expeditions now began Tuesday or Wednesday, when a shipment of ice arrived from the city. Fishing lasted four days, as crews traveled far north of their former fishing grounds, to fish in offshore waters of the villages of Sauipe and Subaúma. Returning Friday or Saturday, many fishermen spent the weekend drinking alongside the visitors from the city.

On my first 1980 Saturday in Arembepe, the morning was rainy; but it cleared by afternoon, and a stream of automobiles ran in and out. There were even more cars Sunday, when we counted 309 automobiles and 3 buses in an area that had only 16 cars and 1 bus the next Monday. In 1973 I had been shocked to see a road sign marked "Arembepe." The 1980 equivalent was my difficulty finding a Sunday parking place in Arembepe itself.

One Saturday Alberto complained of an especially busy Friday night. People had sat on his doorstep until seven in the morning drinking beer and liquor. The weekend offered other diversions. Music blasted all day Saturday from a discotheque in the central square, but the heavy dancing began at nine in the evening and lasted until four in the morning. The square and beach even had "Bahianas"—the elaborately costumed women who bedeck street corners in Salvador, selling Bahian foods (part of the region's Afro-Brazilian cuisine). Dora, our former cook and now a barmaid, was one of many women working for wages in bars and restaurants, and for tourists. Her labor netted her about $10 per weekend.

By no stretch of the imagination could Arembepe be identified as the predominantly fishing village I had studied in

I had trouble finding a parking place in Street Down There one Sunday in August 1980. (Courtesy Jerald T. Milanich)

A Bahiana sells cooked food in the central square, while weekend tourists wait for a bus. (Courtesy Jerald T. Milanich)

the 1960s. In 1980 just 40 percent of its adult men, and only a third of its total work force, made their living from fishing (see Appendixes 2 and 6). Arembepe had become a tourist town. As one informant remarked, there were bars every-where. A Sunday stroll along Street Down There showed just how complete the transformation had been, providing firsthand illustration of the statistics on occupation I subse-quently collected. One out of every three occupied houses sold something.

The proliferation of bars had contributed to the breakdown of community solidarity. In the 1960s there had been few bars. *Cachaça* by the glass was available at the two large stores near the central square. Returning fishermen often tossed down one or two shots before their evening bath in the lagoon, going home for dinner, and joining the men's group on the chapel stoop. By 1980, men had picked up the habit of drinking in bars close to their homes, where they socialized with neighbors and the bartender's family. Rarely did they venture over to the chapel stoop, which was now usually vacant in the evening. The neighborhood—and even more narrowly, the subneighborhood group of about a dozen houses whose residents drank at the same bar—had replaced the whole-community evening interaction of the past.

Alberto and Carolina were now accustomed to the business success they had found psychologically disturbing in 1973. Their oldest daughter, Maria José, a bright and hard-working woman of twenty-five, was living with Ivan, an ambitious migrant from interior Bahia. Ivan hoped to open his own commercial establishment, preferably a restaurant, in Arembepe. Meanwhile, he had moved into Alberto's small house and helped him with the business. Although Maria José and Ivan had formed a common-law union, he slept on a couch in the living room, while she shared a bedroom with her two younger sisters.

Carolina, Alberto, Maria José, Ivan, and Cosma—Maria José's eighteen-year-old sister, whose 1973 spirit possession was described in Chapter 6—each sold something different. Alberto sold beer, Arembepe's coldest because of his excellent freezer. Normal wintertime Sunday sales of 100 liters brought him a profit of $25. He and Carolina also sold cigarettes, shots of *cachaça,* fruits, vegetables, spices, herbs, razor blades, aspirin, and matches. Cosma was in charge of soda pop. Maria José sold bread, sweets, and roasted peanuts. Ivan made money from cocktails (he had tended bar before coming to Arembepe); and he and Maria José prepared our meals during our stay. Ivan supplemented his income doing odd jobs, painting, plumbing, and electrical work, mainly for summer people.

The business savvy that Ivan hoped would bring success in the tourist trade led him to suggest to Alberto that they build a porch at the back of the house, directly overlooking the Atlantic, which sometimes lapped the foundation of the house at high tide. The fishing fleet now anchored picturesquely right behind Alberto's house. Larger boats needed deeper moorings than the old sailboats. This had forced abandonment of the old reef-protected harbor for the slightly rougher area just south, right behind the seaward side of Street Down There. Ivan and Alberto were correct in thinking that the fresh air and harbor view would appeal to outsiders. Each weekend, city people drank beer and ate seafood snacks in Alberto's outdoor bar.

A few houses down, Aunt Dalia's juice bar also sold beer

but specialized in juice and ice cream. Dalia also had a porch and a view. Her success had been built on sales to hippies in the late 1960s and early 1970s. Young outsiders, along with the dozen former hippies who had stayed on, still brought Dalia substantial business in 1980.

The gap in construction that had formerly separated the end of Street Down There from the summer houses farther south was being filled in. A new restaurant, Arembepe's fanciest, with bow-tied waiters, had just opened on the site where Francisca, Arembepe's slaveowning landlord, had once defended her coconut trees against the pranks of village boys. A former hippie, now considered a permanent resident (*morador*), ran a restaurant, bar, and rooming house just beyond. He rented (filthy) indoor rooms and bamboo cabanas just seaward of the restaurant, under the coconut trees. All of these were occupied one Sunday afternoon. Since I saw few bathers in the nearby Atlantic, I assumed that these shacks were the local version of the "motels of high turnover"—places for rapid sexual encounters—located near the beaches of Salvador and Rio de Janeiro.

It was still true, I was told, that the number of city people who came to Arembepe on Sundays in August was "nothing" compared with summertime tourism. Amy, who ran Claudia's Restaurant, reported that her clientele consisted almost entirely of outsiders. Tibrás officials came two or three times a week throughout the year. Although Amy never knew in advance when they would come, electricity and refrigeration let her store fish and cook when her customers arrived. Unlike the slow winter trade, Amy reported good business even on weekdays in summer. In winter, she served twenty-five to thirty Sunday meals. The number doubled in the summer. Illustrating the extent of villagers' monetary reliance on outsiders were complaints about reduced business during 1980, attributable to a gasoline shortage. Arembepe, too, felt the global energy crunch of 1980. Business had been much better in winter 1979, people said.

Worlds Apart

There was still a difference between weekend visitors and other outsiders who sought leisure in Arembepe. The owners of the comfortable vacation homes on the town's northern and southern fringes were wealthy outsiders who belonged to a separate and distant social world. They maintained their aloofness from villagers and from the outsiders who did their tourism in the village proper. At the end of the northern rectangle, just north of houses owned by wealthier villagers, but still south of landlord Jorge's *casa grande* (which marked Arembepe's northern boundary), stood a row of attractive two-story summer homes, with sea views; many had enclosed garages. When we asked villagers about renting one of these houses for our brief stay, their answer was always the same: "They wouldn't rent." Arembepe's highest-ranking municipal official, the former policeman and naval carpenter, who prided himself on his connections to important outsiders and lived nearby, knew little about these wealthy outsiders. He couldn't even tell us their names. They were said to come to Arembepe on weekends, though we saw little evidence of it in 1980. Villagers assured us that people with such wealth would have no reason to rent.

The same applied to the owners of the houses south of Arembepe, where we had lived in 1973. This area was less isolated than before, because construction had filled in the gap between these houses and the village, and because the summer people now maintained employees who lived in caretakers' quarters or garage rooms. One caretaker told us that the new owner of the most opulent house, built originally by a high state official, came just once or twice a year but surely wouldn't rent. Our 1973 landlord was in Arembepe, recuperating from an operation. Only one house, whose owner, a wealthy woman from Rio, was said to be traveling abroad, could be rented through a lawyer in Salvador, for $700 a month. It was in poor condition, and we decided to seek lodging elsewhere.

Prudencio, who for decades had represented the landlords in Arembepe, had died during our absence. No single individual had replaced him. Some of his roles had disappeared, and others had been split up among several people. For example, because of lotting, the landlords had divested themselves of many of their coconut trees, removing the need for someone to oversee their harvest and sale. In 1980 an immigrant who ran a newsstand at the entry to Arembepe also took care of several of the summer houses. He knew more about the summer people than any other Arembepeiro, since they usually stopped at his stand when they arrived.

Subdivisions

As lotting progressed, Jorge had opened a real estate office in one of the new streets that paralleled the northern rectangle to the west. Although he often visited Arembepe on weekends, Jorge rarely did business there himself, leaving such matters to his younger brother and brother-in-law. One villager told us, insightfully, that with so many social ties to Arembepe, Jorge found it hard to say no to villagers when they asked for special consideration—for example, an extension of the deadline for a monthly payment. His brother-in-law acted as the hard-nosed landlord.

Jorge, educated and upwardly mobile scion of the landowning family that Arembepeiros had known for generations, would forever be considered the village patron. But with Prudencio, his longtime local agent, no longer available as buffer and mentor, Jorge found the patron's role more uncomfortable than ever. After all, he told us, "I'm a professional (engineer)." His increasingly successful career demanded frequent travel, often abroad. Tiring of real estate, Jorge complained, "I don't make much money selling lots. Prices are low and there are all kinds of subdivision expenses. For example, the law says you have to build roads to provide access to each lot. That eats up most of my profits."

In place of villagers' previous uncertainty about the lotting scheme was general acceptance of continued immigration, sales to outsiders, and growth. A few people complained. One woman thought that outsiders were being favored in lot sales. Some, she said, had bought up two or three lots, leaving little choice for villagers who wanted to live near their relatives. "You'd think he might leave land for people from here," she said. Jorge told us that he wished to do just that, but his relatives, who were much more involved in sales than he was, appeared to be less concerned with social ties and more interested in immediate economic gains.

In August 1980, lots were selling for 35,000 cruzeiros (about

AREMBEPE in 1980

$600) cash, but most buyers were putting down 10,000 cruzei-
ros and paying 2,000 cruzeiros monthly for two years. The
landowners had just announced an increase in the down payment to 15,000 cruzeiros (about $250). Because of economic
changes to be described in Chapter 8, this put lot ownership
beyond the means of most of the fishermen.

Local real estate values had increased faster than inflation.
As the national economic miracle had continued, though
slowed down a bit, the flow of cash through the community
had permitted many villagers to improve their homes. Only 15
percent of the houses surveyed in southern Arembepe in 1980
were wattle and daub, whereas most had been in the 1960s.

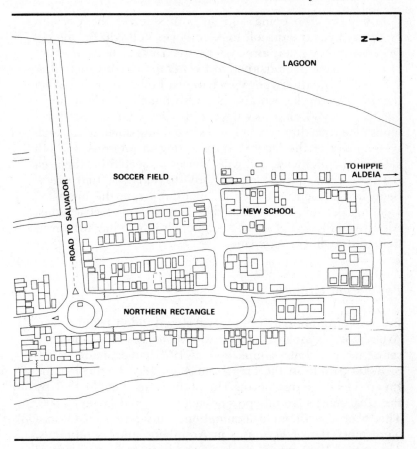

Most were brick with tile roofs. Housing had also improved in Caraúnas. Most of that settlement's one hundred houses (a doubling since 1973) were brick. During our stay, one sold to city people for the equivalent of $600 cash, well beyond the income of an ordinary fisherman. One reason that houses in Caraúnas were more substantial was the increasing number of salaried workers. Many of these were local Tibrás employees, who now numbered forty—17 percent of Arembepe's adult male work force. Outsiders, too, were buying in Caraúnas, in the new satellite village of Volta do Robalo, and throughout the area being subdivided, viewing any developed land near the beach as a good investment.

Lots were also being sold on both sides of the Coconut Highway near the turnoff to Arembepe. Volta do Robalo, on the northeast corner, already had two rows of houses, about twenty-five completed, another twenty under construction. A successful captain-owner who had just built a house in Volta overlooking the lagoon and had also bought three adjacent lots for his children, was enjoying his view while it lasted. He envisaged row after row of houses extending down to the high water mark of the lagoon. With lotting in progress on both sides of the highway, and with houses projected for the area between Volta and the lagoon, Alberto remarked that Arembepe would soon be a city. At nightfall, from the highway, viewing coconut palms outlined by hundreds of electric lights, Alberto and I agreed about Arembepe's impending urbanization, and its lingering beauty.

Population Growth

Because of the brevity of my 1980 stay, I didn't try to census Arembepe. Talking with the head statistician in the municipal seat, I learned that a sample done in 1977 had estimated 2,500 to 3,000 people in the area from Arembepe to the Jacuipe River, 11 kilometers north. The statistician thought that by the 1980 census Arembepe's population would exceed 2,500. This was a reasonable assumption, considering that there were more than 600 houses in Arembepe and its satellites. The actual 1980 census figures turned out to be 617 houses and 1,561 people, which seemed low to me.

Arembepe's population remains difficult to census accurately, because so many people who own homes in the village live there only part of the year. I did my own quick census[2] and survey of 130 houses in southern Arembepe (just 29 less than the total number of dwellings in 1964). This included both sides of Street Down There plus the new streets to the west, where houses had been built right up to the high water mark of the lagoon. Confirming the importance of outside and absentee ownership, 58 percent of the 130 dwellings belonged to non-Arembepeiros. Just 47 percent of the houses were inhabited year-round by anyone, owner or renter. Rentals were prominent in southern Arembepe, as they were throughout the village. In winter 1973, when the pattern of tourism and part-time residence was beginning, just 10 percent of the houses were rented, and only 34 percent had been rented at least once. By 1980, these figures had risen to 30 and 50 percent, respectively.

Familiar Outsiders

The outsiders who have built, bought, or rented houses in Arembepe proper are not the aloof elites of the northern and southern edges. Most belong to the lower middle class, and thus are similar both to weekend tourists and to the fallen gentry with whom villagers have dealt for decades. There has been no dramatic change in the class affiliations of the outsiders with whom Arembepeiros most often come into contact. Although encounters with outsiders are more regular and take place for different reasons now, villagers' behavior with them isn't very different from what it was during the 1960s.

Most Arembepeiros haven't begun to kowtow to city folk, as a few observations from Alberto's bar will illustrate. One Sunday a group of strangers walked up from the beach to Alberto's porch and asked if cold beer was available. Alberto's daughter and "son-in-law" ignored them, continuing an animated conversation with a regular customer, Milton, a city man who rented a house across the street for weekend use. When Alberto's daughter eventually offered to take the strangers' orders, they asked for seafood snacks to accompany their beer. She told them that the crabs that Alberto usually bought on Sunday from river fishermen hadn't arrived that week; the tourists then left.

The interactions of Alberto and his family with Milton also illustrate that villagers maintain their customary, nonobsequious behavior patterns, developed in an egalitarian community, with most outsiders. Alberto called Milton his buddy *(camarada)*, and their joking suggested a familiar and long-term relationship. Milton told me he had first visited Arembepe during the 1940s, when he had met Alberto. Once the village opened up, he had rented a house for weekend and summer use, and he always drank (many hours each weekend) at Alberto's bar. Because of Milton's leathered and sunburned skin and lack of teeth, I was suspicious of his claim to be a member of the middle class, especially when he urinated off Alberto's porch, announcing to me that he was "just looking at the ocean."

Behind the western side of Street Down There are several new dwellings, most belonging to city people. Many owners use them only in summer, and some houses have mammoth gates that are chained and padlocked. Following an urban Brazilian custom designed to deter thieves, some houses are surrounded by high masonry walls with broken glass cemented to the top. This gives them, to paraphrase archaeologist Jerald Milanich, a concentration-camp atmosphere. Similar homes had been built due west of all of Arembepe's traditional streets.

I had trouble appreciating the tourist appeal of this zone. None of the houses had ocean views, and their placement below the sandy ridge where the old village stands cut them off from the sea breeze. Some did face the lagoon, which dries up in summer, more now than in the past, since Tibrás uses its water in manufacturing. Villagers said that mosquitoes, which had never been a problem in the old Arembepe, were a nuisance for residents of the western zone, particularly in the rainy season. Caraúnas had a similar problem.

The Rental Business

Other outsiders, including Milton, Alberto's buddy and weekend neighbor, had worked out long-term agreements to rent quarters for weekend and summer use. Several houses belonged to city people, some of whom had built them only as rental investments. Other rental units belonged to villagers. As in 1973, many Arembepeiros had sold or were renting their beachfront houses to people from Salvador. Some still followed the pattern of building duplexes; but by 1980 most villagers had decided to stay in the front, generally more comfortable, and to rent the rear portion, reversing the 1973 pattern, as demands to rent increased.

Tomé, the spectacularly successful fishing entrepreneur of the 1960s and early 1970s, had left his wife for a hippie woman (see Chapter 11). They shared a rental house with another family, with only a curtain separating the two households. Tomé cited a housing shortage. He and his partner had been looking for several months for a dwelling, for which they were willing to pay up to $125 per month. But outsiders had cornered the market.

Arembepe's permanent immigrant population (from my household survey) had swollen from 24 percent in 1964 to 41 percent in 1980. Some were people renting beach quarters while working elsewhere. For example, the back of a house in the northern rectangle was rented to a young man who worked in Camaçari's booming petrochemical industry. The municipal seat was now just a forty-minute commute, compared with two to three hours in 1973. Other renters included bus drivers, Tibrás workers, artisans, and others attracted by jobs in the expanding local economy.

Laurentino, the reputed devil worshipper, had sold his store and made his living from rentals. Operating in Street Down There, he had made money catering to hippie needs. He rented them rooms; he had also built a rooftop tank to catch rain water and rented shower stalls. His business had prospered, particularly during the pollution crisis of 1973. Although Laurentino's devil worship was believed to continue, it appeared no longer to bother other villagers. In 1980 he owned several rental houses. The smallest one, just one room, brought $50 a month. For the larger houses, with two bedrooms and a living room, he got twice as much.

Several villagers had grown suspicious of still another rental pattern, in which villagers and outsiders agreed to long-term rental contracts. For example, after a run of bad luck that forced him to sell one boat and one house, Tomé asked his mother to vacate the home he had built for her so that he could rent it to a man from Salvador. They signed a five-year contract, which (lamented Tomé, himself seeking rental quarters in 1980) still had a year to run. One homeowner in northern Arembepe complained to me that "rich outsiders" were renting villagers' homes and then treating them like their own. Some city folk had even hired lawyers, claiming that they had contracted to buy in installments, rather than simply to rent the house. Although no one had yet lost title to a house through such a rental agreement, this was feared, given the renters' clout in the external legal system.

Boxcar Apartments

Mapping and a household survey of southern Arembepe revealed new facets of settlement pattern and population
growth. In 1973 the poorest villagers, formerly concentrated
in flimsy shacks at the northern and southern ends of Arembepe, had been moving to Caraúnas. By 1980 there had been
a partial reversal of this trend. Caraúnas had become more
prosperous. The average brick house (with lot) there cost
$600; almost all the houses had electricity, and some had
indoor plumbing. Although just 5 percent of the real estate in
Caraúnas had been bought by city people, more and more
outsiders were seeking land there.

As real estate prices rose in Caraúnas and Volta do Robalo,
and as all the lots were sold in those satellites, the poorest
villagers were giving up hope of affording a home. They were
taking up temporary residence with relatives, building shacks
adjoining the more substantial houses of their kin. Shacks had
been built behind many of the houses facing Street Down
There, even on the narrow Atlantic side of the street. Just a
few of these were rented. Most were occupied by relatives,
often the married children of the owner of the better house in
front.

On the western side of the street, with much more space for
rearward expansion, the developing compound pattern was
particularly obvious. Dora, our former cook, lived down an
alley in a crude, two-room wattle-and-daub hut with her common-law husband, their two children, and her two youngest
sons by previous unions. The shack just west of Dora was
home to her aunt's former husband. The aunt in question,
Dora's mother's sister, had a shack on the other side of Dora;
Dora's oldest son slept in the aunt's living room. Seaward of
the three shacks, and facing Street Down There, was the brick
house constructed by Dora's aunt and uncle before they separated. This more substantial structure was rented by a city
person for weekend and summer use.

This new labyrinthine settlement pattern was most obvious
in the southern part of the village. Still, the trend toward
poorer people living in backyard hovels attached boxcar style
to more prosperous homes facing a street was visible through-

out Arembepe. This settlement pattern expressed population growth, the huge demand for rental property, completed sale of nearby lots, and increasing socioeconomic stratification. The major economic reasons for growing class divisions are discussed in Chapter 8.

Resident Hippies

The hippie period in Arembepe's history had ended by 1980. Villagers remembered that the first hippies had appeared in the summer of 1966–1967, but the main hippie years were 1968–1971, particularly 1970 and 1971. I met fewer recognizable hippies in 1980 than in 1973; just nine had stayed on. In the opinion of many villagers, these people were no longer hippies; they had become permanent residents.

Always more numerous than females among Arembepe's hippies, males had found it easier to be accepted as locals. A ten-year resident from interior Bahia whom I remembered from 1973 had persuaded his whole family to move to Arembepe. He operated a restaurant, bar, rooming house, and cabanas in southern Arembepe. His three sisters helped with the business. His parents had retired to a rental house in Street Down There, and his brother worked for Tibrás.

An Argentine couple, also long-time residents, ran a bar in the northern rectangle. Another Argentine, a craftsman, had lived in Arembepe for six years. His rental house adjoined Aunt Dalia's juice bar in Street Down There, which had always been the preferred hippie neighborhood. Three Brazilian hippies, two men and a woman, occupied separate households in Caraúnas. The woman made clothes, and the men made handicrafts. One of them was reputed to do especially good work. He sold things locally and in Salvador and had done well enough to buy a lot and build a house. Three other hippies lived in Street Down There, one in a small shack that he used as shop and weekend bar, at the southern limit of the village.

Unique among the hippies was a young man from Salvador who had been in Arembepe for three years. Formerly a craftsman, he had become a jack-of-all-trades and even fished—the only hippie to enter Arembepe's traditional economy. Villagers had mixed feelings about him. Some accepted him as a serious fisherman and full human being; others disparaged his attempt to fish, considering all hippies to be silly, childlike creatures who could do nothing worthwhile. Illustrating acceptance was the retired captain who told me that the young man's parents had visited Arembepe. Such kinship ties provided villagers with evidence of the hippie's roots and humanity; another hippie's status had also risen when his parents and siblings moved to Arembepe.

Longest-term resident was Sonia, a middle-class native of São Paulo, whose education included some college. Because of her ongoing affair with Tomé, Sonia had become Arembepe's most notorious and stigmatized hippie. Their story is told in Chapter 11.

The Hippie Handbook

By 1980 I had overcome my previous resentment toward the hippies. Rather than ignoring their presence, I spent some time investigating their current life style and activities, and trying to understand their place in local history. The few hippies who had decided to stay on as permanent residents were now just one among many intrusive elements figuring in Arembepe's transformation.

Although the media had lost their former fascination with Arembepe's hippies, the hippies' arrival still loomed large in villagers' perceptions of change. For Arembepeiros, the hippie invasion divided local history into eras, before and after. By 1980 many villagers were expressing *saudades* ("homesickness," "nostalgia") for the old days—the prehippie, untransformed Arembepe. They had lost their fascination with the new. I was happily surprised to discover that they remembered us, members of the anthropological field teams, as part of the increasingly romanticized past.

How, specifically, did Arembepeiros now view hippies and their historical role? First of all, how does one identify a hippie? I found that villagers attributed certain stereotypical traits to hippies, and that even former hippies did exhibit characteristic ways of acting and thinking that set them off from other villagers. In other words, a hippie subculture was still discernible within Arembepe. One Sunday afternoon I sat talking with a sixty-year-old woman on the stoop of her brick home in Street Down There. Through the open window of a house across the street, I saw a blonde woman who looked like an *ippa* from Rio I had met in the Aldeia (the hippie settlement to the north, described further in the next section) a few days previously. My informant denied that this women was a hippie. But she had no hesitation using the label for a couple who approached us looking for Sonia, Tomé's stigmatized hippie lover (and my informant's neighbor), a few minutes later. The man, who spoke with an Argentine accent, was wearing expensive clothes and didn't look like a hippie to me. My companion focused on his beard and his request for information about Sonia in identifying him. Guilt by association! Furthermore, as an expression of her own hostility toward the hippies, particularly toward Sonia, for "taking another woman's husband," my informant knowingly lied in answering the man's question.

For villagers, important traits of hippies were hair and dress. Hippies had long hair; men with beards were hippies. Hippies went around "half-naked"; men wore just loincloths; women used brief halters and wore no bras. Males and females bathed together nude in the Caratingi River. (Boys from Arembepe liked to bathe there too, to catch a glimpse of naked *ippas*.)

Speech and diet gave additional subcultural clues. Foreign hippies had accents. More significantly, hippies spoke more slowly and softly than normal people did (reminiscent of "laid-back" Americans). Hippies also differed in diet and consumption patterns. "Bread," I was told, "is the food of hippies." Villagers recounted that during their heyday, Arembepe's hippies had subsisted on bread and soda pop. Villagers also knew that hippies were supposed to smoke marijuana. There were rumors that certain Arembepe hippies were regular cannabis users. "Walking around stoned" was mentioned as another hippie trait.

Villagers seemed more resentful of hippies than in 1973. This was part of a more general pattern of hostility that had developed since my last visit, as change became less novel and more bothersome. One man who prided himself on his social ties to outsiders chided me for calling the northern hippie settlement "the Aldeia."

"Don't use that hippie name," he said. "Caratingi is its proper name; call it that."

Villagers scorned the handful of village youths who were known to hang out with hippies. "What a shame," remarked Dora of a twenty-year-old native, "that she has associated herself with that *ruindade* [low life] of the hippies."

Many villagers expressed low opinions of hippie morality. "Hippies even rob each other," I was told. (On a visit to the Aldeia, I did meet an *ippa* from Portugal spending a few days there who complained of having had $300 in traveler's checks stolen the night before.) For traditional Arembepeiros, robbery is highly stigmatized antisocial behavior. Both in 1973 and in 1980 I was repeatedly warned of robbers and assailants. The thief is a symbol that has come to summarize many fears and uncertainties that villagers have about the outside world. To classify hippies as robbers is to assign them a place outside normal social life. As I was often assured, Arembepeiros do not rob and have nothing to fear from each other: "We may be poor, but we're not thieves." Hippies, by contrast, don't just rob; they steal from *each other*. In telling me this, Arembepeiros were like vegetarians distinguishing between meat eating and cannibalism.

Another symbol, speech, was also used to establish hippies' lesser humanity. As we know from our own culture, we feel most comfortable with people who talk the way we do. Arembepeiros used the hippies' speech to diagnose something more subtle—not just a social difference but an incomplete humanity. Drugged, foreign, or both, people who uttered words without seeming sure of their meaning were seen as parrots (*papagaios*), creatures capable of speech but not of understanding.

Until the arrival of the hippies, a German priest and American anthropologists had been the only foreigners villagers had known. All of us were initially classified as *papagaios*. During my visits in the 1960s, I always felt that fieldwork in Arembepe was a linguistic struggle. Why, I wondered, was my ability to speak and understand Brazilian Portuguese so good in Rio and São Paulo, but so bad in Arembepe? Only later did I realize that talking like an Arembepeiro was as different from conversing in formal Brazilian Portuguese as the speech of a worker in Liverpool is from BBC English. Cut off from foreigners, outsiders, and even from the national speech patterns that can now be heard each day on radio and television, traditional Arembepeiros were as much linguistic chauvinists as any similarly isolated people. To speak was to talk like an Arembepeiro; anything else smacked of parrot talk.

When Alberto, informed of my return, rushed to Claudia's Restaurant to welcome me in August 1980, his enthusiastic but tactless greeting was, "Oh, my *papagaio's* come back." Toward the end of my stay he commented that I used to be a *papagaio*, but now I spoke "more or less right." This evaluation may have been based on an actual improvement in my speech. More likely, it reflected Alberto's (and Arembepe's) growing familiarity with alien speech patterns.

Consider a final illustration of the stigma attached to alien speech in traditional Arembepe. Part of contemporary village lore is the story of a woman who, in 1964, refused to give us full information when we were attempting to complete our interview schedule with all 159 households. Villagers insist that her daughter, born soon after our departure, never learned to speak like a native Arembepeiro. With speech that was "all mixed up," the girl talked just like the foreigners to whom her mother had been inhospitable. The girl's plight was somehow her mother's punishment. The moral seems to be that in traditional Arembepe, *papagaios*, though less than human, should still have been treated courteously.

Despite the view of hippies as robbers, *papagaios*, vagabonds, and incompletely human, many villagers simultaneously held a more positive image of the hippie life style. One woman, after lamenting that some village youths were mixing with hippies, went on to say that there were good hippies, too. Those people worked making handicrafts, behaved with decorum, spoke respectfully, and minded their own business. Unlike the unreliable transients, these were mostly the hippies who had become locals. If they were not fully part of the village social system, at least they didn't mock its values.

Nature and Culture in the Hippie Aldeia

The hippie Aldeia has grown up near the Caratingi River, a thirty-minute walk north of Arembepe. One makes the trip along the beach or inland, wading through the lagoon. In summer the lagoon dries up, making it possible to get there by car. Accompanied by Alberto and the 1980 field team, I visited the Aldeia for the first time on a Friday afternoon. Alberto was surprised to find so few people there. His estimate that the settlement had once contained 200 people corresponded with that of the municipal statistician in Camaçari.

The Aldeia had three separate sections. The southern area, the settlement's core, had ten substantial wattle-and-daub huts with palm-frónd roofs. Just north of this area was a coconut grove with flimsy lean-tos made entirely of palm fronds. A bit further north was the river, where we saw two pup tents.

Two hippie couples and João, a twenty-one-year-old man who normally lived alone, made their homes in the southern

The southern part of the hippie Aldeia, a beautiful site that has attracted young people from all over the world. (Courtesy Jerald T. Milanich)

area. All made their living from handicrafts, but one man also painted. Three of these people had gone into Salvador that day, one for medical attention, the other two to sell their wares to agents of the city's thriving tourist industry. Two native men—brothers, one single, the other married—also lived here, and there was a native Arembepe woman who washed, sewed, and cooked for the hippies.

Considered a bit deranged by Arembepeiros and hippies alike, she habitually prayed to ocean and woods, and occasionally made an appearance in Arembepe proper, where she drank too much *cachaça* and sometimes removed her clothing in public. A would-be entrepreneur from Salvador had recently opened a bar where he sold rum. Using a team of animals, he had just brought the Aldeia its first refrigerator, powered by bottled gas. He planned to sell cold beer to tourists on weekends. This would supplement his earnings from the butcher shop he ran in Arembepe on Fridays.

The next part of the Aldeia was a poor person's version of a European youth hostel. No rent was collected for the palm-frond hovels, which barely provided shelter from sun and rain. Lacking owners, the lean-tos were kept up in a desultory fashion by a stream of temporary occupants. This was a transient area, where, we had been told by an Arembepe hippie, we could find American, English, German, Italian, and Danish hippies. It turned out to be the hangout of the "low-life" hippies that villagers vilified, the place where the Portuguese transient, said to be rich, was robbed of her traveler's checks. Everyone I talked to here was scantily attired; marijuana smoke (which Alberto had never smelled and didn't recognize) wafted through the walls of one hut.

A bit further north was the Caratingi River, on the banks of which two tents had been set up. One belonged to a young man from Salvador, out for weekend camping. Standing in front of the other was a slight young man in a jump suit. This *paulista* (person from São Paulo) had come to Arembepe to vacation and to *lose weight*. His daily routine was to walk north to the mouth of the Jacuipe River, a three-hour round trip. He reported that his weight had fallen from 90 to 65 kilograms. Two Amazon-sized women, his camping companions, then arrived. Now I understood why he needed to diet, since the pup tent looked hardly big enough for one. One of

A hippie resident of the Aldeia in 1980. (Courtesy Jerald T. Milanich)

the women sat down and leafed through a photo magazine
with pictures of women with bare breasts the size of her own.
The other woman entered the tent and started giving orders
to the man.

These people, whom Arembepeiros still classified as hippies, are perhaps more appropriately called "campers." Participating in an international culture pattern, they travel to
the warmer beaches of northern Brazil for the winter, just as
young Americans make springtime visits to Florida. Although
I had trouble determining the socioeconomic background of
the hippies and young transients, Arembepeiros insisted that
it takes money to be a hippie. Villagers believed that many
hippies were rich, which made it particularly hard for them to
understand why hippies lived the way they did, eschewing
the consumer goods that natives had done without until recently, and now found tantalizing.

It does take money to adopt the hippie life style. Although
he spent most of the year in the Aldeia, twenty-one-year-old
João used his earnings from making mobiles and curtains to
travel to other hippie beach settlements. He trekked from

Belém, at the Amazon's mouth, to the extreme Brazilian south, a distance of more than 3,000 kilometers. João had last seen one of his friends, also from São Paulo and spending a few days in the Aldeia in 1980, in a beach settlement in southern Bahia. This young *paulista* knew something about anthropology and told me he had taken part in an archaeology dig in Mato Grosso (west-central Brazil)—information suggesting upper-middle-class status.

There was no doubt of the privileged background of the young woman who was temporarily living in João's house. This *ippa* claimed to have been born in Egypt of Jewish parents, to have moved to Brazil when she was five, to have attended French schools in Rio, and to have lived in an Israeli kibbutz as a teenager. Besides the fluent Portuguese and English she spoke with us, she claimed to speak French with her parents and to know Hebrew and Italian. The reason she spoke so many languages and traveled so much, she told anthropologist Maxine Margolis, is because she was Jewish. To the amusement of Maxine—who is Jewish, speaks several languages, and travels a lot—the *ippa* explained that "all Jews speak many languages and like to travel." (There are fewer Jews in Brazil than in the United States. Our informant felt we needed to be enlightened about Jewish characteristics.)

The young woman spoke of how she had given up the career she had begun in Rio after getting her university degree, in order to live a "purer life" away from the city. This was her second visit to Arembepe. She was convinced that world civilization would be destroyed by a nuclear war in three years. She was seeking some place safe from radiation where she could live on a communal farm. She knew that the Aldeia was unsuitable for farming but planned eventually to settle in the interior, near the city of Goiânia as Doomsday approached. (This turned out to be an irony, because Brazil's first radioactive accident occurred in Goiânia, in 1987.)

Along with her rejection of urban life and her search for purity and a communal life style, her dietary preferences helped her to fit into hippie subculture. Like those of João and many other hippies, her meals were usually vegetarian. She and João shopped in urban supermarkets because macrobiotic foods were available there and because prices were cheaper than in Arembepe. She was concerned about her health, boiling all her water (which she drank in tea) and wearing shoes as a precaution against foot borers (common in rural Brazil). Less characteristic of other Arembepe hippies than her vegetarianism was her belief in spiritist religion, which is increasingly popular among Brazil's urban elites (see Brown, 1979).

This *ippa's* interaction with Alberto shows her ignorance of the local social system and reveals that she retained certain prejudices from the urban south. As we left the Aldeia at sundown, I was surprised to discover that the unusual sight 50 meters to the west, which I had initially interpreted as a whitewashed coconut-tree stump, was actually a prostrate woman dressed in white. It was Lucia, the hippies' washerwoman, praying—apparently to the woods or the setting sun, as we had been told was her practice. When Alberto and I asked João's guest what Lucia was doing, she offered enlightenment by informing us that it was Friday.

"Friday," said Alberto. "What's so special about Friday?"

"What," replied the *ippa*. "You, a black man from Bahia, don't know that Friday is the day of Oxala?" (Oxala is a deity in *candomblé*.)

"No," huffed Alberto. "I have nothing to do with *candomblé*." (Alberto's wife has participated in *candomblé*, but he has always expressed adamant opposition to it.)

The *ippa* was stereotyping: Because Alberto was a dark-skinned rural Bahian, he must, she thought, be a believer in *candomblé*. She didn't realize that *candomblé's* popularity, though growing, had traditionally been slight in Arembepe. She was also trying to show Alberto that she was no spiritual ignoramus, that she was knowledgeable about his presumed religion. Besides these false assumptions, the *ippa* had also used racial terminology inappropriate for Arembepe. Residents of Brazil's southern cities see race in terms of black, white, and *mulato*, with fewer terms and distinctions than in Bahia generally and Arembepe specifically. Although Alberto's skin is darker than that of most villagers, he was usually classified as a *moreno escuro* ("dark brunet") or simply as *escuro* ("dark"), rather than as *preto* ("black").

Despite these cultural faux pas, João's *ippa* guest contrasted sharply with the transient hippies in the palm-frond shacks, all of whom had facial lesions, suggesting malnutrition. She was a decorous, educated, and apparently healthy transient. Because she and João shared certain goals that had led them to a hippie life style, she can be seen as a more sophisticated version of João himself. A gentle, articulate, slow-speaking young man, João did a good job of encapsulating the ideology of Arembepe's hippies. A runaway from his parents in São Paulo, he had accompanied another family to Arembepe in 1974, at the age of fourteen.

The key elements of hippie thought are apparent in his unfavorable comparison of present and past Arembepe. João was one of several hippies who told me that it had been better in Arembepe before electricity and the boom in weekend tourism. "Things were more natural, simpler, more peaceful then." When I told him that I had begun to study Arembepe in 1962, he seemed envious. "Were there hippies here then?" he wondered. When I replied no, that I had been in Arembepe before all that, he concluded, with wonder in his drawl, "You were here, then, when it was really natural."

João went on to lament the loss of the community spirit that had once thrived in Arembepe and especially in the Aldeia. He recounted the origin myths, the stories of the House of the Sun on the sand dunes near the river, of visits by Janis Joplin and Roman Polanski, of the year that Mick Jagger had spent traveling back and forth between England and Arembepe. At one time, João asserted, Arembepe had been the drug capital of Brazil, with all kinds of drugs: cocaine, marijuana, hashish, heroin, LSD, mushrooms, and other hallucinogens. Now drugs and rock stars had all but vanished and community spirit had failed. (Archaeologist Jerry Milanich's inspection of the garbage dump uncovered evidence of large-scale consumption of cognac and *cachaça*.) João remembered a few of the hippies I had met in 1973, but most were gone without a trace. He had little to do with the transients who slept in the lean-tos and seemed a bit wary of their presence. He had fished with the old fishermen and loved their stories. He preferred the really old captains. Even Tomé, at age forty-seven, was too young for his taste. Young fishermen knew too little lore.

In Arembepe, as João saw it, community spirit and generosity had been replaced by self-interest and capitalism. Villagers were no longer as they had been when he arrived. For example, Aunt Dalia's husband, once a good friend and João's landlord, had changed: "His best friend now is capitalism. He sits in front of his house counting his roll of 500-cruzeiro [$10] bills."

João complained that although he had tried to do things for villagers, to be friendly with them, he had given up because they didn't appreciate his efforts. More than before, he kept his distance.

His interaction with Alberto, whom he respectfully addressed as "Seu [Mr.] Alberto," is instructive about the clash of cultural values. When we arrived, João was making a curtain out of sea shells and snail shells from the lagoon suspended on nylon fishing line. We had been told by a hippie in southern Arembepe that such a curtain, to be hung in a doorway or window, sold for the equivalent of $150. This seemed expensive in view of the meager labor invested. After collecting the shells, João had been working on the curtain for six hours and was almost done. Two completed curtains were hanging nearby, one in a window, another inside his house.

Alberto scrutinized the curtain and asked João if he was going to paint the shells. João said no, that natural was best. Alberto suggested that it would look better if the shells were painted a bright red. He then pulled me aside, but still within João's hearing, and remarked that this was the kind of thing (junk, he meant) that tourists buy. "Why don't you buy it," Alberto teased, "to take back to the United States?"

Alberto also appraised João's living quarters. To my eyes, the house was clean and furnished in attractive, if modest, hippie style. Straw mats made of palm fronds covered the floor, and there were two sleeping hammocks. Alberto found the scene absurd. For decoration drawn from nature, João had brought in a dead bush, which lay (awkwardly) in his living room. "Is that tree alive?" asked Alberto. He gave me a knowing wink. Who but a loony hippie would have a dead tree in his living room? João and Alberto got into an argument about pollution, João citing the (obvious) pollution of the ocean, the yellow foam, which Alberto claimed (incorrectly) had always been there. Alberto played down the danger of Tibrás's sulfuric wastes; João saw Tibrás as part of the assault on paradise.

These interactions between young hippie and old villager

made me think of Claude Lévi-Strauss's (1967) discussions of the opposition between nature and culture, addressed in the myths of many societies. The French structural anthropologist has pointed out that people everywhere are concerned with the contrast between that which is natural and that which, manufactured by humans, is artificial, a cultural product. All their behavior showed that Alberto and João were engaged in a debate about the merits of culture versus nature, about economic development versus tradition and preservation. Alberto stood for culture—for lights, electricity, roads, cars, tourism, business—changes that had, he thought, made things better for him. João lamented the loss of the natural, the simple, the primitive. He maintained a romantic vision of a traditional Arembepe that he had never known, whereas Alberto was very sure that his own life style had improved. Some villagers shared Alberto's opinion. Several others, unexpectedly, given their fascination with novelty in 1973, agreed with João. Reasons for dissatisfaction with change will become more apparent in Chapter 8.

A Dimming Symbol

The hippies' era was ending in Arembepe, as it had throughout the world. The subculture survived in such people as João, the hippie artisans of Arembepe and the Aldeia. Having become permanent residents, they, like many other villagers, catered to the tourist trade, making handicrafts and running bars. As we worked on our household survey in Street Down There, even Alberto, an observant man astute about social differences, couldn't say whether or not some recent arrivals who rented nearby were hippies. The distinction was becoming less salient. Villagers who knew them well said that hippies no longer liked to be called by that term. Those who had settled in Arembepe preferred to be accepted as ordinary villagers. Furthermore, outsiders now had difficulty identifying hippies in Arembepe, since many kinds of people milled around the village every weekend.

The hippies were only a part, and today are a small fraction, of the many outsiders who have come to Arembepe because of its beauty, seaside location, increasing accessibility, and tourist economy. Yet the hippies have a decided symbolic importance, because their arrival separates two eras in local history. They provide a reference point that sets traditional Arembepe apart from the here and now. The media accounts published since 1970 have focused on the hippies, according them attention disproportionate to their numbers and importance in village life. Even in 1980 a film crew doing location photography drove straight to one of the hippie bars in southern Arembepe. For urban Brazilians, the image of the hippie still holds more fascination than that of a rural worker or a weekend picnicker in a honky-tonk town. As one municipal official told me, the Aldeia's rock concerts, drug traffic, and nudity created a furor when reported in newspapers and on television. With pollution and hippies to catch the media eye, no wonder the villagers were ignored.

Yet many other changes, although less sensational, have affected Arembepe. The following chapters explore the more profound alterations, undetected by the media, including a major transformation in the fishing industry that is part of a general change in the pattern of local economic and social life.

8 If You Don't Fish, You Work for Tibrás

A hallmark of Brazilian economic development, according to Sylvia Hewlett (1980), has been the coexistence of great and growing wealth with deepening poverty. Although real income has increased for most Brazilians, the rich have done much better than the poor have. The rich include the upper and middle classes—30 percent of the population in the industrial south but just 20 percent in Bahia and the northeast. In 1976, the top 1 percent of Brazilians had a larger share of total national income than did the bottom 50 percent. In 1980 a third of Brazilians had incomes below the minimum needed for family subsistence (Hewlett, 1980). In Arembepe by 1980, local manifestations of growing wealth disparities were visible to the naked eye. Social classes had formed in a once classless community. The poorest people were getting poorer, and the rich dramatically richer. Nowhere were the changes more obvious than in the fishing industry. Fishermen were getting fewer fish per day's labor[1] than they had received in the 1960s, while boat owners were drawing ten times their previous profits.

Arembepe was firmly entrenched in a world political economy, partaking through the mass media and direct contact with outsiders in a planetwide process of cultural amalgamation. Mules and donkeys had become rarer than automobiles. Television antennas bedecked even modest homes, conveying transoceanic messages. Soon the international telephone system would reach out and touch Arembepe. These developments mirrored what was happening throughout Brazil. Nationally, the percentage of households with TV sets had increased from 7 to 51 percent between 1964 and 1979 (*The Economist*, 1979). Almost all Brazilian households had at least one radio. Brazil had become the world's fifth-largest user of communications satellites, for phones and TV transmissions. Through "the magic of electricity" villagers enjoyed the advantages of irons, water pumps, refrigerators, and freezers. Local people were licking their chops at the inventory of consumer goods offered by "the civilized world." Future archaeologists excavating Arembepe of 1980 would surely uncover hundreds of different products designed and marketed by corporations based thousands of miles away.

The paved highway had done the most to end Arembepe's isolation. Originally planned by an ambitious landlord to increase tourism and enhance land values, the road's early completion, coinciding with the hippie diaspora of 1969–1971, was assured by Tibrás. A flood of tourists from Bahia joined the hippies and spurred the rise in property values and rents. The end of isolation transformed Arembepe's entire economy, bringing occupational plurality while changing the nature and role of fishing. Direct sale to tourists and easier access to wholesalers allowed ambitious villagers to replace outside fish marketers.

Profits were plowed back into more costly fishing technology, including larger and much more expensive boats. As the value of property increased, so did the owners' share of the catch. This increased wealth differentials so much that old leveling mechanisms became ineffective. Social relations in the fishing industry grew less social, more purely economic; owners became bosses instead of coworkers. Given their traditional ideology of equality, Arembepeiros resented these changes. Many stopped fishing, but a swell of immigrants helped fill the void.

By encouraging occupational plurality, differential rewards from fishing, and immigration, the new economy produced new social cleavages. As the economy became more complex, so did local social structure. Arembepe was now divided by social class, occupation, neighborhood, provenance, and religion. Social deviance appeared and flourished. This chapter considers the most significant economic changes. The social consequences are examined in Chapters 9 and 10.

Some reasons for occupational diversity have been mentioned. Tourism created new jobs in construction, food preparation, lodging, and sales. Appendix 2 compares male employment in 1964, 1973, and 1980. It shows, for example, that just 40 percent of Arembepe's employed men fished in 1980, versus 74 percent in 1964. Competing for second place in 1980 were factory employment (17 percent), construction (16 percent), and business (14 percent). Forty Arembepeiros now worked for Tibrás. Just a handful were fishermen who had shifted jobs. Most were young men, better educated than the past generation, who were working for the first time. With wages ranging from just over $100 to just under $500 per month, factory workers made much more than fishermen did in 1980. Factory work also had more fringe benefits, and pay was regular—not the fisherman's fluctuating and uncertain income.

It wasn't just new opportunities on land that drew villagers away from fishing. There had been striking changes in fishing itself—most notably in the relations of production. Reversing the trend of increasing access by ambitious fishermen to the means of production (which had prevailed between 1962 and 1973), the gap between boat owners and ordinary fishermen had widened enormously. To be sure, the cost of purchasing, outfitting, and provisioning a fishing boat had risen, but the owner's profit had grown disproportionately. In 1965 the captain-owner had drawn 230 percent of the earnings of the ordinary fisherman for a day's fishing. By 1973 his share had increased to 300 percent. By 1980 the figure was 800 percent; a captain-owner now got 75 percent of the catch. Understanding this dramatic break with traditional local egalitarianism requires discussion of major changes in fishing. Villagers were simultaneously being enticed away from fishing by better land-based opportunities, and being driven away from it by changes in production and marketing.

Larger Boats and Long-Distance Fishing

One obvious contrast with the past was that fleet size had diminished and boat size had increased. Only nineteen boats were fishing in 1980 (versus twenty-six in 1973 and thirty-one in 1965). Two other boats were working for Tibrás, their captains and crews helping to lay pipes to carry the factory's industrial wastes farther out to sea. Four other vessels were being repaired. Tomé, who owned two other boats, couldn't afford to repair his motors and was fishing as an ordinary fisherman with his sister's husband.

Only one of the old-style open sailboats still fished in 1980—with a small motor. All the rest were classified as *barcos* rather than *saveiros*—the term that for decades had been one of the most common words in daily discourse. Although the new boats were much larger than the old ones, with bigger motors and on-board ice chests, the main difference was the enclosed cabin, which slept three people, under cramped conditions.

Most of the 1980 boats had been bought after 1973. With the cost of just a new motor at more than U.S. $2,500 in August 1980, a fully equipped boat cost at least $5,000. Dinho, Tomé's younger brother, who now owned five boats, had just bought a large one for about $10,000. This figure far exceeded anything any villager could have afforded in the 1960s. With three or more boats, four villagers, including Dinho, were millionaires, in cruzeiros. Even Tomé, with two inactive boats and two houses, had property worth more than 2 million cruzeiros ($35,000)—testimony to inflated values of motorboats and real estate, both vital means of production in the new economy.

Some of the experimentation with new fishing strategies evident between 1965 and 1973 could still be detected, though the fishing pattern was more set now. With the end of lobstering, only a few villagers still owned trammel nets. One of a handful of old-time fishermen who could still afford to experiment, Dinho had bought a shark net, to take advantage of the recent arrival of "red sharks" in the area. The sharks, whose meat villagers could buy for half the cost of fish, reportedly congregated in the area where the Tibrás residues flowed into the ocean.

Use of gas lamps for nighttime fishing, which began in 1973, had been incorporated in the more general pattern of long-distance fishing—"ice fishing." Begun by Tomé in 1973, when he bought the first large motorboat with an enclosed cabin, "ice fishing" involved travel to banks eight to ten hours north of Arembepe. Boats left Tuesday or Wednesday, after loads of ice came in by truck from Salvador. During the three or four days they were gone, most fishing took place at night, using bottled gas–fueled lamps. Fish were stored in the boat's ice chest. When the boat returned to Arembepe, the fish were taken to the owner's refrigerator, freezer, or ice vault. They stayed there until they were sold locally or to wholesalers from Itapoan—now just a twenty-minute ride away. Most of the fleet was back in the harbor by Saturday evening, ready for Sunday socializing and a Monday of resting and taking care of obligations on land.

By 1980, crews had plumbed bottoms and marked spots in the waters offshore from Sauipe and Subaúma. Neither of those northern fishing villages had a harbor to protect sailboats or motorboats, so that raft fishing with small crews was customary there. As Arembepe's fishing territory incorporated these waters, their fishermen, particularly from Sauipe, migrated to Arembepe. By 1980 they comprised a significant proportion of the fishermen in Arembepe. Most fishing was still done over the continental slope, less than 15 kilometers offshore in northern Bahia, as in Arembepe.

Although most boats did long-distance fishing, two captain-owners preferred the old daytime fishing pattern. One was Fernando, the captain-owner whose excessive drinking, intense fear of outsiders, rumored *candomblé* participation, and habit of carrying a gun were mentioned in Chapter 6. Fernando had come to terms with the insecurities that had plagued him in 1973. He was content to pursue a relaxed style of fishing, leaving at eight-thirty in the morning and returning around five in the afternoon. Motorization allowed him to reach the banks on the slope in ninety minutes, compared with four to six hours in the 1960s. Often Fernando fished closer to shore, where he caught smaller fish that could be used by the ice fishermen as bait for larger species they sought over the slope. The catches of Fernando and the two ordinary fishermen who accompanied him gave them food and some cash, but their annual catch was less than half that of the "ice fishing" boats. Alberto called Fernando's fishing style "silly," though it was based on a decades-old pattern. The new fishing style was much more productive, more than doubling a boat's average annual catch in the 1960s.

Another option was overnight fishing close to Arembepe. One of the boats hired by Tibrás for pipe laying did overnight gaslight fishing when it wasn't being used by the factory. In rough weather, many captains stuck closer to home, fishing overnight instead of making the long trip north. The new pattern relieved pressure on local banks, perhaps allowing some recuperation of the fish supply near Arembepe. Note that in 1980 only two small crews fished regularly in the banks that had once sustained the families of more than 100 fishermen, yielding more than 100,000 kilograms of fish annually.

Motorization and the Cooperative

Even more striking than the change in the fishing pattern, to one familiar with Arembepe's history of egalitarian social relations, were changes in the allocation of fishing profits and in the relations of production. As noted in Chapter 6, government loans, through the fishermen's cooperative, had facilitated the rapid motorization of the fleet, permitting industrious fishermen (captain-owners who already owned boats) to add expensive motors. Also discussed in Chapter 6 was a pattern in which successful fishermen were repaying their debts, then withdrawing from the cooperative and marketing their own fish. Tomé had made this move and was sending his fish to be sold in Itapoan. His next younger brother, Dinho, was about to do the same thing.

It had been my impression in 1973 that the cooperative's days were numbered, since the price it offered for fish was lagging and since Arembepe's traditional entrepreneurial pattern had always been one of pursuing individual self-interest. Because there had never been much community spirit, cooperatives could not succeed in Arembepe if their goal was presented as community welfare. Success could come only if individuals believed they were benefiting personally. Villagers had been willing to avail themselves of loans to increase their productivity and have access to ice, bait, gasoline, oil, and fishing supplies. But when more profitable options appeared, members felt no strong loyalty to the cooperative.

The predicted failure of the cooperative came soon after my 1973 departure. After Tomé and Dinho abandoned their agreed-on support to seek individual advantage, all the successful captain-owners eventually withdrew from the cooperative and sought alternative marketing arrangements. Some bitterness was generated by the collapse. Fernando, who stayed a member to the end, complained that city-based employees had robbed the fishermen. Most villagers disputed this story, citing general withdrawal as the reason for failure.[2]

Marketing

Since the 1960s Tomé had been Arembepe's most innovative fisherman. The first fisherman to own his own sailboat, to buy an enclosed boat, to do "ice fishing," and to use a seafloor map to locate new fishing zones, Tomé also started a new marketing pattern. Unfortunately, for reasons spelled out in Chapter 11, it was not Tomé but his brother Dinho—an equally enterprising follower—who reaped the benefits. In late 1973, rather than selling either to the cooperative or to local land-based entrepreneurs, Dinho arranged to have his catches taken to Itapoan, where a fish store offered a more profitable deal. Like Tomé, Dinho reinvested his profits in a second (large) fishing vessel.

Unlike Tomé, Dinho used this new source of income to retire from fishing, which he had always done reluctantly, both in Rio and Arembepe. Unlike Tomé, who spent four days a week fishing many miles north of Arembepe, Dinho could now devote full time to fish marketing. Dinho joined two other nonfishing entrepreneurs who had also bought boats with enclosed cabins and hired captains to pilot them to the new, distant fishing banks.

One of those other two businessmen still farmed and marketed coconuts. The other ran a store and restaurant, rented small houses and rooms, and also farmed. Dinho, by contrast, devoted his full attention to fish production and marketing. By 1980 he had become Arembepe's most successful fish marketer and its richest resident. Owner of five boats, Dinho had just paid the equivalent of $10,000 for the largest one. The first floor of his opulent two-story house (a second story was a new local status symbol) was his fish store. It had Arembepe's only ice vault, plus freezers and refrigerators (other fish merchants had just the last two appliances). Besides his own five boats, Dinho also bought fish from others and arranged transport to Itapoan of fish that weren't sold locally.

Other Arembepeiros had a similar relationship with a second Itapoan fish store. No longer did agents from Salvador come to Arembepe, since marketing opportunities were ample in Itapoan and Arembepe itself. Representatives of two other Itapoan retailers also came on Fridays and Saturdays, when the fleet returned, hoping to buy fish. Another agent drove in from the county seat. One immigrant rented his pickup truck to Dinho and other local merchants to take surplus fish to Itapoan when the fish stores sent no agents. The same man also used his truck to bus Arembepeiros to Camaçari, where many now picked up monthly pensions.

Across the street from Dinho's house, in the shack where the cooperative had been housed, was another fish store, jointly run by a captain-owner and two nonfishing owners. The shack had three large freezers, where the catches of five boats could be stored. Like Dinho's fish store, this one had several scales, checked regularly for accuracy by municipal officials. (This was one among many examples of the increasing penetration of village life by the nation-state, a prominent aspect of changing Arembepe that is examined in Chapter 9.) Fish were still unloaded in the old harbor. Then the boat anchored in the new, deeper harbor, just to the south. In the past, fish had been placed on the beach and divided among fishermen and owner. Now they were carried directly to one of the fish stores, where they were laid out on the cement floor. Another difference from the past: half (by weight) of each fisherman's catch was now turned over to the owner. Gone, along with the joint line system of pooling small fish, was the fiction of "the boat's fifth." By 1980 the owner's share was more accurately called "the boat's half."

A Double Profit

As Alberto explained, the owner now made a double profit. "First, he gets half of each fisherman's catch. The captain gets to keep his entire personal catch; so that captains get twice the ordinary crew member's share. But even here the owner profits, because the captain, like the ordinary fisherman, must sell his fish to the owner for 70 cruzeiros per kilogram [$1.17 at 60 cruzeiros per dollar]. The owner always sells the fish for

As part of the new marketing system, trucks transport fish to Itapoan. Other fish is sold in the local fish store, shown here to the extreme left. Also note the 1980s fleet in the new harbor. (Courtesy Jerald T. Milanich)

much more than he pays the fishermen. Sometimes he finds local buyers for the fish, at 120 cruzeiros per kilogram. Sometimes he has to sell some fish to one of the Itapoan fish stores for just 100 cruzeiros." Assuming half local sales and half exports, the owner's average resale profit (at 110 cruzeiros per kilogram) was 40 cruzeiros.

Illustrating this differential allocation of the rewards of fishing is division of the catch of a boat that returned one Saturday in August 1980 after four days' fishing near Sauipe with a five-man crew. The owner also acted as captain. Weighed in his fish store, the total catch was almost exactly 200 kilograms. Each fisherman saw his catch, now identified with his "mark," weighed separately. The weighing was done in the fish store by a salaried employee who also recorded the weight in a notebook. Each fisherman would eventually be reimbursed for half his catch, at 70 cruzeiros per kilogram, after loans were subtracted. (Fishermen often asked boat owners for advances against the week's work, money for their wives to buy food during their absence.) Assume, to illustrate simply, that the five fishermen, including the captain-owner, had each caught 40 kilograms. Each ordinary crew member would receive only 1,400 cruzeiros (less than $25) for nearly 100 hours of grueling work on the open sea. The captain-owner would add the 80 kilograms turned over by his crew to his own 40 kilograms. Sold for an average price of 110 cruzeiros per kilogram, these 120 kilograms would bring the captain-owner 13,200 cruzeiros. Add to this 3,200 cruzeiros—the owner's profit between paying fishermen 70 cruzeiros and selling their fish for 110 cruzeiros—and the captain-owner's income amounted to 16,400 cruzeiros. Once owner's expenses (4,000 to 6,000 cruzeiros per trip for fuel, bait, ice, food, and drinking water) were deducted, the profit was 11,000 to 12,000 cruzeiros, or about $200. This was eight times the earnings of the ordinary fisherman. That adds up to $10,400 versus $1,300 annually.

From various measures of Arembepe's fishing productivity,[3] actual annual earnings were only about 85 percent of these figures ($9,000 and $1,100, respectively). Depreciation of the boat and the owner's much greater risk (none of the boats was insured) have not been taken into account. Nor has the fishermen's "subsistence share": Crew members could keep 3 to 5 kilograms of their fish before beginning to share equally with the owner. Still, Dinho and other owners of two or more boats were making much more money than ordinary fishermen. No wonder Dinho could afford to pay $10,000, one year's profits from one boat, to buy another one in July 1980.

The hope of making enough money from fishing to buy a boat had been realistic for an ambitious fisherman in the 1960s. By 1980 it had become an impossible dream. A boat now cost five to ten times the ordinary fisherman's annual income. Just to repair a boat in July 1980 cost over $300— more than an ordinary fisherman made in three months.

Arembepe had always had intelligent and successful entrepreneurs. A particular group of men, however, just happened to make their fortunes at the right time—when the wealth entering the village was greater than ever before, when entrepreneurial efforts could be parlayed into permanent assets. In a once egalitarian community, as the volume of wealth had grown and as the traditional leveling mechanisms had become less effective, separate socioeconomic strata had appeared,

and people were very much aware of their existence. Because
of property and class, the Weberian Protestant ethic could no
longer ensure a fisherman's success.

The Genesis of Stratification: Capital and Land Time

The roster of successful Arembepeiros didn't change much
between 1965 and 1980. Tomé had been replaced by his
brother Dinho, and some new fortunes were being made in
tourist-oriented businesses. Still, the surest predictor of success in 1980 was success in 1973, and even as far back as 1965.
Most of the 1980 boat owners had owned vessels for more
than a decade. The conversion of a ranked hierarchy into a
stratified hierarchy happened like this: People who had
worked hard and innovated intelligently during the 1960s had
acquired productive property. They were good risks for loans
during the early 1970s and were able to motorize. Motorboats
cost much more than sailboats, and (reflecting the higher
price and operating costs), owners took a larger share of fishing profits to compensate for their greater investment. The
differential between boat cost and fisherman's earnings never
stopped growing.

As capital (initial wealth) had been a factor in continued
success, the new fishing pattern accentuated the value of a
new input—time—to devote to a series of new land-based
concerns. Dinho's decision to retire from fishing to work full-
time on the land side of the fishing business was critical in his
success, for several reasons. First, the new pattern demanded
that all fishermen, including the captain-owner, spend three
to four days per week at sea. This left just one workday,
Monday, to attend to essential land-based concerns of the
fishing business. One day wasn't enough.

Arembepe's fishing industry had relinquished the auton-
omy that wind power, locally manufactured supplies, seasonal
adjustments in fishing strategy, low consumer demands, and
production for immediate consumption had permitted. Like a
thousand other Third World communities, Arembepe's life
style was becoming more like our own, as villagers gave up

more and more of their self-sufficiency. The whole fishing operation now depended on external supplies. For example, each fishing expedition required thirty sacks of ice, at a total cost of $35. Crews had to await ice trucks from Salvador, which often arrived behind schedule, forcing delays in fishing. Much of the bait used in 1980 was shrimp from faraway São Paulo. Villagers no longer relied on casting for schools of tiny bait fish in the harbor. Local casting experts and netmakers had let their skills lapse, and no youngsters had replaced them.

Shopping for a new boat or motor might require several trips to Salvador. Borrowing money from banks or through government programs was also time-consuming. If one wished to market his own fish, he had to supervise weighing, keep records, arrange transport to Itapoan, and maintain relations with the fish stores there. A hundred other minor matters filled a boat owner's time in 1980. Tomé complained that as owner and marketer for two boats and captain of one, he had never had enough rest.

The new pattern of long-distance fishing plus dependence on external inputs posed almost impossible demands for captain-owners. Realizing this, Dinho retired from fishing to devote his full attention to landside matters, and make a fortune in the process. Of the other three multiple-boat owners, none fished. One had fished briefly in 1973, but quit when his wife's inheritance allowed him to buy two more boats. The other two had never been fishermen.

Still, a few men had found ways of combining the duties of captain with the owner's responsibilities. Two captain-owners did only daytime fishing. Another captain-owner, who did long-distance fishing, hired a man to weigh and sell his fish, keep records, and do the simpler jobs on land. When this owner had unavoidable business on land, he cut fishing to three days or fished for even shorter periods in nearby waters. Most captains couldn't change their fishing habits so easily, since their crew members depended on four days at sea and the better catches available in the northern waters. But this one was close kin with two of his crew members, his son and brother-in-law. Sometimes he trusted them to use his boat without him, or he told them and his third crewman, not a relative, to find another boat to fish in that week. This use of kinship was a successful strategy for keeping the roles of captain and owner of a single boat, and two others used it.[4]

Thus increased demands on land placed limits on the once-common dual role of captain-owner. Nor, in economic terms, were an owner's efforts as captain particularly cost-effective. Assuming the same 200-kilogram catch previously used for calculation, the owner, by employing a captain, would have cut his gross profits by 17 percent, and his net profits by 25 percent ($47) per trip. Still, the value of the dual role of captain-owner had never been simply economic but also social. As was discussed in Chapter 4, owners who were also captains, who shared daily fellowship, inconvenience, fatigue, and dangers with ordinary fishermen, had traditionally commanded greater crew allegiance than nonfishing owners did.

New Crews: Strangers and Debtors

The matter wasn't nearly as simple in 1980. The special expertise of the captain was less valuable, since crews fished in strange waters and since almost all the fishing was now done over the slope. There was little landmarking of the sort that was once believed to separate captains from ordinary crew members. Also, the differential rewards of owner and crew had become much too obvious to mask behind any captain's "ordinary-fellow" behavior. Unless crew members were kin, resentment was inevitable. How could strain be absent when everyone knew that fishing owners got ten times the ordinary fisherman's share for the same day's work, and when even captains made twice as much?

Another change in the relations of production was that fishermen no longer had set places. Because the loyalty of crew member to captain and owner had diminished, there was more shifting. Its extent reflected fishing strategy, with greatest crew fluctuation on short-term expeditions. For example, one fisherman arranged to fish overnight in another craft when his regular boat was hired out to Tibrás. I saw several crews assembled on the spot for daytime or overnight fishing.

Long-distance fishing had more stable crews. Owners and fishermen counted on a four-day workweek. The owners had to make larger investments in perishable ice, bait, and food, and therefore needed to ensure that fishing would take place. One way of keeping crew loyalty was to give cash advances. This indebtedness had become a new way for owners to keep their crews. This provides one more example of the ongoing and pervasive shift from social to economic relations of production. That is, by 1980 many men fished for someone not because he was a relative, friend, or *compadre*, but because they owed him money.

Given these changes, fishermen were fascinated by television reports about a fishermen's strike in southern France, going on during my 1980 visit. "We have grievances, too," fishermen told me. For instance, the price of fish hadn't risen fast enough. Although sympathetic to the French strike, Arembepeiros couldn't understand how those fishermen could afford to stop working. "They must have some kind of insurance," one villager surmised; "in Arembepe there's no such thing."

Another grievance was living conditions during long-distance fishing. Men who for years had done daytime fishing in sailboats found the new style unpleasant. "Grown men have to try to sleep in crowded quarters alongside a noisy motor. And the cabin holds only three men, so that the other one or two have to sit outside. Sometimes it's cold, especially when there's a wind." Fishermen also faced the danger of sudden storms in distant waters. Although owners didn't directly share this risk, they did fear the loss of their investments.

In August 1980, coinciding with the unusually high and low tides that accompany a full moon, Arembepe had an unseasonable storm, one of the worst I had ever seen there. Most of the boats had returned by the evening of August 29, but a few were still out. The churning waves brought Tibrás residues close to shore. The ocean was yellow and strong, making entrance to the harbor very dangerous. "On a day like this," one fisherman said, "the cold at sea slaps you in the face."

"There are people out there," remarked Alberto, "thinking they're going to die if their motor fails."

Alberto's nephew stood for hours on Alberto's porch, trying to sight his boat, which he had allowed an inexperienced captain to take out for the first time. The young man had just borrowed money from a bank in Salvador for a new motor.

He'd barely begun to make payments and now, lacking insurance, like all Arembepeiros, he faced loss of his means of livelihood.

Alberto's nephew, whose boat soon arrived without mishap, was luckier than another owner, who got the news that two of his craft, not daring to risk returning to Arembepe, had anchored in Praia do Forte, 25 kilometers to the north. The owner's son drove him up in their car. The boats were undamaged when they arrived, but the owner made the mistake of tying them to one another in the harbor. That night the storm threw them together, causing damage that would lead to the loss of several days fishing time. The two crews thought the owner silly to have tied the boats together and had warned him against it, but he had never been a fisherman and made a mistake. His crew feared pressing the point, since he was a rich owner. They were just fishermen.

From Fellowship to Exploitation

The shift in Arembepe's fishing industry from social to economic relations, detectable in 1973, had proceeded rapidly. From start to finish, fishing had become a business in which an owner (usually not a fisherman) expropriated more than half the labor product of the fisherman. No longer independent producers, fishermen had become employees. They resented captains and owners, and lacked trust in each other. Unlike 1973, when a few crews had still used the joint line system, every fisherman now marked his catch individually. Each crew member had his mark, cutting one side of the tail, both sides, the head, or the area below the throat once or twice. It was rumored that some fishermen stole from others by adding a second cut to the neck, or an extra slash in the tail, if that was their mark. Concern with the individual share continued on the land, as fish were weighed separately.

Division and weighing of the catch had moved inside, from public space (the beach) to private space (the shacks and fish stores owned by land-based entrepreneurs). With boats coming and going at different times, the daily public ritual of the 1960s had ended. No longer did the village assemble to greet the boats as they returned in the late afternoon and watch the fishermen pool their catches, deciding how much would be sold, how much kept for their families, and how much given away to destitute onlookers. The village poor still begged; but often now they were cursed or ignored altogether, and they rarely got pieces of fish.

The 1980s pattern of social relations in fishing may not continue indefinitely. Given other opportunities to make a living, most Arembepeiros will not continue working for fellow villagers under conditions that contrast so sharply with tradition. In fact, the 1980s pattern was dependent on immigration and couldn't have developed in its absence. Villagers' perception of the industry's reliance on fishermen from outside was even more obvious than the actual dependence. I was told repeatedly that most of Arembepe's 1980 fishermen were immigrants, people from the northern coastal village of Sauipe in particular. As noted, Sauipe lacks a good harbor, and its only fishing vessels are small rafts. As Arembepe's fishing expanded to include the slope offshore from Sauipe, the northerners began moving to Arembepe, to catch more fish and make more money than before, riding boats from Arembepe to their own fishing grounds. Farther from a city than Arembepe, Sauipe's traditional fishing economy had been less cash-oriented. Sauipeiros were willing to work for less than Arembepeiros were, because their cash incomes still exceeded what they could make back home.

Stepped-up immigration and job seeking also reflected rapid national population growth. In 1980 the population of Brazil, the western hemisphere's second most populous country, had an annual growth rate of almost 3 percent. It tripled between 1940 and 1977 and was about 130 million in 1980. Arembepe's own population had doubled between 1964 and 1980. Because of immigration and the new relations of production, the percentage of natives among the fishermen had fallen from 79 percent in 1973 to 63 percent in 1980. The proportion of fishermen from Sauipe in 1980 (20 percent) about equaled the percentage of all immigrants in 1973. Sauipe's representation among 1980 captains was even greater: 26 percent, versus 57 percent native Arembepeiros and 17 percent other immigrants. This reflects Arembepeiros' own reluctance to work as underpaid at-sea agents of the nonfishing owners they had grown up with. There was another reason to hire captains from Sauipe: They knew the waters where Arembepe's boats now did most of their fishing. It was too early to tell whether these Sauipe immigrants would live permanently in Arembepe or were simply working temporarily for cash, as Arembepeiros themselves once did in Salvador, Rio, and other ports.

Where Are the Arembepeiros?

Such relations of production could continue only as long as immigrants kept on arriving and accepting low wages. One thing hadn't changed: Boat owners couldn't profit from fishing without fishermen, and Arembepeiros *were*, as any villager would agree, deserting fishing for other jobs. The number of native fishermen in 1980 (fifty-seven) had fallen to less than half the 1964 figure.[5]

Many villagers said the trend was for fishermen to go to work for Tibrás, but statistics didn't bear them out. Data on the 1980 occupations of the 105 fishermen[6] who had lived in Arembepe in 1973 are tabulated in Appendix 4. Only 8 of these had shifted to Tibrás jobs by 1980.[7]

To be sure, one aspect of Arembepe's economic transformation was that more native sons (although not more ex-fishermen) were doing factory work (17 percent in 1980 versus 11 percent in 1973 and 2 percent in 1964). Of the forty Arembepeiros employed by Tibrás in 1980, 80 percent were natives. This differed sharply from fishing, where just 63 percent were natives. Most of the Tibrás workers were younger than thirty. Some of them, of course, would have fished in the old economy. But many would have sought jobs other than fishing, in Arembepe or outside. Tibrás workers are less likely than fisherman to have a family background of fishing. Only 49 percent of the 1980 Tibrás workers had fathers who fished, compared with 80 percent of the 1980 fishermen.

The Basis of the New Order

The dramatic shift from social to economic relations in fishing can now be seen in a larger context that includes Arembepe's general economic transformation, increased immigration, and growing heterogeneity. Gone with the wind was the socially cohesive kin-based crew of the 1960s. Only four 1980 crews had close kin ties, compared with over twenty in the 1960s. In factories, construction, business, and tourism, covillagers who would in the past have labored alongside one another in a fishing boat were now working separately in varied locales. Crews were relying more and more on recent immigrants, with weak local social links. Nor did immigrants have much time to forge such ties, since they spent four days each week at sea. The immigrants remained strangers, emerging from their usual isolation only to partake in weekend drinking. The outsiders, in turn, resented other villagers, particularly the nonfishing natives who exploited their labor. Distrust pervaded social relations in crew and village alike.

Related to these changes, the Fishermen's Society had declined in importance. It had fewer meetings, and the candidates for president in 1980 were both nonfishermen. Boats no longer gave as units. Each fisherman was supposed to give 200 cruzeiros [less than $5] for the annual *festa* of Saint Francis in February. Villagers lamented that the festival had become an affair mainly for tourists. "The *festa* used to be the fishermen's thing. Now it's for outsiders. You can't imagine the people who come here in February. The cars park along the road all the way to Volta do Robalo. If you get here on the eve of the *festa* you're trapped till it's over. The cars are so thick no one can get out." Business people now played a major role in the Society and in organizing the festival. And of course they reaped far larger profits.

Thus by 1980, the increased costs of an industrial technology, along with cupidity, had bloated the owner's share of fishing profits from less than 25 percent to 75 percent of the catch. More productive fishing had also raised profits. The annual catch of the average boat had risen from 3,500 kilograms in 1965, to 5,500 kilograms in 1973, and 9,000 kilograms in 1980—through long-distance fishing. In 1965, the cost of a fully equipped sailboat had equaled the sales proceeds from just 400 kilograms of fish. The motorized leviathan of the 1980s was worth 5,400 kilograms of fish. The most glaring contrast, however, was between the owner's share of the annual catch and the ordinary fisherman's: 6,750 kilograms for the owner and 500 kilograms for the fisherman, compared with 850 and 600, respectively, in 1965.

Arembepe's history between 1973 and 1980 was the local version of a generalized and concurrent Brazilian development. People lucky enough to have been prosperous when the "economic miracle" began became its prime beneficiaries. In Arembepe, as throughout Brazil, the poorest people, after a few years of increasing real incomes, found themselves worse off than in 1968. By 1980 Arembepe's ordinary fishermen were getting to sell fewer fish than they had sold in 1965 (500 versus 600 kilograms),[8] while the owner's share had increased eightfold. No wonder Arembepeiros were leaving fishing to outsiders. No wonder people who used to deny wealth differences now carried purses and called each other millionaires.

Things could get worse—not just for Arembepe's poor but also for its *nouveaux riches*—if chemical pollution continued to threaten fish supplies. Fishermen said that Arembepe's old spots had fewer fish than they used to. The harvest of the horse-eyed bonito, which usually accounted for half the an-

Owner of three boats, the man with the purse inspects and helps unload the catch from a four-day fishing trip. (Courtesy Jerald T. Milanich)

nual catch, had been below normal in 1980. Fishermen contended that the more distant banks produced larger catches than their traditional territory had. An increase in annual fleet production from 108,000 kilograms in 1965 to 130,000 (average of SUDEPE figures for 1977 to 1979) bore them out. Fishermen didn't agree about why the northern waters were more productive. Tomé thought that overfishing was becoming a problem all over. Northern yields per trip had been better when he started fishing near Sauipe in 1972 than they were in 1980.

Some fishermen blamed Tibrás for declining fishing productivity. In a heated argument with a skilled painter who worked for Tibrás, one captain-owner contended that Tibrás was destroying local fishing. He had seen dead fish, and he knew that pollution had driven fish from their homes. The Tibrás worker retorted by citing an observation made by other fishermen: mackerels now congregated near the end of the Tibrás pipes, where they apparently feasted on the wastes. "Isn't mackerel fishing better than ever?" he asked. Others told of yellow (sulfur-covered) turtles and red sharks that seemed also to enjoy their seafood with sulfur spicing.

The experts I consulted in Salvador had no doubt that Tibrás's pumping of sulfuric acid 2.5 kilometers out at sea, just 3 kilometers south of Arembepe, was affecting Atlantic waters to the north and to the south. The yellow foam that was so obvious in Arembepe's ocean could be detected several kilometers up the coast. It may have affected yields as far away as Sauipe. One marine biologist attributed a series of recent sea gull deaths to Tibrás pollution and thought that the effects of pollution would soon begin to show up in fish. Arembepeiros complained only about declining yields. They hadn't noticed deformities in the fish they caught.

The problem of ocean pollution seemed less immediate than the lagoon scandal of 1973, because the ocean is much vaster and destruction takes longer to show up. Still, many tourists will eventually conclude that bathing in Arembepe is unhealthy. Evidence for contamination of fish, and of the people who eat them, can be predicted. Tibrás pollution probably has played a role in the changing fishing pattern, even as the factory has also changed the local economy by providing jobs for villagers. Much more than in 1973, when its attitude seemed to be "let Arembepe be damned," the Tibrás of the 1980s had worked hard to improve its local image.

Factory Work at Tibrás

Providing well-paying jobs for young men who had finished junior high school, the titanium dioxide factory, Tibrás, 5 kilometers from Arembepe, employed forty Arembepeiros in 1980, 80 percent of them native sons. After fishing, factory work just exceeded business and construction as the second most common male job. Most villagers working for Tibrás had unskilled positions—kitchen work, gardening, sweeping, and cleaning. The factory's public relations head told me that Tibrás gave preference to locals (people from between Itapoan and the Jacuipe River) for such menial work. Most of the skilled workers were bused in from Salvador. Of the 1,032 people working for Tibrás in 1980, about 20 percent (195) came from the local area.

The public relations man said that since 1974 he had been working with a German priest in Abrantes, the district seat, which is almost as close to Tibrás as Arembepe is. Their aim was to provide better educations for local children so that they might one day fill higher-paying jobs. The public relations man complained about the cost of bringing 800 workers from the city. Eighteen busloads came each day for the shift that began at 8:00 A.M. and ended at 4:00 P.M. One company plan for cutting gasoline and bus maintenance costs was to build, near Abrantes, a new town with 400 two- and three-bedroom houses. Workers' purchase of these dwellings would be financed by Tibrás, with monthly installments payable over fifteen years, the amount to be determined by salary level. The aim was to get skilled workers to move closer to the factory.

Tibrás began operation in 1970. South America's only titanium dioxide factory, its 1979 output was 22,000 metric tons. 1980 output was 50,000 tons, 60 percent of national consumption, scheduled to rise to 70,000 tons in 1984 or 1985. An increase in the work force to 1,300 was projected by 1985. This would create at least twenty-five new jobs for Arembepeiros.

The reputation of Tibrás had improved substantially since 1973, mainly because of the services it provided for nearby communities. As noted, the factory had worked with the priest to improve the school in Abrantes, the base of his parish. Although educational opportunities had improved in Arembepe, where there were now competently staffed elementary and junior high schools, certain subjects, physics, for example, were taught only in Abrantes. Twice each week, Tibrás bused over 100 children from the Arembepe-Jacuipe region to study physics in Abrantes.

The factory provided several other services. Although Arembepe now had its own medical post, where a physician from Salvador spent two days a week, villagers preferred the medical care available at Tibrás. Two doctors worked at the factory each weekday morning, and one in the afternoon. Registered nurses covered the lighter shifts, from 4:00 P.M. to midnight and from midnight to 8:00 A.M. The Tibrás medical staff treated not just factory employees but any local resident. In theory the Tibrás clinic was for emergencies, but in fact people went there with routine maladies. In extreme emergencies, factory vans had taken physicians to nearby villages, and an ambulance was available to take people to hospitals in Salvador.

Phone service had not reached Arembepe by 1980 but was projected soon. Meanwhile a token-operated phone stood at the corner of the highway and the turnoff to Tibrás. When it wasn't working, phone calls to the city and even long-distance calls could be made (free of charge) in the factory. Still sensitive to the water-pollution issue, Tibrás had a faucet outside its gates where anyone could get purified water certified as drinkable by the state health department. The public relations officer I talked with explained that the lagoon problem had been solved by treating factory wastes and sending them out to sea. Pipes now extended out 2.5 kilometers in the ocean and had reached a depth of 30 meters. He downplayed the current marine pollution problem but told me of the company's plan to end the pollution potential "once and for all," by using tankers to carry wastes 12 to 15 kilometers out to sea. The tankers would be loaded from a floating platform seaward of the factory. My informant didn't mention the likely end to any remaining tourist appeal of the seaside summer houses just north of the projected loading area.

Publicity about its community services was a major part of the Tibrás campaign to improve its image. Factory tours were also available, and I found the public relations official I interviewed very cooperative. The factory itself was a world apart, its security maintained by armed guards. To enter, one had to leave a passport or identity card. Arembepeiros warned me to wear long pants; shorts, the usual male dress in Arembepe, weren't permitted. Once inside, I was impressed by the physical plant. Gardens made the inner courtyards attractive. Workers could do their banking at a branch of the Banco Econômico here. I passed a lunchroom where a waiter in white shirt and bow tie was setting out slices of melon, fried fish, and abundant quantities of rice. Decorative plates, vases, and clean tablecloths contributed to the pleasant atmosphere. Next door was an activity room, where workers could play pool; some men played checkers at a table outside. No sulfur wastes or job hazards intruded on this comfortable ambience; they belonged to another part of the plant. I was passing the area where workers could relax.

Arembepeiro Jaime, an old friend of the anthropological teams of the 1960s, a boy of eight when I first met him in 1964, was now a married man and a semiskilled (grade 3) Tibrás worker. Jaime's mother had died when he was two, and his father had remarried, leaving Jaime and his brother to be raised by an ancient great-aunt. Anthropologist Carl Withers, who led the Columbia University Brazil field team in 1963, had found Jaime charming and bright. Knowing that Jaime's chances of being educated were poor without outside support, Carl sent money for years to pay for Jaime's education in Salvador.

My 1980 trip gave me a chance to see the results of Carl's support. Jaime had studied beyond junior high school and held a grade 3 Tibrás position, for which he received more than $300 per month, including double pay for overtime. Jaime had worked for Tibrás for five years. He had married in 1979 (legally and in a religious ceremony) and was the father of a month-old boy.

Because of his good education, Jaime had never been a grade 1 worker. This category, in which most Arembepeiros were employed, included unskilled custodial tasks. Still, even the grade 1 salary ($115 to $150 per month) was twice the minimum wage. Grade 2, in which Jaime had begun, paid

$215 monthly. The highest positions (grade 4) paid a monthly salary of $500 to the most skilled workers. Some also received special pay for hazardous work, and wage indexing provided between one and three inflation raises annually.

Jaime seemed neither pleased nor displeased with the nature of his work. Like Arembepe's forty other Tibrás workers, Jaime went to work each day in vans sent from the factory. He usually worked the daytime shift but sometimes chose to make double pay from night work. The benefits of Tibrás employment showed up in his life style. The good company lunches were obvious in his girth. His new brick house in Caraúnas (now a more respectable neighborhood than in 1973) had a refrigerator, black-and-white TV, gas stove, and bathroom. His plumbing system awaited running water; his well would be finished soon. When I visited his house, his well-dressed wife was ironing with an electric iron on a real board—novelties never seen in Arembepe in the past, when women had ironed on tabletops, using charcoal-stuffed irons.

Jaime had become an investor and a consumer. He had bought some land and was looking for a car; he asked me about costs of particular models. He knew that a used Volkswagen beetle could be had for about $1,500. He had bought his refrigerator for the equivalent of $250, and his television for half that. Jaime earned less than the owners of the most productive boats did, but his work was less risky than fishing. His salary was regular, with protection against inflation. His fringe benefits included good retirement, widow and child benefits, and disability insurance. Nor was Jaime's income reduced by tax. "No one in Arembepe pays income tax," he contended. "No one makes enough money." (He was wrong about that but right that no villager paid.) Although income tax was deducted from Jaime's wages, he could file for reimbursement in Salvador, since his salary was below the taxable level. Thinking that anyone could get their tax payments back in this way, he saw taxation as a functionless bother.

Like other villagers, Jaime knew much more about the outside world than previously. He asked me about strikers in Poland and about the 1980 presidential elections in the United States. He had followed news of strikes in São Paulo but reported no union activity or strikable grievances at Tibrás, or in the Salvador area. Like a few other villagers, Jaime had moved into the upper working class. His life style contrasted sharply with that of most fishermen. Arembepeiros saw Tibrás, as they had viewed the national oil company in the 1960s, as a step up.

This became apparent one Sunday afternoon when two villagers, a captain-owner and a skilled Tibrás employee, tried to involve me in their argument about the value of Tibrás versus fishing as a profession.

"I'm proud to have a better job than my father," said Pedro, the Tibrás worker. "I wanted to be better educated than my father, just as he wanted to have a better education than his father. Don't you want your children to do better than you?"

Valter, a captain-owner, provided the counterpoint: "You may be doing well at Tibrás, but it's bad for Arembepe. The fish are leaving, and they are dying."

Pedro argued that fishing would eventually end in Arembepe, that the new economy was better. His grandfather, he said, had been a fisherman, but he would have been proud of Pedro for advancing himself. "Fishing is unskilled work; anyone can catch a fish."

Valter defended his work. "Here's my card showing I'm a professional fisherman. Do you have such a card?" he asked Pedro.

His will to defend the fishing profession enhanced by several beers, Valter insisted on the value of his work. "I'll take you out in my boat tomorrow. Let's see if you catch anything. Let's shake on it."

They never shook, and Pedro seemed unconvinced, though he ended the discussion peacefully, contending that he had nothing against fishing—some of his best friends. . . .

Tibrás had influenced behavior, life styles, values, and opinions in Arembepe in many ways. Villagers—not just those employed by the factory—relied on Tibrás for services and for jobs. Arembepeiros sold prepared foods to the workers who came each morning from Salvador; they got the business of Tibrás employees in their bars and restaurants; and some hired out their boats and labor to lay pipes for Tibrás on the ocean floor.

Although Tibrás had restored the lagoon and been forgiven for the scandal, tourism and fishing, two major components of the local economy, remained vulnerable to pollution. So did the health of Arembepeiros and other Bahians—from rural people in small coastal settlements to diners at elegant seafood restaurants in Salvador, which bought some of the fish caught offshore from Arembepe and its neighbors.

In the long run, Arembepe's fate would be determined by Tibrás's activities, and the future remained a mystery throughout the 1980s. The factory had filled the gap left when the national oil company stopped hiring Arembepeiros because they lacked secondary educations. Much more accessible, Tibrás worked to improve the education of local people, to stock a cost-effective pool of laborers close by. Still, as I listened to Jaime talk of television and Volkswagens, I wondered what Carl Withers, now dead, would have thought if he could have seen what his investment in Jaime's education had wrought—a contented, well-fed factory worker with an all-American appetite for consumer goods. Jaime's story may be one of the happier chapters in the assault on paradise, but it does provide one more illustration of Arembepe's dependence on external forces and of the quickening erosion of cultural differences. Taxes, government forms, pensions, and national wage indexing—all are aspects of the increasing presence of the state in local life. The impact of Brazilian nationhood, particularly on Arembepe's public health and family life, is the subject of Chapter 9.

9 The Web of Government

One of the most evident contrasts between the 1960s and the 1980s was Arembepeiros' growing familiarity with external services and institutions. This reflected nationwide improvements in transportation and communication, and increased government efforts to enhance health, education, and welfare. Through their improved access to Salvador, Arembepeiros could take advantage of new and expanded national programs. The role of government in villagers' lives had become much more prominent. Benefits were funneled through municipal seats. Bus service now linked Arembepe and Camaçari, and a local man sold rides there in his pickup truck. More than a dozen villagers went to the municipal seat to collect monthly pensions. Although glad to have these federally sponsored benefits, which just one villager had drawn in the 1960s, people complained about having to stand in line to get their stipends, the amount of which varied from month to month, averaging about $40 for a retired fisherman.

Welfare and Education

The age at which eligibility began had just been reduced from sixty-five to sixty years. The availability of government pensions was one of the main reasons why many men (14 out of 105) had retired from fishing between 1973 and 1980. During the 1960s, about 10 percent of Arembepe's fishermen had been over seventy, and 31 percent over sixty years old. The new fishing pattern would have been especially taxing for older men. Pensions allowed them to opt for a more leisurely life style.

Women also drew government stipends, some as fishermen's widows, others as retired businesswomen. More would do so in the future. For example, Alberto's wife, Carolina, and their two grown daughters, who worked in their parents' store, all made monthly payments of about $10 each to ensure social security and retirement benefits. Most local business people did the same thing. The even more ample benefits available through factory jobs have already been mentioned.

Villagers went to Camaçari for many other reasons. The town had grown enormously since my last visit there in the 1960s. New jobs had fueled this growth. A booming petrochemical industry had developed on the outskirts of the municipal seat—like Tibrás, a local manifestation of Brazilian national development goals. Small amounts of oil had been found in Camaçari and adjacent municipalities, but much more important were the factories that transformed petroleum into products like polyurethane. A few men from Arembepe commuted (an hour's round trip) to work in the petrochemical industry. Camaçari now had one-way streets, two supermarkets, a "commercial center," several pharmacies, doctors' offices, labs, and other medical services. The head of statistical services for the municipality told me about plans for the national census, scheduled to begin in September 1980. Would he send me the results for Arembepe? "Certainly," he replied. "Or better yet, take down my number and give me a call next year. I'll give you the information on the phone." Remembering the sleepy county seat of the 1960s, I had trouble imagining myself sitting down in my Ann Arbor office and making a long-distance call to Camaçari, Brazil.[1]

Camaçari also had a dozen lawyers' offices, testimony to increasing litigation, which extended to Arembepe. Our former cook Dora, for example, accompanied me to Camaçari to see the attorney who had agreed to represent her in a suit she had brought against a former neighbor. The case originated in Dora's decision to tear down her old wattle-and-daub hut in northern Arembepe, to build a brick house on the lot she rented from the landowning family. Before construction could begin, the man who owned the brick house in front of her built a fence around her lot, claiming it as part of his property. Trying to avoid a feud between her relatives and his (both belonged to large local families), Dora took the case to court—an ambitious move but probably a lost cause given her inexperience with the law.

One example of Arembepe's penetration by the nation-state is the registration of boats. (Courtesy Jerald T. Milanich)

Many Arembepeiros now paid licensing fees to the municipality for their stores, bars, and restaurants. This was another contrast with the 1960s, when only the owners of the two largest stores had paid those fees. Municipal officials inspected weights and measures, and there was regular mail delivery. The streets now had formal names, street signs, and house numbers. The names were those of the landlords who had owned particular parts of the village. Even residents of Street Down There were abandoning this traditional designation for a new, landlord-derived name.

The numbers had been there in 1973, when they facilitated my village census. They had been painted on each house during a malaria-eradication campaign by the state health department. Additional numbers had been added later, as in Caraúnas and Volta do Robalo.

Arembepeiros themselves were now identified in the more detailed and impersonal terms of the nation-state. Full names were used in legal documents, and people were more familiar with the last names of fellow villagers. Most adults now had identity papers. Alberto's whole family, including his twelve-year-old daughter, carried them when they left Arembepe.

Alberto told me that people could be jailed if they were stopped by police and lacked an ID. The military and police presence in Bahia was less evident and seemed less ominous than on my 1973 visit. Then, on my visits to the city, the ubiquitous teams of rifle-wielding agents of the military government had depressed me. The military police even invaded Arembepe briefly in 1973, seeking drug dealers (and probably political undesirables) among the hippies.

Another new pattern was for Arembepeiros to join the armed forces. After junior high school, many local boys now presented themselves to the army, air force, or navy. (Military service is, in theory, required of all healthy young men in Brazil.) Along with education beyond primary school, a stint in the armed forces provided experience and documents that helped young men find jobs with Tibrás and other externally managed organizations. Jaime, the Tibrás worker introduced in Chapter 8, had joined the army after completing some high school. Both experiences helped him get his semiskilled job at Tibrás.

State and municipality had combined to bring better educational opportunities to Arembepe. This reflected implementation of the Basic Education Reform Law of 1971, which mandated eight years of education (in primary and junior high school). The new law also set a national core curriculum of general studies, including practical courses to determine vocational aptitudes (industrial, commercial, agricultural, and domestic) in grades five through eight. Preparation for employment was a main goal of educational reform. Arembepe's new junior high school and its two elementary schools had a total of five competent teachers—two local people and three outsiders. Two were state employees, two municipal. The principal, an Arembepe native who had graduated from a teachers college in Salvador, was paid partly by the state and partly by the municipality. The classroom of the 1980s differed radically from the educational setting of the 1960s. Back then, kids had wandered in and out of the crowded one-room school, where they had been poorly supervised and barely taught by a local woman with just a third-grade education.

Schooling had become a much more serious, and costly, matter by 1980. Children now had to wear uniforms, pay fees, and buy books and supplies. They paid attention in the classroom, where trained teachers instructed them. Education beyond junior high still eluded most villagers. Just one native was a college graduate, having passed the difficult "vestibular" exam, on which the success rate in Bahia was barely 10 percent.

Public Health

Health services had also improved, but were still inadequate. Besides the Tibrás clinic, health benefits were financed by various levels of government. A local medical post set up in 1978 was supported by Fundo Rural, the agency in charge of social services for fishermen. The two practical nurses who staffed the post full time were municipal employees. Fundo Rural paid the salary of a physician from Salvador who spent two days a week in Arembepe and three in Abrantes, the district seat. Preferring the Tibrás clinic, Arembepeiros complained about this doctor, saying he did little to help their health problems and just wrote prescriptions. For emergencies, villagers had to go to Tibrás or a city hospital. Arembepe still lacked a pharmacy, although the medical post kept a small selection of free medicines. Aspirins and other simple remedies could now be bought in local stores. Many prescriptions still required a bus ride to Itapoan, where there were several pharmacies. The physician came to Arembepe Tuesdays and Thursdays. He worked a six- to seven-hour day, scheduling sixteen appointments in the morning and an equal number in the afternoon. As at Tibrás, consultations were free.

Urine, blood, and stool specimens went to labs in Camaçari for analysis. With the lab results, the doctor wrote prescriptions, often for worms, still viewed as the main local health problem. The head nurse at the post told Maxine Margolis that most local kids had intestinal parasites, which she believed came from their playing in the lagoon, making reinfection likely. The nurse also mentioned dysentery, measles, and schistosomiasis as health problems. As Tibrás pollution of the lagoon ended, the snails returned. With them came more frequent diagnoses of schistosomiasis. According to the nurse, schistosomiasis was a much greater threat in 1980 than it had been in the 1960s.

Many changes in knowledge and customs had enhanced

local public health, but problems remained. A lingering effect of the pollution scandal was greater caution about lagoon water. Many villagers got their drinking water from deep wells that had been dug throughout the village; these had electric pumps. Others preferred water from wells in Volta do Robalo—farther from the ocean and lagoon—or got their drinking water from the faucet at Tibrás. Few villagers would risk a drink of lagoon water, but many had returned to their old bathing spots. Others continued to avoid the lagoon; they had built showers in their homes and used well water for bathing and for washing dishes. Alberto, for example, took care of a summer home across the street and drew water from its well for bathing, dishwashing, and even his toilet. People whose homes, like Alberto's, directly bordered the ocean had to rely on others for well water. These seaside houses stood on an inland extension of the sandstone reef, and it was too rocky to dig wells. These villagers hoped the municipality would drill for a public fountain in the central square.

Sanitation problems remained. The municipality employed four men to keep the village clean, but much of the garbage disposal rested on traditional agents—animals and tides. Buzzards still ate fish innards on the beach. Horses, donkeys, chickens, and ducks scavenged garbage dumps throughout the village; but local livestock had dwindled, given easier access to animal products in supermarkets. Villagers still put their garbage on the beach to be taken out by the tide. Toilets heavily outnumbered septic tanks. Alberto's toilet simply poured onto the beach, where sanitation was left to the high tide that lapped the foundations of his house twice a month.

Villagers without toilets still used the bushes on the edge of the lagoon to relieve themselves, but construction had cleared many of these once-favored areas. The reef was another favorite spot. One day Jerry Milanich saw a boy defecate on the reef near Alberto's house, then wipe his rear end on the rocks. A few minutes later a man arrived with a basin and began washing dishes with sea water in the same place. These are some of the public health practices that maintain parasitic infestation, dysentery, and resultant malnutrition among Arembepeiros.

Still, there had been progress in combating some diseases. The government had sponsored a campaign to control malaria by mosquito spraying. When we arrived in August 1980, the media were urging parents throughout Brazil to take their kids for their second dose of oral antipolio vaccine. In this successful campaign, medical people went into rural areas with the vaccine. German measles control had been less successful because many children had not received the vaccine. Some doctors discouraged males from being vaccinated, since, they pointed out, the danger of rubella is mainly to pregnant women. The disease will continue to be a problem, of course, if vaccination is not universal.

Although Arembepe still lacked facilities for full prenatal care and medically supervised births, childbirth was much less of an adventure than it had been in the 1960s. Most deliveries then were done by two native midwives, who had learned their skills locally. Betty Kottak was present at a childbirth in 1964. This proved a harder delivery than most; the mother was in labor several hours. As she endured contractions, the room filled with smoke from the midwife's pipe. Thinking birth was imminent, the midwife splashed her hands with alcohol, but relit her pipe after it turned out to be a false alarm. There was no second dousing when the baby finally emerged.

Current conditions are more sanitary, and more impersonal. By 1980 pelvic examinations were available in Abrantes, but women went there only if a pregnancy appeared risky. Most women had never had a pelvic exam, which they feared. One of the local midwives still practiced; the other had retired in 1975. Most women now went to the maternity center on the road to Salvador, less than twenty minutes away, to have their babies. Villagers' only complaint was that the maternity center did routine episiotomies, for which Arembepeiros saw no reason.

By 1980 Arembepeiros routinely went outside for many other health-related services. They visited the nearest dentist, in Itapoan, to have teeth pulled, but there was no preventive dental care, nor were teeth ever filled. Even the poorer villagers now bought vitamin syrup for their children. This had helped correct the malnutrition that had been so marked in the 1960s, when Alberto and Carolina had lost ten of their thirteen children to illnesses exacerbated by a poor diet. Use of antibiotics, which could have saved many lives in the 1960s, had also increased. Avoidance of lagoon water brought other health benefits. Most mothers now breast-fed their babies. There was less use of bottles and powdered milk than before. I was also struck by the number of villagers with eyeglasses, prescribed and ordered in Salvador.

New government programs and the expansion of others also made it possible for villagers to get specialized care in city hospitals. A few had even been treated for mental problems in Salvador. Hospital benefits for fishermen (through Fundo Rural) were less ample than those provided by INPS (Instituto Nacional de Previdência Social), the national social welfare fund, into which local business people paid. The medical benefits through factory jobs were even better. Indigents and unemployed people were eligible for free hospitalization.

The case of an infant born with a club foot illustrates inequities between benefits available to fishermen versus other rural producers. Examining the baby two weeks after its birth in 1974, a physician recommended consultation with specialists at a children's hospital in Salvador. Once there, the parents (a fisherman and his wife) were told that the boy needed an operation but that their hospital didn't accept payment by Fundo Rural. They were sent to an adult hospital that did take fishermen's benefits, but the baby was kept there for two months without any operation. During this time the child, still less than a year old, was visited by his parents, who had to take the bus in from Arembepe, and by his godmother, who lived in Salvador. The parents tired of waiting for the operation and removed their son from the hospital. They eventually found a physician who certified (falsely) that the father was a farm worker so that the operation might be done in a children's hospital that accepted the benefit program for farm workers. The operation, which required just two days' hospitalization, was declared a success. The child was fitted with orthopedic boots, which were supposed to be replaced each six months.

All this necessitated many trips to Salvador, which taxed the time and energy of the parents and their relatives. In 1980 they were told a second operation would be necessary. The mother lamented that she hadn't been able to replace the boots at the prescribed time because of another pregnancy, her sixteenth, at age forty-two, six years after the birth of her last child, the one just discussed. Of course, one might argue that Arembepeiros, because of their proximity to Salvador, were fortunate, despite the obstacles, to have access to these benefits. Use of hospitals by rural Brazilians in more remote areas was much less practicable.

Enhanced medical awareness was another aspect of Arembepe's growing familiarity with the outside world. One woman told me that her father had died of a heart attack and her mother of pulmonary edema. Villagers would not have used those terms in the 1960s, nor did many people know the cause of death of their relatives. Alberto's father, a man of seventy, had dropped dead on the beach while loading his fishing gear one morning in 1965. Villagers suspected a heart attack; but there was no postmortem, since the nearest doctor was in Salvador, then three hours away. Lack of a death certificate later prevented Alberto's mother, who had been legally married to his father, from getting the fisherman's widow's pension to which she was entitled.

Besides new diagnoses, there were new causes of death. Traffic accidents and drunken weekend brawls had created safety hazards in Arembepe, as throughout the "civilized" world. A woman who cleaned house for me in 1962 was one of two villagers who had been run over by road-construction trucks. Automobile traffic had affected child-rearing practices. Previously, small children had taken care of their even smaller siblings, since Arembepe contained few dangers. One day in 1980 I heard a fisherman yell at a hippie couple that they should do a better job of looking after their toddler, who was wandering in the street at the point where the road entered Arembepe. The arrival of strangers and their machines has made the job of supervising children much harder.

There had been little change in birth-control methods since the 1960s. Four village women had undergone tubal ligation. One of them had twelve living children out of twenty live births, including four sets of twins. One thirty-year-old woman with five children had asked for a tubal ligation (which could be done at the maternity center) after the birth of her fifth child. A doctor tried to dissuade her, arguing that she was still young and might one day regret not having a larger family.

The medical-post doctor used to prescribe birth-control

pills. Like many other physicians, he stopped doing so after a national campaign publicizing health hazards of the pill. He warned one woman that the pill might be bad for her varicose veins. At forty-two, after sixteen pregnancies, with a new daughter a year younger than her youngest grandchild, this woman hoped she would soon go through menopause, which she saw as her best chance for birth control. Another woman had heard of a male contraceptive pill, but she doubted that local men would take it. Nor did radio encourage population limitation: "Stop taking the pill," crooned a male vocalist singing the nation's number one tune, "I want my child to be born."

Faced with poor access to the more humane means of limiting population, a few villagers took extreme measures. Soon after my 1980 arrival, I asked about an old friend, a woman who would have been in her late thirties, and learned she had died. A very poor woman married to an alcoholic, she had drunk a remedy designed to abort the fetus she discovered she was carrying. The abortion worked, but the woman got violently ill. She never recovered, and died after a few months. The old woman who told me this sad tale ended it with a proverb: "One kills a child in order to eat" (that is, to feed oneself and one's family). But, my informant concluded, "The woman who aborts her own child may herself die."

Despite such cases, the trend was toward better health and reduced infant and child mortality. Immigration had also contributed to Arembepe's rapid population growth, a doubling in less than two decades. Increasing government impact and immigration had also transformed relationships based on kinship and marriage.

Marriage and the State

Important changes in marital arrangements occurred in Arembepe between the 1960s and the 1980s. The main reasons for these changes lay in Arembepe's increasing participation in external systems, including the social welfare programs of a nation-state. Compared to the 1960s, when almost half (47.3 percent) the marital unions in the village had been formally sanctioned (by state or church, usually both), there were fewer (34.8 percent) legally sanctioned unions in 1980 (see Appendix 5). Several villagers told me about the decline in formal marriages—the more striking in view of much easier access to agents of both state and church, including a justice of the peace and a priest in the district seat, now just minutes away. Saying that marriages had become rare events, one woman could recall only three local people who had married during the past two or three years. Ivan, the *noivo* ("fiancé") of Alberto's eldest daughter, said he had no plans to make their union official. He had little use for formal marriage, calling it "something for old people." "Nowadays," he said, "young people are *amaziado* [they have a common-law ar-rangement]." I asked Arembepe's highest-paid municipal employee, who is also the village's most devout male Catholic, about my perception that there were fewer formal marriages in 1980 than previously. After reflection, he agreed, saying that some young people now lived together for a few years and then married, while others didn't even bother to marry.

The decline in formal marriage had several causes. Most significantly, government rules for pensions had discouraged many people from marrying because a married couple could not draw two pensions simultaneously. Alberto, for example, was eligible for Fundo Rural benefits as a retired fisherman. Carolina, his common-law wife, made monthly payments to INPS, from which she expected retirement benefits at age sixty. Alberto wasn't sure whether he and Carolina could both get their pensions if they married legally (which they had no plans to do). They might still be eligible, he thought, since different government programs were involved. Other villag-ers were sure that a widow couldn't receive her own INPS benefits and also inherit her husband's Fundo Rural benefits. Nor did my informants think that two spouses could draw benefits from INPS.

Villagers obviously didn't control national welfare laws. Nor were they sure about all the legal ramifications of formal marriage. Because of this, government regulations (as villag-ers interpreted them) reinforced a traditional pattern. Com-mon-law unions had never been unusual in Arembepe. Al-though such living arrangements had lacked the prestige of formal marriage, they had never been particularly stigma-tized. Now, however, the common-law arrangement guaranteed that both partners could draw retirement benefits. This consideration was more important now because of growing female participation in the changing economy. Many women, not content with the benefits due a fisherman's widow, wanted their own (better) pensions as owners and operators of stores, restaurants, and bars. Ambitious single women thus avoided formal marriage, because it might threaten their future benefits.

Along with pensions, Arembepeiros also considered inheritance rights in making decisions about marriage. Brazilian law grants legal spouses equal survival rights. In Arembepe of the 1960s wives usually outlived their husbands and men were the main producers. This meant that young women wished to marry formally. They tried to preserve their virginity as a commodity to be traded against eventual inheritance rights. This consideration was less compelling in the 1980s, with business opportunities that permitted women to prosper in their own right.

Arembepeiros have always been well aware of which spouse owns property. Women were especially adamant in remembering that women, rather than their mates, owned particular items. Dora, for example, pointed out that the boats that most village men considered to belong to her brother really belonged to his (legal) wife. He had bought them with his wife's inheritance from her father. Dora complained about her sister-in-law, calling her a domineering woman who constantly issued orders to her husband. After the wife got her inheritance, Dora's brother gave up the common-law union he had maintained "on the side" for years, although he did employ one of his illegitimate sons as a fisherman. In marriage as outside, in Arembepe as elsewhere, differential wealth entails differential power.

A legal marriage was necessary only to guarantee the inheritance rights of spouses. If children of a common-law union were registered in both parents' names, they could inherit from either, and the other parent usually had access to their inheritance. Because of this, there was no incentive for Alberto and Carolina to marry legally, he told me. Their only significant property consisted of their two houses, one in his name and one in hers. Since they had registered their children in both their names, their daughters would jointly inherit the property of whichever parent died first. If Carolina died first, Alberto would still have access to her house in Volta do Robalo through the children.

By 1980 some people were even questioning the special inheritance benefits of formal marriage. They had heard that a stable common-law union of at least two years' duration might also confer inheritance rights on the partners. If true, this would remove the main economic incentive to marry legally. Still, few villagers had the knowledge, connections, or money to litigate for such rights. Because Arembepeiros lacked legal experience and political clout, even legitimate rights based on formal marriage were sometimes denied. For example, Alberto's mother had been trying to get her widow's pension for years. Although she had marriage papers, government officials refused to approve benefits because no death certificate had been filled out when her husband died—years before there was ready access to doctors, coroners, and state officials.

A final cause of the decline in formal marriages may have been villagers' observation of hippie life styles. Even during the 1960s Arembepeiros had partly modeled their decisions about marriage on external norms. Wealthier Arembepeiros, who were more likely to marry legally than poorer villagers,[2] weren't just ensuring inheritance rights. They were also emulating the norms of middle-class and upper-class people. Later, villagers had regular contact with hippies, whom they considered "rich"—and who often were young people with middle-class backgrounds. These outsiders placed little value on legal marriage and permanent relationships, forcing villagers to revise their opinions about external norms of sex and marriage.

An anthropology textbook axiom is that marriage is a mechanism for creating alliances—social ties beyond the particular spouses. In the old Arembepe only formal marriage had created obligations between spouses and their families. A common-law spouse was not one's "husband" or "wife," but one's "man" or "woman." "In-law" relationships came only with formal marriage. To avoid marriage was to avoid the extended social obligations (particularly to the wife's family) that accompanied the legal bond. More people were avoiding marriage, and hence social obligations, in the 1980s than in the past.

Certain social conventions did act to support stable common-law unions. For example, customs about naming children could be used symbolically to strengthen a union. Parts of each parent's name could be incorporated in their children's. For instance, the children of Aldo and Odete, who had a long-term common-law relationship, included Alzete, Valdete, and Crispina. Only the name of Crispina, a twin, did not combine her parents' names. Twins always got mythical names, like Cosma and Damiana (Cosme, Damião for males) or Crispim, Crispina, and Crispiana. The naming system symbolically separated twins (who rarely survived as a pair) from other children.

Ritual kinship (*compadresco*) offered another way of shoring up common-law arrangements. Fernando's daughter, aged twenty-one, wasn't formally married to the father of her two children. The couple had eloped but said they planned eventually to make the union legal. Asked if he was pleased with the relationship, Fernando said he couldn't help being pleased, since his daughter's mate was his godson, as was their first baby. The union lacked legal status, but Fernando was still godfather to his daughter's partner and to his own grandson, and *compadre* to his daughter and her partner. Thus the *compadresco* system could provide close social ties between a woman's family and her partner and children when there was no legal bond. Similarly, when I asked Dora if she considered her niece's common-law mate, whom she spoke of often and warmly, to be her nephew, she said no. But he was her *compadre*. Dora had asked her favorite niece and her husband to be godparents of her youngest son. Thus *compadresco* relationships could, and often did, take precedence over in-law relationships in common-law unions.

Although ritual kinship can provide compensatory social links, the decline in formal marriage (and thus in the alliances it creates) may contribute to the increasing atomism and social fragmentation noted in previous chapters. There were already signs of this in the 1980s: affinal (in-law) links between fishing crew members had decreased along with kin ties. However, yet another change—a reversal of the sex ratio, so that males now outnumber females—may help counter the pressures toward marital instability.

The Sex Ratio and Female Status

This surplus of males reflects a final factor—immigration—that helped change marriage and household composition in Arembepe between the 1960s and the 1980s. Arembepe's 1964 population was 49 percent male and 51 percent female,[3] and 17 percent of the village's 159 households had female heads. By 1980, in the sampled area of southern Arembepe, there were 164 males (52.4 percent) and 149 females (47.6 percent). Of the 61 households in the survey area, only 4 lacked a coresident adult male, and only 6 (9.8 percent) had female heads. These figures confirm a pattern that became obvious to me after a few days of talking with old friends. Almost all the women who had lacked a permanent, coresident partner in the mid-1960s had one by 1980. Dora, for example, now lived with an immigrant fisherman from Sauipe. Another of our former employees had established a stormy but stable common-law relationship with a bricklayer.

An expanding and diversifying economy, attracting men to Arembepe, had brought breadwinners to many women. Although few of these were formal unions, the social status of the women involved had improved markedly. Most had previously been scorned as village prostitutes (*raparigas*) by other villagers, especially women, because they lived off other women's husbands (in secondary, unstable unions with polygynous males). With "husbands" of their own, no longer posing a threat to other families, such women as Dora (see Chapter 11) were no longer regarded as *raparigas;* they had become ordinary village women. Polygyny, too, had declined because of male immigration. Women's greater economic prominence, coupled with the surplus of adult men, may preserve marital and household stability despite opposing pressures.

10 Social Differentiation and the Origin of Deviance

Because of the new surplus of males, the label *rapariga* ("village prostitute") had lost most of its salience as a social category. This ran counter to a general trend in Arembepe toward more social divisions and greater social complexity. Several factors had produced new divisions in this once fairly homogeneous and egalitarian community. For example, people who had moved to Caraúnas and Volta do Robalo were no longer considered to be Arembepeiros. Occupational diversity also meant different activities and associations for villagers. And many kinds of outsiders played regular roles in local life.

The process of social change in Arembepe provides clues about the means by which any egalitarian or simply ranked society is transformed into a stratified social order. Not just in Arembepe but more generally during such a process of sociocultural evolution, attributes that once were associated with particular *individuals* come to be considered markers of different social *groups*.

For example, during the 1960s a handful of villagers had had psychological problems. They were classificatory oddities. Other villagers didn't know what to make of them, how to explain their behavior. So people just ignored them. In other words, during the 1960s, the *role* of the "mentally ill person" was undeveloped. By contrast, the mentally ill had become a salient social category with characteristic generalized behavior by 1980.

In the realm of religious expertise, too, the idiosyncratic perceptions and special talents of individuals had found no social reinforcement in the old Arembepe. By 1980 they had. For example, no one cared in 1965 that one woman claimed to be able to discern in dark corners faces that others missed and to receive spirit possessors. A niche for her, and others with similar talents, had opened up—in *candomblé*—by 1980.

Another individual trait that had evolved into a social category by 1980 is linked closely to the development of socioeconomic stratification out of a hierarchy of graduated wealth contrasts. Although there were relatively wealthy Arembepeiros in the mid-1960s, villagers had always insisted that no one in the community was really rich. By 1980, by contrast, "rich people" had also become a salient social label.

The Rise of the Bourgeoisie

Arembepeiros used the term *burguês* ("bourgeois") to describe wealthy people, including some fellow villagers. Alberto said that a *burguês* is someone who makes more than 50,000 cruzeiros (about $850) per month. He assigned some boat owners and, somewhat jokingly, one Tibrás worker to this category.

Although many people, including Alberto, appeared to be more comfortable with success than they had been in 1973, others were wary of the rapidly broadening wealth differentials. One man complained, "There are so many rich people here now that it scares you."

Two of the most characteristic statements of the old Arembepe—"We're all relatives here" and "We're all equal here"—were no longer heard. Immigrants, tourists, summer people, and hippies were certainly not relatives of native-born Arembepeiros. Men like Dinho and a few others who carried purses and owned cars and large boats were clearly not the equals of an ordinary fisherman. The huge income gap between boat owner and crew member—a relationship at the heart of the traditional economy—was particularly impressive to villagers. It led some of them to exaggerate owners' profits and local wealth contrasts. Alberto, usually accurate in his estimates, told me that rich boat owners could gross 100,000 to 200,000 cruzeiros ($1,700 to $3,400) *per day* from their fishing interests. I told Alberto those figures were impossibly high. After we had figured out the actual profits (see Chapter 8), he saw his error. Still, his mistake is indicative of villagers' heightened perception of local wealth differences.

Since there had been too little time for such wealth contrasts to be transmitted across the generations, some familiar themes continued in local explanations for success. People still cited luck as a major factor in economic ascent and decline, especially in fishing. Through a series of minor incidents, luck could erode. As Alberto put it, "Someone loads up his boat with ice, leaves port, and the motor breaks down. He loses all his ice and that day's, or week's, fishing. This happened to Tomé, who then started fishing in his other boat, only to have the same thing happen a few weeks later." While Tomé's luck was declining, that of his younger brother Dinho was rising, said Alberto.

Villagers were right: Luck (chance, more accurately) along with entrepreneurial activity did still contribute to success. Certainly, as we shall see in Chapter 11, Tomé had been mistaken to overextend himself financially and to rely too much on external resources. He was just as definitely *unlucky* to lose both his motors at the same time. Boat owners wouldn't have become as wealthy had there been no fishermen from Sauipe to replace natives who had qualms about having nonfishing covillagers as their bosses and, besides, could find more lucrative work on land. Even the business success of Alberto and Carolina rested as much on luck as on their hard work, foresight, and innovation. They were among the first villagers to electrify their homes. This allowed them to buy a reliable refrigerator and freezer and sell cold beer. But they had controlled neither the arrival of electricity nor the harbor shift that enhanced their view and made their bar especially attractive to outsiders.

An Irrational Fear of Robbers

Use of such terms as *burguês* and *ricos* ("rich people") suggests that consciousness of local class differences was developing, but villagers still defended Arembepe's social integrity. Many projected their hostility toward the rich against outsiders. One Friday afternoon as boats returned, I saw a small man clutching a purse near the fish weighing stations. Alberto identified him as a fish buyer from Itapoan. "A gunman's going to come and take that purse away from him," suggested

Alberto, but that assailant would surely *not* be an Arem-bepeiro. The man who said that rich people scared him also focused on outsiders. Just one local boy was recognized as having gone astray. First he became a marijuana-smoking hippie, then a vagabond and a thief. Still, he had left the village and thus become an outsider. Although the life-style contrasts they saw each day made villagers envious of each other, they projected onto outsiders their unconscious wish to level wealth. Strangers, not natives, would be the poor who robbed from the rich.

Both in 1973 and in 1980 I found the local fear of robbers way out of proportion to reality, especially since, remarkably, no Arembepeiro had ever been robbed or assaulted by a gunman. The only armed robbery that had taken place locally involved outsiders. A couple, emerging from Aunt Dalia's juice bar one Sunday, was accosted by a gunman. He demanded their car keys and drove off, leaving them stranded. The only other incident in the past several years was even milder: Some Sunday visitors in the beach-home area south of Arembepe had their trunk pried open and their money and documents taken.

Arembepe in the 1980s still lacked law enforcement. The local "policeman" was feebler than ever. Outside officers came from time to time—for example, in June 1980, as part of a widespread search for a man who had raped, robbed, and murdered in a suburb of Salvador. He was later caught near Itapoan.

Given actual happenings in Arembepe, I was a hundred times more likely to be possessed by a spirit than to be robbed. Still, my old friends reiterated the warning "Don't give rides to *anyone*." Beware, they said, of men who dress as women and hitch rides with the intent to rob. Alberto insisted I park my car in front of his house or near that of an acquaintance so someone could watch it. "In the old days," reported Aunt Dalia, "no one locked their doors. Now, everyone does, even when they walk across the street." Knowing I had lived in Africa (Madagascar), Alberto asked me if *candomblé* and robbers existed there. I explained that people I knew in Madagascar feared witches. He found their fears reasonable and promptly declared such witches to be perpetrators of evil magic.

I think that one reason for the exaggerated fear of robbers is that this preoccupation with external threats provided an outlet for envious wishes toward covillagers. Part of Foster's image of limited good (see Chapter 3) is that wealth differences are allowed if they come from outside the community. In Arembepe almost all the wealth generated since 1970 had come from outside—from tourists, hippies, summer people, factory jobs, and the cheap labor of immigrant fishermen. This may be the main reason why, even in a village with a history of egalitarianism and leveling mechanisms, the envy associated with emerging class consciousness was still projected onto outsiders. The fear of robbers may also have expressed resentment against outsiders for the radical changes in local life.

There was another reason for local fears. My 1980s visits to Rio de Janeiro, conversations with urban Brazilians, perusal of newspapers, and television newscasts all convinced me that most Brazilians were more worried about crime than before. Military hard-liners blamed a purported surge in crime on government liberalization. It was unclear whether it was actual crime, or mainly media attention to it, that had increased. Whatever the reason, the national concern with crime, which villagers could share through their exposure to the mass media, reminded me of the preoccupation with "law and order" in the United States during the Nixon years. As in the United States, the effect of a disproportionate interest in crime was to direct national attention toward offenses against individuals and away from social problems. This outlook, of course, was perfectly compatible with Arembepe's traditional worldview.

Alcoholism and Mental Illness

While fearing outsiders, Arembepeiros remained fairly tolerant of unusual behavior by covillagers. No definite social sanction had yet been applied to the wealthiest boat owners. Disapproval of "village prostitutes" had abated as most of the women who once bore that label established unions with immigrants. There was more alcoholism than ever. Villagers had always recognized that certain people drank too much.

They used the term *bebado* ("drunk") for people whose alcoholism kept them from holding steady jobs. By 1980, membership in the category had swollen. The new weekend drinking pattern was turning many fishermen into alcoholics.

Constant drunks seemed to be everywhere in 1980. They wandered around seeking odd jobs and doles to buy another drink. It was almost impossible for me to avoid them when walking in Arembepe, even on weekdays. Villagers were starting to see "the alcoholic" as a social category with characteristic (role) behavior, instead of viewing excessive drinking as simply an idiosyncratic problem for a few individuals. Local theories about alcoholism were just developing. Some villagers saw alcoholism as an illness, but most viewed it as a character flaw, which alcoholics could repair if they wanted.

Alberto reported that a few people started buying *cachaça* from him at 5 A.M. and were drunk by 10 A.M. One of them was a jobless loner who, said Alberto, was waiting to die. Alberto considered this old man and the other constant drunks reprehensible. There was no stigma yet attached to

Illustrating the weekend drinking pattern that intensified between 1973 and 1980, tourists drink several bottles of beer in a shack overlooking the old harbor. (Courtesy Jerald T. Milanich)

heavy weekend drinking, and those who did it (including some captain-owners, fishermen, and business people) weren't labeled "alcoholics" (though many would have been in the United States).

Anthropologist Mac Marshall (1979) found that on the Pacific island of Truk, where he did an ethnographic study of drinking, alcoholics were powerless people. The same was true in Arembepe. But by contrast, whereas on Truk the powerless were young people, their Arembepe equivalents were women and older men. Most were single or separated; none was financially secure. Most of Arembepe's *bebados* were passive bums; few seemed angry or belligerent. They usually tried to ingratiate themselves, becoming maudlin as they begged for money.

Arembepeiros believed that character defects, including alcoholism, could run in families. For example, Dora blamed separate angry attacks (not alcohol-related) by two brothers on other villagers on the defective character of their mother's (immigrant) family. There were several sets of alcoholic brothers and at least one mother-daughter pair of heavy drinkers. Alcoholism was also linked to participation in *candomblé*, which is described in the final section of this chapter.

Like violence and alcoholism, mental illness also seemed to run in families. Villagers regarded two middle-aged brothers as mentally ill. One had a monthly disability stipend through his former factory job. He checked himself in and out of a mental health facility in Salvador, as needed. His older brother, never institutionalized, was a recluse who paced constantly indoors and talked to himself. Villagers also blamed the uneven behavior of their sister and the psychological problems of one of her sons on the family history of mental problems.

Many mental problems were traced to a mother's death or to childbirth. The wife of one captain-owner "went crazy" after the birth of her first child during the 1960s. She had recuperated and was considered normal in 1980. The mental and alcohol-related problems of two of Alberto's nephews started soon after their mother's death.

The most dramatic local case of mental illness was that of Julia, a hippie-like young villager with a penchant for nudity. We met Julia the first day we entered Arembepe in 1980. As we ate lunch in Claudia's Restaurant, we were startled to see an almost naked woman saunter up to the window. At first I suspected that this young woman, whose head was shaved and body painted orange, might be an international *ippa* (female hippie) who had been misinformed that a photography team from *National Geographic* was in town. Instead, she was a local girl who had become mentally disturbed in adolescence, after her mother's death.

Julia had been institutionalized several times, including once during our stay. She always managed to escape or talk her way out during periods of rationality. She was considered particularly adept at convincing mental health specialists she was sane. Back in Arembepe she would revert to deviance. Julia had burned her father's identity papers and had entered some homes and destroyed possessions. Her most common expression of deviance was nudity, which flouted Arembepe's double standard for male and female dress. Although villagers considered an unclothed female much more offensive than a naked male, they were used to Julia's behavior. No one appeared to notice her each day as she drifted through the main part of town, clothed in a skimpy towel, or less.

Normal until adolescence, after her mother's death in 1975 Julia began removing her clothes in public—at first occasionally, then, after the birth of her baby, often. Villagers told me that a totally naked Julia used to carry the baby around Arembepe. The deviance of other villagers was also expressed in nudity. The hippie Aldeia's washerwoman, nature worshipper, and *candomblé* participant, mentioned in Chapter 7, had gotten drunk and removed her clothes in Arembepe. A middle-aged man had also run amuck nude through the village.

Birth and death can engender feelings of inadequacy and guilt in Arembepe as elsewhere. Indeed, we shall see that imagery drawn from kinship and reproduction was important in *candomblé*, to which many insecure and potentially deviant people gravitated. The burden of guilt fell heavily on twins. Twin births were common in Arembepe, but few twins survived as a set. Surviving twins were especially likely to have psychological problems, probably expressing their irrational feelings of responsibility for their twin's death. For example, Alberto's daughter, a surviving twin whose spirit possession was described in Chapter 6, had a history of mild mental

disturbance. She found solace in *candomblé*, with its prominent sets of spirit twins. Her uncle, also a surviving twin, was
Arembepe's highest-ranking *candomblé* member. Another
twin was an authentic lunatic. When the moon was full, he
started fighting with people and threatening to kill them.
Other times, he was normal and had a regular place in a
fishing crew.

From Individual Idiosyncrasy to Group Label

Most studies of conformity and deviance (which scholars usually see as opposite sides of the same coin) have been done in
social systems more stable than Arembepe. There has been
little research on the origin of social deviance. Arembepe
sheds new light on this matter. Developments there suggest
that as new groups, including potentially deviant ones,
emerge within a formerly undifferentiated social system, attributes once seen merely as idiosyncratic personality traits of
individuals serve as models for the construction of the new
(deviant) social categories. Thereafter, individual behavior of
a certain sort is used to assign many people to a particular
category. Once people are so assigned, and as they accept
their new "label" or social identity, their behavior becomes
more restricted and more stereotypical of their category.
They acquire a "role personality," to use a term from "labeling theory" (see Lemert, 1951; Becker, 1963; Farrell and
Swigert, 1975). (For one illustration of this process, see Dora's
case in Chapter 11.)

Anthropologists interested in social evolution have tended
to base their theories of culture change on such major, genera-
tions-long changes as are revealed by the archaeological record or chronicled in historical documents. There is also value
in studying sociocultural *microevolution*—the change process
that Arembepe has experienced. Some of the more intimate
and gradual changes in individuals' experiences, attitudes,
and behavior that accumulate over the years, so that they are
finally perceptible as major structural changes, can be observed in a living context in places like Arembepe, where the
forces of change are working rapidly and dramatically. It is
likely, for example, that the modeling of social categories out
of individual idiosyncrasies—as is illustrated by this discus-

sion of the rise of social deviance—is an important generalized characteristic of social microevolution. It is probably one
of the most powerful mechanisms by which social complexity
grows.

Thus, by 1980 the behavior of unusual people in Arembepe
was no longer seen as idiosyncratic but as diagnostic of membership in newly recognized social groups: the rich, alcoholics,
the mentally ill, *candomblé* participants, and so on. This process of social differentiation was ongoing, not yet complete.
The new categories were neither fully nor consistently stereo-
typed or stigmatized. Their members were not yet recognized
as full-fledged social deviants. Villagers were still building the
stereotypes to go along with the new labels.

Missing in the evaluations of unusual covillagers were the
criticism, anger, and outrage that in other places accompany
a clear image of deviance as rule violation, as going beyond
acceptable social behavior. Arembepeiros devalued two social
categories, but neither described a native villager. Partly stigmatized were the hippies and the other "parrots" who spoke
incompletely or inappropriately. True outrage was reserved
for just one label, the robber, always an outsider. Their images of hippies and robbers helped Arembepeiros distinguish
their own social system from the outside world, since no such
labels set one group off from another among native villagers.

Another reason why full-fledged social deviance had not
yet emerged is that deviance requires conformity, in which
Arembepe has always been deficient. Arembepe had never
fully fitted Robert Redfield's (1948, 1960) stereotype of the
"folk society" or "little community." Like the folk society, the
old Arembepe *had* been small, relatively isolated, homogeneous, and nonliterate. But unlike the folk society, Arembepe
lacked a strong sense of social cohesion. To identify and stig-
matize deviant behavior and individuals, strong community
solidarity is needed. People must agree on social rules and
appropriate behavior. Arembepe had never had the uniform-
ity, the cohesion, and the shared standards necessary to stig-
matize internal deviance. Arembepe had always been an individualistic village with divergent views. Furthermore, after
1970 it witnessed very rapid change, through contact with
varied models of behavior associated with many external
groups.

In Arembepe of the 1960s, with its wide personality variation, there were almost as many *types of individuals* as there were people. There had been no "typical Arembepeiro." In the 1980s who could say what category was normal or typical: business person, boat owner, fisherman, captain, immigrant, factory worker, construction worker, hippie, weekender, summer person, alcoholic, twin, mentally ill, *candomblé* participant, landowner, anthropologist? Deviance, labeling, conformity, and the setting of group boundaries are discussed further with reference to Tomé and Dora in Chapter 11.

Race Relations and Gender Roles

One noteworthy feature of the old social structure, race relations, seemed mostly to have escaped the process of social differentiation. Villagers still didn't discriminate on the basis of skin color or recent slave ancestry. For example, Dinho, Arembepe's richest native, had very dark skin. Working for him as a fish hauler and washer was one of the lightest men in town, the brother of a prominent storekeeper. Two other very light men also worked as menials for much darker boat owners. A teacher who would be considered "white" in the United States had a common-law liaison with a very dark merchant, to whose baby she had just given birth. Although villagers still employed multiple racial labels in the 1980s, fewer such terms were in common use than in the 1960s. Local racial terminology seems to be changing through contact with outsiders who make fewer, but more consistent, racial distinctions.

Gender roles were in more obvious flux. Women's dress was more informal and revealing than in the 1960s, when Betty Wagley Kottak had been embarrassed about wearing even a one-piece bathing suit to take a dip in the Atlantic. By 1980 bikinis and halter tops were common sights. One afternoon I saw Alberto's twenty-five-year-old daughter washing dishes outside in her bathing suit while a young neighbor disco danced on her porch, wearing a skimpy halter and shorts.

Women's work, like men's, had become less communal. Formerly, after the men left to fish, the women would take the pots and pans from last night's dinner down to the lagoon to wash. In the afternoon, before the fishermen returned, the women would use the lagoon to do their laundry and bathe. In the 1980s washing was no longer as social; women with access to well water washed at home.

Men still controlled public space, as my observations of behavior around the fish stores one afternoon reveal. As the boats were unloaded, I wandered in and out of the two fish weighing stations just south of the chapel. This whole area has always been male territory. Men used to sit on the chapel stoop in the evening. The only females who would approach them were elderly women and little girls sent to get their fathers.

In 1980, the broken strings of kites littered the electric wires here. Only boys played in this area, the behavior of juveniles foreshadowing the sex-linked privileges of adulthood. In the shacks, men engaged in mock homosexual play and called each other *viado* ("queer"). Said Alberto to a little boy wandering by with no pants, pointing to the child's genitals: "If you walk by my house like that I'll castrate you." Male territory. Only certain females could enter.

One such woman was Dinho's wife, who sat in front of their fish store. This well-to-do woman wearing glasses and an

Adeli, a successful businesswoman, in her restaurant–boarding house. (Courtesy Jerald T. Milanich)

attractive dress seemed to have left old gender roles, which limited female access to outside social space, behind. Another woman who was comfortable in this area was Amy, daughter of Claudia, the founder of Arembepe's most successful restaurant. Along with the restaurant, Amy had inherited her mother's right to move through male social space. Amy strode into the fish store and soon got a choice fish. On the counter where the fish store employee cut up and sold fish sat his five-year-old step-daughter. Some slightly older girls came to fetch fish, but they were shy and soon left. An old alcoholic woman stood in the crowd of would-be buyers. She was pestering the fish store employee for a dole, but he got tired of her raucous pleas and called her a slut.

The most spectacular female entrance was that of Julia, the psychotic nudist. She had returned that day from Salvador, having once again talked her way out of the psychiatric facility and taken a bus home. Scantily dressed as usual, she began dancing (to no audible music) outside the fish store. Gradually she took off the towel wrapped around her upper body. She lit a cigarette and continued dancing. I was distracted by the arrival of a van marked "Civil Police," which pulled up near Julia. As three officers stepped out, I had visions of Julia being taken back to the city. But this intrusion of the state on Arembepe's internal affairs was not to be. The police officers had come to buy fish. They ignored Julia, who, deciding not to test her luck, wandered off. The news spread rapidly of Julia's return and her near encounter with the law. Other villagers, including Julia's aunt, said they had been as apprehensive as I had.

These women—Dinho's wife, Amy, Julia, and the alcoholic beggar—illustrate the limits of local gender roles. Public space was still a male domain where just a few women felt comfortable. The females with greatest access to public space were businesswomen, small girls, alcoholics, and the mentally ill. In the old days, "village prostitutes" had also dared to encroach on male territory.

The Birth of Religion

Although deviant categories had not fully formed, potentially deviant individuals had one thing in common: They were more likely than others to take part in *candomblé*. *Candomblé* participants included alcoholics, twins, former "village prostitutes," audacious women, Arembepe's only known native male homosexual, and troubled immigrants such as Fernando, who had a strong fear of outsiders (see Chapter 11).

The growing interest in *candomblé* was one more aspect of Arembepe's opening to the outside world. Several *candomblé* participants lived in Arembepe by 1980, compared with none during the 1960s, when, however, two natives were learning about *candomblé* in Salvador. One, Crispim, came back to Arembepe in 1973. By 1980 he had become the main local *candomblé* master. Crispim was a full-fledged *pai de santo* ("saint's father"), with a reputation extending beyond Arembepe. The *filhas de santo* ("saint's daughters") who assisted him came from Arembepe and nearby villages. There was even a tourist from Rio de Janeiro studying *candomblé* with Crispim—for a fee of about $165.

The other native who had been active in *candomblé* in Salvador in the 1960s was Maria. She had moved back to Arembepe in 1964 but couldn't show her skills as a recipient of spirits until the arrival of a saint's father (Crispim) almost a decade later. By 1980 Maria, the mouthpiece of twenty-one spirits, was regarded as merely the most talented of Crispim's dozen acolytes.

Crispim had some competition as Arembepe's spiritual leader. An equally competent *mãe de santo* ("saint's mother") also began holding *candomblés* in Caraúnas in the mid-1970s, but she was a native of Salvador and was still building a local social network. Crispim could draw on his social links as a native Arembepeiro. Two other saint's mothers visited occasionally. One had a *candomblé* house in Caraúnas, active part of the year. The other woman practiced *candomblé* only in Salvador; in Arembepe she was just a "summer person."

One Tibrás worker, an immigrant, was viewed as dependent on a young male *candomblé* expert, who shared his house in southern Arembepe. This would-be spirit father was biding his time until he could move to Jacuipe (the village at the mouth of the Jacuipe River, 10 kilometers north), where he planned to study further with a spirit father there. As part of his training, he planned to shut himself in a room and make special foods, dictated by his instructor, for his saints. He hoped to emerge as a full-fledged spirit father with his own *candomblé* house, perhaps in Arembepe.

I was surprised at the extent to which *candomblé* illustrated increasing local involvement with external systems. *Candomblé* members, it turned out, weren't autonomous individuals but part of a much larger group. To call oneself a spirit father or mother and to open a house of *candomblé,* Crispim and the others had to be licensed. They had official cards from a central *candomblé* organization in Salvador. Licensing followed instruction from a member. Maria and the other saint's daughters lacked these cards. They could practice only through attachment to saint's fathers and mothers.

Religion's new prominence reflected both local and regional changes. Through the 1960s, Arembepeiros had rarely seen agents of organized religions. Even the Pentecostals, who had won converts in nearby Abrantes, had avoided Arembepe, which had just one Protestant. A Catholic priest settled in Abrantes in 1974 and started visiting Arembepe regularly. He gave weekly Monday night masses and a daytime mass one Sunday a month. Also around 1974, a group of nuns moved to Caraúnas. Villagers, led by the former policeman (who had become Arembepe's highest municipal official) built their house for them. He felt strongly attached to the church as the godfather of "more than a thousand" children.

The nuns, he said, had been good for Arembepe. They had helped old people get pensions. Villagers had come to see the sisters as part of community life. (Replacement nuns were sent every few years.) No one thought it strange that the nuns often attended *candomblé,* to enjoy the festive atmosphere. Many villagers see Catholicism and *candomblé*—both of which are local manifestations of larger religions—as different systems rather than competing religions. The Catholic church in Bahia seemed to have absorbed the prevailing urban opinion of *candomblé* as part of traditional Bahian culture—like regional cuisine, good for tourism and no threat to Roman Catholicism. Indeed, the syncretism of Catholic, African, and Native American behavior and beliefs in *candomblé* is well known.

Greater local ceremonial activity rested not just on better access to external religious systems but also on the new economy. In the 1960s villagers had too little money to support spirit fathers or pay for instruction in how to get possessed. Increased local cash flow brought access to several curing systems: spiritual curers, medical doctors, pharmacies, hospitals, and government health and retirement programs.

As in other societies, ceremonial activity intensified in the prosperous season, the summer, which always has been Arembepe's festive period. Villagers complained that the February *festa* for their patron saint, Francis, had become an affair for tourists. It was now managed mainly by local business people instead of by the fishermen, who in the past had formed a procession of boats and made offerings to supernatural entities associated with the sea. Still, villagers could now enjoy the large *candomblés* of December and January. During these months, rarely in others, the spirit father and mother in Caraúnas were possessed by the goddess Oxun, representing a higher level in the *candomblé* pantheon than the lesser spirits (*cabóclos* or Indians) who came regularly.

Local *candomblés*, which lasted no more than three days

With more disposable cash, Arembepe in the 1980s could support both Catholicism and Afro-Brazilian cult activity (candomblé). Shown here is the decades-old chapel and the newer Hotel de Arembepe. (Courtesy Jerald T. Milanich)

even in summer, couldn't rival those of Salvador, where they might last a month. And Crispim was a piddling *pai de santo* compared with masters in the city. His house, made of unfinished wattle and daub, didn't have an air of prosperity. His "saint's room" was considered worthy enough, but women complained that he should be more generous with his acolytes. He and Maria argued over her complaint that he called on her only when he needed her services and never did anything in return. Like a "big man" in a tribal society (see Harris, 1974), a *candomblé* leader was expected to share with other members of his spiritual community. This was especially true in a traditionally egalitarian setting such as Arembepe, where potent leveling mechanisms could operate against arrogance and stinginess. Maria lambasted Crispim to his face for his lack of generosity.

One woman who had also assisted Crispim during the 1970s, though she had yet to receive a spirit, had curtailed her participation because he never gave her anything. "He never got me a saint," she complained. "His saints never gave me anything, and the saints he got for other people never gave me anything." She was especially bitter after a saint at one of his ceremonies called on her to "kill the animal." The person who kills the sacrificial chicken or lamb usually gets some of the money from the sponsors, but she got nothing.

Candomblés were often part of a curing process that might also require a few days' fasting. The spirit father or mother gave the person for whom the *candomblé* was being held a list of items to be supplied, including food and money. The spiritual leader was supposed to use some of the cash to buy ceremonial paraphernalia, and to share the rest with his or her saint's daughters.

Arembepeiros saw *candomblé* as complementary rather than opposed to other curing techniques. Many people turned to *candomblé* only after unsuccessful attempts at cures by physicians. Similarly, many religious people, especially women, hedged their bets by attending mass, taking part in *candomblé*, and holding prayer meetings *(rezas)* for Catholic saints. The *reza*, a small-scale prayer session attended by female neighbors and kin, had been the most common local religious event in the 1960s.

Some *candomblé* masters prescribed cures on their own,

but others, like Crispim, let their spirits diagnose and treat. Although both the masters in Caraúnas received several spirits, each had a regular *cabóclo* used for curing. The diagnosis was done by tossing and studying shells. Patients weren't supposed to name their affliction. If the *candomblé* master, in the client's opinion, correctly identified the problem from the shell pattern, the patient would follow that master's advice. This usually entailed fasting and sponsoring a *candomblé*. Patients then got specific information about curing procedures by filling spirits' requests for beer, wine, rum, or chicken or lamb blood. Usually spirits also wanted cash. "The spirits are like children," said one woman; "they expect their demands to be satisfied no matter what the circumstances." Curing was just one reason for a *candomblé*. Others were held on special occasions, such as the leader's birthday. Many sponsors might contribute to the large-scale summer *candomblés*.

Candomblé could be used for both good and evil. Alberto contended that people used *candomblé* to get rich. He said that Laurentino, the arrogant storekeeper described in Chapter 4, had abandoned *candomblé* but still used the devil dog he had relied on all his life. *Candomblé* could summon evil spirits *(diabos)* to cause sickness and death. Our former cook Dora had heard of soul loss: When victims' souls were extracted or imprisoned by a *candomblé* master, they could weaken and eventually die. Release and survival could come only through *candomblé*.

Alberto's statements to me about *candomblé* were very negative, though he admitted he sometimes attended "just to enjoy." Ashamed of his wife's participation, he called *candomblé* "a bad thing that can lead to ruin." "People *say* they get possessed," he asserted suspiciously.

Dora, an occasional participant, was more positive. She, Maria, and others told me about the social structure and cosmology of *candomblé*. The only formal local male role was that of spirit father (but many spirits were male). There were no sons, just daughters, of saints, though Crispim had once had a male assistant. *Candomblé* thus continued the traditional local male avoidance of religion.

Women were routinely possessed by male and female spirits, but Crispim received just one female being, the goddess

Oxun. When male spirits possessed females, the women's voices deepened. The same spirit might flit from person to person, and the same human might receive several saints in one session. Possession followed hours of drum beating, drinking, and dancing—often to the point of exhaustion. Sometimes possession was quick; at other times it took hours.

"A wind comes and enchants the saint's daughter. It makes her enter a trance and become receptive to the spirit world."

"Everyone has a spirit within, a guardian angel," explained Dora, "but some people also have the ability to receive spirits. Unfortunately, I don't."

Spirit possession rested on a talent that some people were born with, others acquired, and many never got. Recognizing their talent, some people decided to enter *candomblé*. Maria, for example, reported that as a girl she had always been spiritually adept. In the shadows of domestic corners she discerned the faces of spirits that other people never saw. Though she recognized her supernatural abilities, they lay dormant until her daughter entered adolescence. Then Maria turned to *candomblé* in earnest; by 1980 she had hosted twenty-one saints.

An interesting feature of *candomblé* cosmology is its reproductive and kinship imagery. Like Catholicism, *candomblé* uses a kinship model for its spiritual community. The leaders—fathers and mothers of saints—symbolically gave birth to saints by permitting themselves to be possessed. The fathers and mothers also had children in the flesh. These were the "daughters of saints" who assisted their "parents" and were themselves possessed by inferior spirits, who were like the leaders' grandchildren.

Maria's case makes the link between reproduction and spirit possession clear. Though she had always recognized her supernatural talent, she didn't join *candomblé* until her only daughter was twelve years old, when Maria began to have pains. She sought relief in the (urban) *candomblé* community and has been active ever since. Maria despaired of having another child. Unlike most local women, she has been pregnant just once. However, Maria's spirit possession has produced twenty-one symbolic children. (Remember that spirits, with their childish, whimsical demands, were compared specifically to children.)

Maria's own daughter became a saint's daughter after one of her sons got sick. She sought a cure in *candomblé*. At the ceremony, she had a vision that her son would improve and that she would receive a saint. Both came to pass. Unlike her mother, Maria's daughter had received just one saint, but she had many real children. One village woman active in *candomblé* always got possessed during childbirth, again linking this religious system to reproduction. This was also an effective way of dealing with the pain, letting a spirit have the baby.

Villagers' comments suggested that a slight stigma was attached to *candomblé*, even by participants. (They may have thought that I disapproved of this new dimension of local religious life.) Alberto clearly detested *candomblé* and avoided telling me that his wife and daughter had received saints. Because of the people who most often took part, *candomblé* in Arembepe might be characterized as "a training ground for deviance."

Some examples. Laurentino, an unusual villager, who now relied only on his devil dog, had taken part in *candomblé*, as still did his brother, the nude amuck-runner mentioned previously. Maria's ability to see imaginary faces might have been taken as evidence for psychosis in our society, but in hers it showed she had a talent that could blossom in religious activity. Maria and her daughter were incipient alcoholics. Both had once been classified as village prostitutes. Their usual female companions had similar habits and reputations. Assertive and flamboyant, neither mother nor daughter fulfilled local expectations about feminine behavior. They drank, told dirty jokes, and got possessed. When Maria, a large woman, saw me again in 1980, she yelled a greeting from a block away, rushed up, and practically lifted me (180 pounds) with a bear hug: "Oh, Conrado, you've come back to take me to America!"

Women, who have always been less powerful than men in Arembepe, were also much more active in *candomblé*. Twins, people with a history of mental problems, and Arembepe's only known homosexual were also *candomblé* regulars. Were other potential deviants, such as the rich and recent immigrants, also especially active in *candomblé*?

I could find no evidence that villagers still linked economic success to *candomblé* magic, as they had in 1973. No one named boat owners as *candomblé* participants, or even believers. Nor was there evidence for greater participation by immigrants from the northern fishing villages. Those low-paid workers could be expected to be envious of native Arembepeiros and might have sought magical redress through *candomblé*, but they weren't doing so. Instead, they were spending most of their time on long fishing trips and weekend drinking bouts. *Candomblé* remained mainly a domain for a few unusual men and many unusual women.

Although powerless and unusual people predominated among its participants, the stigma attached to *candomblé* was slight. In the old Arembepe there had been diffuse knowledge of, and faith in, aspects of the *candomblé* belief system, but the actual rituals and ceremonies had been absent. By 1980, if Catholic nuns could attend and enjoy *candomblé*, most villagers reasoned there was little harm in it. So, with a local economy that could now support religious activity, villagers were adopting external rituals to accompany and enlarge their preexisting beliefs. The growth of religion was yet another manifestation of sociocultural change, of Arembepe's increasing social complexity.

11 *A Community of Outsiders*

What academics call "social change" is a process lived by real human beings. Of the many Arembepeiros who have befriended me and shared their knowledge, I have chosen four who have been affected by the forces of change discussed in previous chapters. By considering in detail how the lives of a few actual people have been altered, I hope to give concrete human meaning to this story of rapid change.

All four are people I know well. I met Dora, Fernando, and Tomé in 1962. Dora cooked for members of the 1962 field team: Betty Wagley, David Epstein, field leader Marvin Harris, and myself. Fernando, captain and part-owner of a sailboat, was the common-law husband of Dora's only full sister. Tomé had just returned from Rio de Janeiro, where he had spent seven years in commercial fishing. Soon after our arrival, this enterprising captain-owner invited us to a birthday party in his well-furnished brick house in Arembepe's northern rectangle. There we drank vermouth and listened to music on a small battery-operated phonograph, a rarity then in Arembepe.

We saw little more of Tomé during that first stay; but I went out fishing with him in 1965, and we had long conversations in 1973 and in 1980. Dora washed clothes for us in 1964, 1965, and 1980 and was our cook again in 1973. Fernando always enjoyed talking with us but visited us most frequently in 1973, when we lived farthest from his house. He seemed to fancy himself our protector during our stay in the isolated area of summer homes to the south. Beginning a period of problem drinking that lasted until 1976, Fernando also enjoyed our ample stock of beer and Bacardi rum.

I don't remember Alberto from 1962, but he was to become my most trusted informant, best friend, and field assistant. I

Atahydes Alves de Souza—one of the many Arembepeiros who have befriended me and shared their knowledge. (Conrad P. Kottak)

learned about Alberto from Niles Eldredge, a member of the 1963 field team, who had found him an excellent informant and suggested I look him up. Fostering my acquaintance with Alberto and our working relationship as anthropologist and informant was our employment of his younger sister as our cook in 1964. The woman from whom we rented a house that year insisted that we hire this local woman, whom she trusted. Following a pattern he had established with Niles, Alberto visited us almost every night to converse and teach me about Arembepe, especially the fishing industry.

None of these four—Alberto, Dora, Fernando, or Tomé— was a typical Arembepeiro, since, as noted in Chapter 10, there is no such thing. One characteristic they shared is an attraction to outsiders—witness their friendships with us. Although no single story can encapsulate the "typical Arembepeiro's" experience with change, these four personal histories will provide concrete illustration of the impact of many forces on local life. Alberto's story, for example, samples the shift from fishing toward the tourist industry and a more diversified economy. So does Fernando's, but with an added component of the new economy—the Tibrás employment of one of his sons. Fernando's case also illustrates, in extreme form, villagers' hostility toward external forces. Dora's life between 1962 and 1980 shows the impact of male immigration on marital arrangements, the declining significance of the *rapariga* ("village prostitute") label, and the continuing poverty of ordinary fishermen and their families. Perhaps most interesting, the case of Tomé, an unusually ambitious man, shows the importance of innovation and its rewards and pitfalls, the force of leveling mechanisms, and the continuing impediments to class mobility in northeast Brazilian society.

These contrasting stories also illustrate the wide range of personality variation even in an egalitarian community such as traditional Arembepe. The anthropologist must pay attention to such personality contrasts. They influence choice of informants and personal relations in the field, and thus both the direction and the results of ethnographic research. Through these four cases, we may also see that (in Arembepe as elsewhere) a person's fate is determined by many factors. These determinants include "pure chance," idiosyncratic experiences and thought patterns, personal and family planning and decision making, cultural expectations, and socioeconomic limitations—both local and regional.

The Teacher

Born in 1923, Alberto is the oldest of the four villagers considered here. A native-born Arembepeiro, Alberto enjoyed the role of informant about his home community, particularly teaching Niles Eldredge and me about fishing. Alberto started fishing fairly late in life, at the age of twenty-four, after spending a half-year in Salvador, where he worked successively as store clerk and domestic. Before going to the city, Alberto had never had regular employment; he had done odd jobs in Arembepe. Once Alberto discovered that he disliked urban life, he decided to return to Arembepe and become a fisherman.

He began fishing in the same crew as his father, an ordinary fisherman, but soon joined his godfather-uncle, who owned a half-share in a boat and was its captain. This man taught

Alberto most of what he knew about fishing. Later, Alberto fished in more than a half-dozen crews, sometimes with kinsmen, sometimes not. By 1973 he was fishing irregularly, spending more and more time on the store that Carolina, his common-law wife of thirty years, had started a few years earlier. Tired of fishing, Alberto was delighted to work as my field assistant between June and August 1973, for a regular wage.

Alberto's story between 1965 and 1980 was one of improving but unspectacular fortune. His success, fitting Arembepe tradition, came through innovation and luck. In 1980 Alberto said that his life had improved: "Hasn't yours?" he asked me. He attributed his success to electricity and especially to his refrigerator. Alberto and Carolina's household had been Arembepe's third to install electricity, which permitted them to buy a refrigerator and eventually a freezer. Electric refrigerators, explained Alberto, are much more reliable than the old kerosene models that a few storekeepers had previously owned.

Note the element of luck here: old-time business people had invested in kerosene refrigerators before electricity arrived. They held on to their old models and did not immediately buy electric appliances. This created a niche for a shrewd business move by Alberto and Carolina: they sold the farm plot where they had invested profits from their store and used the cash to buy an electric refrigerator. Adding a freezer a year later, they became known for having the coldest drinks in Arembepe, a valuable resource given the increased consumption of alcoholic beverages, especially beer, by villagers and outsiders alike.

Electricity reached Arembepe in 1977. Alberto and Carolina began by buying two cases of beer (each containing twelve 1-liter bottles) for resale. By winter 1980, they were selling 100 liters per weekend, producing a profit of about $25, a figure that quadrupled in summer. Also contributing to their success was the paved highway, which permitted not just weekend and summer people but beer and soft-drink trucks to add Arembepe to their delivery routes.

The success of Alberto and Carolina thus rested on a combination of luck and business skills—enterprise, foresight, opportunism, and hard work. Arembepeiros did not bring electricity or the road to the village. Nor did Alberto and Carolina have anything to do with the shift to larger boats that demanded a deeper harbor, necessitating the move of moorings to the south, which gave Alberto's house its valuable view. Still, in the face of luck, they innovated opportunistically— converting a distant farm plot into a refrigerator, an at-home generator of income. Alberto and Ivan, his daughter's partner, convinced Carolina they should expand their house seaward and build a balcony where weekend tourists could drink their beer. Again, a strategic innovation led to success. Alberto's household continued plowing profits back into the business, adding the freezer, a stereo system in the balcony bar, and a second refrigerator when the first one broke down.

Continued profits allowed Alberto and Carolina to buy a lot in Volta do Robalo and build a house on it, which they were renting in 1980. This house was registered in Carolina's name, but the Arembepe home belonged to Alberto. Alberto and Carolina had been wise not to sell their house in seaside Arembepe to outsiders, as many villagers had done. Along with the view, they had a good location for selling beer. The only nearby competition for beer sales was Aunt Dalia's bar, which specialized in juice, ice cream, and sales to hippies. Alberto and Carolina could sell both to locals and to weekenders who owned or rented houses in Street Down There and in the new neighborhood just to the west. For those willing to wade through the lagoon in winter, Caraúnas was nearer to this part of Arembepe than to the central and northern parts. The best ocean swimming areas were also closest to southern Arembepe. The location of his bar (and his reputation among outsiders for success and reliability) had also brought Alberto the job of caring for a house across the street, owned by a summer person from Salvador. This added about $35 per month to his income, while the summer person's well and electric pump gave Alberto's family ready access to clean water for washing dishes and bathing.

For sales of vegetables and sundries, Carolina and Alberto had competition. One out of three homes in this part of Arembepe sold something. The reselling of limes, onions, tomatoes, herbs, and other produce from the agricultural estates to the west had been Carolina's idea, but Alberto blamed her for not being more aggressive in meeting competition. He complained that she had ignored his advice to buy more fruits and vegetables for resale. To illustrate her shortsightedness, Alberto told me that a man from Salvador had arrived, rented quarters across the street and a few doors north, and begun to sell cheaper fruits, vegetables, and sundries. Their produce sales had fallen off as a result. Alberto knew about the practice of first underselling to try to drive competitors out of business and then raising prices, but he thought that his own seaview and drink sales would shield them from this tactic. Still, he complained, if Carolina had built up a larger sales volume years ago, they could have matched the newcomer's prices and kept their advantage.

Alberto's story illustrates successful adaptation by individuals and a household to Arembepe's transformation from isolated fishing village to economically diverse suburban resort community. Alberto and Carolina's economic advance showed up in their life style. A small house that in 1964 had been mostly wattle and daub was now all brick. Only one room had been plastered and painted when I first met Alberto, and his house had a dirt floor. Years of gradual improvement added up to much more comfortable quarters in 1980. A third bedroom and a toilet had been added, along with the seaward addition. All the inside rooms were plastered and newly painted; the floor was cement; the house was spic and span. Besides the refrigerator, freezer, and stereo, they owned an electric iron, a gas stove, and a black and white TV. This affluence posed a sharp contrast with 1964, when Carolina had cooked on a simple wood-burning grill and ironed with charcoal, when they couldn't afford even the cheapest transistor radio.

Along with their new life style, Alberto's family seemed much more comfortable with their success than they had been in 1973. Carolina took part in candomblé less often than before. Their middle daughter, now a grown woman and a regular candomblé participant, no longer got possessed by unwanted spirits. The health of the whole family had improved. Once a constant complainer about her ailments, Carolina was cheerier in 1980. Alberto attributed his persistent slight afternoon cough to years of pack-a-day cigarette smoking, which he had given up in 1977. He kept his slim and fit-looking physique despite his fifty-seven years and his retirement from the daily manual labor of fishing. His hearing was failing noticeably, and his eyesight, which had troubled him in 1973, continued to be a problem. An opthalmologist we consulted in Salvador in 1973 diagnosed Alberto's problem as his optic nerve, attributing his visual deterioration to years of glare at sea.

Psychologically, Alberto exuded a new confidence. When presenting me to an immigrant neighbor and friend he remarked, "You remember my boss [*patrão*], don't you?" Alberto was openly acknowledging and addressing years of gossip about our relationship. Villagers had always suspected that I paid Alberto for being a regular informant, which I never did, except with occasional presents and departure gifts, until I hired him as a field assistant in 1973 and 1980. Alberto had grown accustomed and felt entitled to his own moderate success; he was less threatened by envy than before. All Arembepeiros were now more familiar with economic success and conspicuous consumption, and these life style changes were often the result of contacts with outsiders.

One afternoon in 1980 as Alberto and I were looking at boats beached for repairs near the fish stores, he pointed to a large vessel that belonged to a man from Salvador and joked with me, in plain hearing of a neighbor, "You're going to buy that boat for me, aren't you?" What a contrast with the 1960s, when he had often complained that covillagers were making him uncomfortable by accusing him of taking money from me to tell their secrets. In 1964 and 1965 I had often wondered why Alberto sometimes didn't appear for our nightly chat; I later learned that he was avoiding me after particularly disturbing gossip attacks. Even in 1973 Alberto had avoided confrontations with village gossip about our relationship. By 1980 his self-confidence had grown immensely.

Of the four people discussed in this chapter, Alberto might be considered the most typical in certain ways. In contrast to Dora, once stigmatized as a *rapariga,* and to Fernando and Tomé, captain-owners, Alberto belonged to no deviant or statistically restricted social category. For about thirty years he had been an ordinary fisherman. Like many others, he had reduced his fishing and then abandoned it in response to new opportunities. His parents and grandparents were long-time residents, having been born either in Arembepe or in one of the estates a few kilometers to the west. His grandparents had been among Arembepe's original settlers. Alberto remembered a great-grandmother who had told him stories of her life as a slave. Like the other three, Alberto would be considered "black" in the United States, but his skin was darkest of the four. My records show that he used various racial terms for himself: *moreno escuro* ("dark brunet"), *escuro* ("dark"), and even *preto* ("black") on occasion. He seemed to be using the last, once heard only rarely in Arembepe, more often in the 1980s. This may have been a sign that the local classification system was being simplified. It may also have been another reflection of Alberto's new self-confidence. He was now freely using a term that was once uncommon locally, probably because it carried over into Arembepe derogatory Brazilian stereotypes about people with very dark skin.

Despite his more typical economic role and native birth, Alberto's individuality stood out in obvious ways. As a youth he had suffered an accident that left him with a minor but easily seen physical disability. Another aspect of Alberto's personality soon became even more apparent to me. This was his interest in teaching. In the 1960s he often mentioned his friendship with the learned German priest who had married one of the landowners. He took me to the man's apartment in Salvador, and I saw that Alberto was indeed friendly with the elderly man and his two sons, both university graduates.

Although Alberto was barely literate, having obtained only the limited schooling available locally during his boyhood, he valued education. He and Carolina had burdened themselves with the expense of educating their oldest daughter, Maria José, in Itapoan, and their youngest daughter, Wanda, was taking advantage of the improved schools in Arembepe. Alberto had often told me that one member of the landowning family had become a high school teacher; and he spoke with pride of the college education of another landlord.

Alberto knew that I planned to become a university professor. He appreciated the fact that I found Arembepe worth studying, and he very much wanted to instruct me. Both Niles Eldredge and I found that he liked particularly to teach about fishing. He labored with both of us on maps of the ocean floor, detailing the zones where different species could be found,

making sure we had the correct names of the zones and pointing them out when we went out fishing. In 1973 he went over
the ocean floor map in my doctoral dissertation, chiding me
for mistakes and penciling in corrections.

Perhaps other anthropologists have forgotten after long ab-
sences, as I did between 1973 and 1980, the specific talents
and personality attributes of a particular informant that originally led the anthropologist to value him or her especially. In
1980 I found myself rediscovering the full range of Alberto's
special qualities. A key marker of a good informant was Alberto's habit of admitting when he didn't know the answer to
a particular question. Other informants would simply give me
a wrong answer; Alberto would go out that evening or the
next day and discreetly check out the point. Despite (or perhaps because of) his failing vision and hearing, Alberto had
always paid close attention to what he saw and heard.
Through observation of what went on around him, he built a
broad knowledge of village life, and he had a good memory.
I was also struck by the accuracy of his estimates and figures,
particularly since other people who should have known particular facts better than he did were much less accurate.
Accuracy, memory, knowledge, attentiveness, and willingness to admit lack of knowledge are qualities that make a good
informant. Alberto had these in abundance.

A final point: Alberto considered his village's story well
worth telling, and he wanted to make sure I got it right.
Unlike others, who insisted on directing my questions about
their society back at me ("Are there camels in the United
States?"), Alberto pondered even my most naive questions
and usually made a sincere attempt to answer them.

In retrospect, I realize that my association with Alberto was
no accident, no chance throwing together of compatible souls.
Through Niles Eldredge, I had discovered Alberto. On the
other hand, through Niles, Alberto had also found me. In a
community of outsiders, Alberto was the native-born partici-
pant-observer, the teacher searching for a student, probably
as determined to teach as Niles and I were to learn. This book
therefore reflects joint accomplishment of a common goal,
Alberto's and mine—to bring Arembepe's story to the outside
world.

The Village Prostitute: What Happens to the Deviant Once Deviance Disappears

I met Dora, who was born in Arembepe in 1937, two years before I met Alberto. Because Betty Wagley Kottak got to know her even better than I, I have drawn on Betty's knowledge and a published article (I. Kottak, 1977) for material in this discussion. Dora, our employee during each visit to Arembepe, stands out in my memory as an exuberant, sentimental woman with a strong sense of family—a domain in which, until the 1970s, she had little success. Unlike Alberto, an excellent informant, Dora was never a very good one. Often she grew impatient with our questions and cut them off, saying she didn't know things it was obvious she did. One trait she shared with Alberto was a dislike of gossip; she didn't usually like to enlighten us about the soap-operatic details of other people's lives. Neither did Alberto, but he always tried hard to answer factual questions.

Dora did love to visit people; when we planned short trips outside Arembepe, she often asked to come along. In 1980 she still remembered a trip she and her then four-year-old son (whose congenital heart condition killed him at age thirteen) had made with us to Camaçari in 1962. There the boy, Dora's first-born, had met his father for the first time. Earlier, Dora had lived for a few months in Camaçari with the boy's father, whom she had met while working as a servant in a Salvador suburb. She had abandoned him following abuse and rivalry with another woman.

Although she was normally a reluctant and frustrating informant, Dora did often help us by "facilitating"—telling people we wanted to talk with them, arranging meetings, accompanying us, and introducing us to strangers. For example, when Betty told her in 1980 that she was interested in talking to the nuns and to the candomblé people in Caraúnas, Dora wanted to go right over. Visiting was her joy; our hosts could answer the questions.

During our 1980 visit, Dora reported several times "I've had a feeling lately my Americans would be coming." Whereas Alberto needed us to satisfy his wish to teach, Dora had continuing material needs. She had lost the only house she'd ever owned. She wanted a new one, a home of her own, for her growing family, and she was determined we were going to help her get it. From our first through almost our last conversation in 1980, she insisted on this, until she got what she wanted. Persistence was another of her traits, which is why she always managed to arrange meetings with hard-to-contact people.

From the mid-1960s through the early 1970s, when Dora began living with her common-law spouse—an immigrant who worked as an ordinary fisherman—she had been one of a dozen village women classified as *rapariga*, village prostitute. This uniquely stigmatized category lost its significance as most women so labeled found marital partners among the flood of men who migrated to Arembepe in the 1970s. More than the few alcoholics who were socially stigmatized as "drunks" (*bebados*), *raparigas* had been objects of local scorn. Other villagers attributed the plight of these women to mistakes on their part, rather than to the economic and demographic factors that made a "husbandless" category inevitable. That is, the village economy gave women few ways to make a living for themselves, and the marriageable population had a surplus of females. The stigma of being a "manless" woman reflected Arembepe's general poverty, competition for resources, and the belief that obligations associated with legal marriage and the nuclear family took precedence.

These conditions changed during the 1970s, when women's job prospects improved, many males migrated to Arembepe, and legal marriage became less frequent. In this context the deviant status of *rapariga* all but disappeared, although the term was sometimes heard as an insult. The following discussion, of how Dora got to be a *rapariga* and of what happened to her as that deviant category lost its salience, is based largely on an article by Isabel (Betty) Kottak (1977). That article applied "symbolic interactionist" or "labeling" theory to Dora's case. Betty analyzes Dora's deviance in terms of Edwin Lemert's (1951) eightfold progression—from primary deviation (first departure from a norm) through ultimate acceptance of deviant status and role.

Dora's primary deviation, getting pregnant, occurred when she was twenty. Note that her deviation was not sexual intercourse, which many young women had before elopement or marriage, but pregnancy. The obvious anatomical change removed Dora from the virgin (*moça*) category and motivated her to seek a mate. She joined her lover in Camaçari, but their common-law union lasted only eight months; she moved back to Arembepe with her infant son. In ironic contrast to villagers' later view of Dora as a *rapariga* seeking to live off other women's husbands, she had actually tried hard to improve her economic and social position. She had ventured into an unknown world outside Arembepe, where she had obtained employment as a domestic. Like many other local women, she had an affair with an unmarried man—lighter in skin color and wealthier than most men back home. She had hoped for socioeconomic advance. But luck, which had contributed to the rise and fall of so many Arembepeiros, was a factor in Dora's subsequent plight: an inexperienced young woman away from home, she chose the wrong man.

Dora returned to Arembepe and moved into her grandmother's wattle-and-daub house, where her childless brother and his wife also lived. Although these people helped Dora care for her son, her chances of attracting a man had been reduced by childbirth. Young men preferred younger women than Dora and generally avoided acquiring stepchildren. The partners that Dora was able to find were "losers." The father of her second son (who lived only two years) was an alcoholic. Following this brief affair, Dora took up with the father of her oldest surviving son, born in 1962. This was an unsuccessful fisherman, and again the union didn't last.

Dora suffered further penalties and social rejection, which are common aspects of a deviant career. Her needs increased as her children grew older. Dora's brother's wife began to have children, and the support of Dora and her children became more burdensome for her brother. Dora realized that she and her children were draining resources that her brother (a nonowning captain) needed to buy his own boat. To increase her independence, she took various steps: She sought work from the few outsiders, like us, who filtered into Arembepe in the mid-1960s. She became more aggressive in meeting men and trying to obtain their support. She began to associate less with her brother's family and more with women like herself, unmarried females who lived alone. She flouted canons of proper female behavior by visiting the beach as the boats returned in the evenings, by staying out late on festive occasions, and by dressing garishly. In short, she began to act like a *rapariga*.

As a final step, in 1965, she began her first affair with a married man, a successful captain-owner, whose two sons she eventually bore. Other villagers began to regard her as someone who was depriving a legal wife and family of their rights. To make her affair (as secondary wife in an informal polygynous union) easier and to relieve tension in her brother's home, Dora left that household in 1966. With her consort's help, she built a wattle-and-daub hut (the first "home of her own") in northern Arembepe. This hut was blatantly located near her consort's primary home, in a neighborhood where Dora had never lived before. She was regularly abused by her lover's relatives and in-laws, who lived nearby. When she fought with her lover's wife, her own relatives didn't take her side. The stigma applied to Dora had become generalized and community-wide. The label *rapariga* was applied to her more often. "Decent women" told their children not to play with hers.

Dora's relationship with her consort gradually deteriorated. As he gave less and less to feed Dora and her children, she began "entertaining" men for money and food. This became easier, as Arembepe's access to outsiders improved. Such behavior hadn't been possible when Dora lived with her brother. By 1970, Dora mainly associated with other members of the *rapariga* category (including Maria and her daughter, the *candomblé* participants discussed in Chapter 10). Dora became a leader in the *rapariga* group—smoothing over arguments between other members and using her facilitating skills to help them find jobs. (The economic opportunities open to such women were also increasing by 1970.) With Dora's support and encouragement, the *raparigas* would occasionally invade male territory, visiting the beach, where they would laugh, joke, and poke fun at fishermen and fish buyers. Dora had become more aggressive and was regularly visible in domains not ordinarily open to village women. She moved at will through public space, entering stores and bars and freely interacting with outsiders, including tourists and anthropologists.

By 1973 it was clear that Dora's role as *rapariga* and the

deviant behavior associated with it had intensified, as had her labeling by covillagers. Dora's *rapariga* status excluded her from the usual female areas of social participation: normal home life, an adequate diet, the possibility of advancing in socioeconomic status through a husband, the likelihood of good health, legitimacy, and inheritance rights for her children. This exclusion caused Dora much anguish, especially with the deaths of several of her children. Still, as is generally true of membership in deviant social categories, Dora's role as a member of a subculture opened compensatory areas of social participation normally closed to ordinary women. For example, along with other *raparigas*, Dora became active in *candomblé* in the mid-1970s.

Members of any social system are concerned about deviant people only if and when there are well-established deviant roles, and the role of *rapariga* was disappearing from Arembepe in 1980. Dora's social status had risen because her common-law union with an immigrant fisherman had lasted several years, but her life style hadn't improved dramatically. Like other ordinary fishermen in 1980, Dora's husband received low wages. His employer was a wealthy storeowner and local entrepreneur, from whom Dora took weekly cash advances, to be repaid, they hoped, out of the next catch. Dora regarded her partner as a good man. She ignored his excessive weekend drinking and stressed that he was a kind father to their two young children (including Dora's only daughter) and to her three sons from previous unions.

With her husband's earnings, Dora had planned to convert her wattle-and-daub, straw-roofed hut into a brick house; but a former neighbor had seized her land, fencing it off and calling it his own when she tore down the hut to start building the new house. Dora was dubious about winning her court case against him. In the meantime she had temporarily lived with another brother, with whose wife she frequently argued. Her 1980 home was a hut loaned by her aunt.

The lives of Dora and her sons had been spent in tiny hovels with mud-wall parasites, bare earthen floors, and leaky, insect-infested palm-frond roofs. By 1980 Dora was desperate for a home of her own, to bring her family together, to have all her children around her. She felt especially sorry for her oldest son, aged eighteen, who slept next door in her aunt's living room. About to finish junior high school, after which he planned to enter the army, get work papers, and eventually find a steady job, Dora's son had no classes until afternoon. Dora lamented, "Sometimes he likes to sleep late because he doesn't have anything to do. My aunt calls him lazy when he does. I wish he didn't have to take that. I want a house of my own so that my son can sleep late if he wants to. I wish my man and my sons had steady jobs. Nowadays fishermen don't earn enough to pay the bills."

"People treat me funny sometimes. They look at me in a strange way. I think it's because I don't have a house. But my boys are all handsome and strong and I have hope for the future."

Dora looked to her sons, particularly the three oldest ones, aged fourteen, fifteen, and eighteen, to bring an end to her continuing poverty. Their future incomes would help her build a house on the lot we helped her buy in late August 1980. With the down payment in hand, she would make monthly payments on the balance. Since a few months before our arrival, Dora had been working in a bar recently opened in the village square by her *comadre* (godmother of her second son). Her weekend wages and tips would pay off her mortgage.

Dora pinned her hopes on kinship—on her sons' eventual success and on that of her *comadre*. Their close ritual kinship had lasted twenty years, despite the premature death of Dora's son whose baptism had created the relationship.

Recalling past taunts and exclusion, Dora said that she trusted few others. She liked the brother with whom she had first lived and his wife and children, her full sister, a half-sister, and some of her nieces and nephews. Besides those people, she claimed to be "close to no one in Arembepe." In 1980 she locked her door each time she left her hut. "You can't trust people not to mess with your stuff," she explained.

Though Dora was no longer a *rapariga*, her former status had left its mark. She thought that "people look at me funny," though she couldn't say exactly why. She felt cut off from most other villagers. Still, in 1980, twenty-three years after the primary deviation of her first pregnancy, Dora, through her sons, could glimpse an end to years of poverty, miserable living conditions, and social isolation. The wish, now a more realistic hope, to escape all this was symbolized in Dora's desperation to bring her children together in a new home.

The Stranger

I first met Fernando, born in 1933 in the Bahian interior, in 1962. His mate, Ivone, was Dora's only full sister (they had two brothers). Fernando was then twenty-nine; he had come to Arembepe in his early teens and had been living with Ivone for six years. After a year of courting, which had begun at the Saint John celebration one June, they decided to elope. One evening Ivone went to her house and packed a few of her things to take to the house that Fernando had been building for his future family. She moved the rest of her possessions after a few weeks. Their first child, a daughter, came a year later. By 1980 they had ten children, and during the almost quarter-century of their union Ivone had miscarried six times. Fernando, an illiterate man with no formal education, remembered that the total number of his progeny was ten; but he had to count names on his fingers to tell me how many girls and boys.

When he was eight years old Fernando had run away from a fairy-tale home, replete with wicked stepmother. Following Fernando's mother's death, his father had taken another wife. Fernando decided to leave home when he saw his stepmother put his younger brother's hand in the fire as punishment for taking something. The runaway skirted Salvador and was taken in by a man in Itapoan, who after eight days beat him, spurring further flight, to Abrantes, Arembepe's district seat.

In recalling his childhood, Fernando stressed incidents of physical abuse. A man in Abrantes had lodged him for four years and beat him for lying. In 1942, at the age of twelve, Fernando moved to Arembepe, where he worked successively as a mule driver for two businessmen. They gave him room and board in their homes in the central square. He liked the first, another outsider, better than the second—Prudencio, the landowner's agent. Fernando recalled another beating—from Prudencio's wife, the old schoolteacher.

Fernando started fishing when he was eighteen. As an

immigrant, he had no kin ties to captains or crews and started fishing with a man from Jauá, whose boat was temporarily fishing out of Arembepe. In 1960 Fernando became captain and half-owner (with a local businesswoman) of a sailboat. In the mid-1960s he joined the other captains who were dissolving their relationships with nonfishing owners for full ownership. "I don't want to have to fish and divide my profit with someone who sits on shore doing nothing while I do all the work. And I'm not the only one who feels this way."

In the mid-1960s, Fernando was a reasonably vigorous and successful captain-owner. He followed a behavioral model provided by people like Tomé. Still, Fernando was never as daring, innovative, or enterprising, and this showed up in his good but unspectacular catches. Fernando maintained a stable crew, using ritual kinship to compensate for his lack of kin ties and legal marriage links with other villagers. Enjoying the good health of a man in his thirties, Fernando fished regularly. He varied his fishing strategy with the seasons, but he never strayed far from fishing patterns set by others and by tradition.

This pattern of following rather than leading persisted into the 1970s, when Fernando was one of the last captain-owners to withdraw from the fishermen's cooperative, which had given him a loan to motorize his boat. In 1980 he was one of just two people still following the old pattern of daytime fishing in Arembepe's traditional banks, while others were doing distant nighttime "ice fishing." In the mid-1960s I shared villagers' impression of Fernando as an ordinary, respected, noncontroversial, good man. My perception changed during my 1973 visit.

Of all the Arembepeiros I spent time with that year, Fernando seemed the most fearful and hostile toward change. Other social scientists have observed that outsiders often exhibit the strongest antipathy toward external forces and people. Fernando provides an excellent example (as does my 1973 reaction to the hippies). So uneasy was Fernando about his nighttime visits to the summer house we were renting south of Arembepe that he began carrying a revolver for protection. To my knowledge, no one in Arembepe had possessed such a weapon in the mid-1960s, and gun ownership was still rare in 1973. More than my other friends, Fernando reiterated that thieves and armed robbers would surely try to storm the domicile of "Americans, who, they think, must be rich." These would be outsiders, of course. "You have nothing to fear from Arembepeiros." Fernando's fear was strong and contagious, and his warnings soon unnerved me. I suspected every set of headlights that crept into our isolated neighborhood after sundown. "Get a gun," he said; "otherwise you'll be killed." In our absence one evening Fernando got the idea of throwing firecrackers from our windows to convince would-be thieves we were armed. Fernando was also more vocal than other villagers in denouncing other outsiders, the hippies, for licentiousness.

Another sign of Fernando's unease was his excessive alcohol consumption, in sharp contrast to his previous habits. In the 1960s Fernando had hardly ever drunk *cachaça*, but in 1973 he requested not just beer but ample glasses of Bacardi rum when he visited us. (Alberto's drinking habits provide a contrast. In the 1960s he always took at least one shot of *cachaça* each evening, to "warm up" after the day's fishing. He remained a controlled and moderate drinker in 1980.) Fernando, by contrast, had gone from one extreme to the other.

In 1973 the people of Arembepe felt insecure about many changes—Tibrás pollution, hippie stragglers, weekend hordes of boisterous outsiders, a booming economy, and a dramatically increased cash flow. Alberto's family expressed its unease through his wife's psychosomatic illnesses and his daughter's uncontrolled spirit possession. Both of them sought relief in *candomblé*, as eventually did Fernando, who often mentioned to me that fishermen had been accusing certain captains of using black magic. He hinted to me that other captains, including Tomé (who never did), were participating in *candomblé* and that this partly explained the dramatic increase in the wealth of certain people. Fernando stood out among villagers in giving a magical explanation for a down-to-earth but unfamiliar process—rapid commercialization and an economic boom.

When I left Arembepe in August 1973, I predicted that Fernando would go on seeking solace in alcohol and in *candomblé*. (I based the prediction about *candomblé* on his belief that it contributed to economic success. I suspected that Fernando, trying to get richer himself and to guarantee his protection against others, would seek the most available magical solution.) My prediction was correct, but fortunately only in part. Other villagers reported that Fernando did drink too much between 1973 and 1976. Although people realized that Fernando was drinking too much, they never labeled him an alcoholic. They reserved that term for someone who worked sporadically, hung out around bars, and drank even at breakfast time. Fernando also became increasingly involved in *candomblé*, the only captain-owner to do so. He eventually became one of the main ceremonial assistants of Crispim, the spirit father in Caraúnas.

On my return to Arembepe in 1980 I was pleasantly surprised to find that Fernando's behavior had stabilized. He seemed as much at ease with himself and his life style as he had been in the mid-1960s. He was no longer active in *candomblé*, and he was clearly not an alcoholic. His drinking was limited to beer on Sunday, now customary for most men in Arembepe.

Fernando had fallen a few notches in covillagers' estimation. Some ridiculed his nonintensive fishing strategy, which usually produced small catches. Yet Fernando and his family enjoyed a pleasant life style supported by boat ownership and fishing, the Tibrás salary of a son who still lived at home, and year-round rental from a brick house behind theirs, built in the early 1970s to take advantage of the tourist and hippie trade.

By 1980 the modest but wise investments that Fernando and Ivone had made in different areas of Arembepe's changing economy had enabled Fernando to withdraw from the rat race that had threatened his mental health in 1973. He and the two fishermen in his crew drew unspectacular profits from a leisurely fishing schedule of eight hours at sea (eight to four) weekdays only. Fernando now had time to spend with his wife, children, and grandchildren. His hostility toward outsiders had turned into ambivalence. One step in his acceptance of change was his acquisition, through the baptism of his six-year-old son, of middle-class *compadres*—a man and his daughter, who resided in Salvador. Fernando and Ivone had gotten to know them when they rented the house next door for weekend use. The godfather, a middle-aged man whose job entailed international travel, offered Fernando the security of a kinlike link to someone from a different social world. For Fernando this tie made the outside world seem less mysterious and threatening than it once had been.

At first I found it curious that Fernando and Ivone had asked the man's daughter, instead of his wife, to stand as *comadre*. On reflection, I realized that the choice of a younger woman ensured that the link between the families would last longer.

Fernando continued to perceive his lack of kin ties to other villagers as a problem. He complained that he had been unable to finance a well to bring running water to his house, since the ground underneath was very rocky. "If only I had relatives nearby," he said, "we could split the cost." Still, Fernando had managed to expand his (ritual) kinship network—through baptism of his ten children, and by standing as godfather for a dozen others.

Despite his ritual kinship web and his economic comfort, Fernando's resentment and insecurity about outsiders had merely abated, not disappeared. Illustrating this was his explanation for Tomé's economic decline (see next section). Fernando told me that the bank had seized Tomé's family home when he had failed to repay a debt. In fact, as Alberto reported accurately, and Tomé later confirmed, Tomé had decided to sell his home and buy a smaller one in order to repay debts and finance boat repairs. The result was the same, but Fernando's interpretation showed a feeling of being directly victimized by outside forces.

Another of Fernando's tendencies was inaccuracy. Prior to 1980 I had concluded that Fernando was a less valuable informant than Alberto, but I never stopped to consider exactly why.

In 1980 I asked Fernando, Alberto, and others some of the same factual questions. Alberto was almost always right, and Fernando often wrong, even about matters on which he should have been the expert, like the cost of diesel fuel. Fernando, the boat owner, was 20 percent off, while Alberto, the bartender, was on target. Fernando's inaccuracy reflected a personality that viewed the world unrealistically and suspiciously.

Fernando's attraction to us was yet another expression of

his ambivalence toward outsiders: He was fearful, but he was also fascinated. Like Alberto and Dora, Fernando's mental health rebounded as he grew accustomed to change, and as he enjoyed a stream of modest but steady improvements in his life style. By 1980, though still suspicious, he was no longer irrationally afraid of the outside world—which had generally been good to him.

As an anthropologist rather than a psychologist, I can only speculate about the reasons for Fernando's extreme reaction to outsiders. Was he obsessed with a fear that some people and deeds he thought to have left behind would follow him to Arembepe? Perhaps, like us—other strangers who had discovered Arembepe in the old days—Fernando was especially possessive about the community where he had made a place for himself. Or did he, as an immigrant, attribute to other outsiders the worst of intentions, as an expression of his own envious and resentful feelings toward his host community? His exaggeration of dangers to us in 1973 may also have disguised a possible (unconscious) wish to seize our wealth and life style for himself. Or was he equating us, as old-time, familiar outsiders, with himself? Did he imagine that people were eager to do to us what he feared they wanted to do to him?

No doubt, multiple psychological factors affected Fernando in the early and mid-1970s, as he dealt with rapid economic and social change. Fortunately, Fernando did eventually manage to adjust. As in many cases, in many cultures, he used a drug (alcohol) and a new religion (*candomblé*) as temporary crutches. By 1980 this stranger had grown more independent and trustful. The outside world and its denizens, though still strange, were no longer overwhelming.

The Innovator

From 1964 through 1973, Tomé was Arembepe's most successful fisherman. He had returned in 1961 from a long period of outside commercial fishing—a brief stay in Salvador and seven years in Rio. In 1964 Tomé still shared his boat with a nonfishing owner, a storekeeper who was his neighbor; but by 1965 he had dissolved this relationship and owned his own vessel. In 1964, from our survey of all Arembepe households, Tomé had the highest fisherman's income. His success rested on a bundle of factors discussed in Chapter 4. More than any other captain-owner, Tomé worked hard, took calculated risks, maintained the loyalty of his (mainly kin-based) crew, and experimented with new fishing strategies. In the mid-1960s, his success led to his election as president of the Fishermen's Society.

Like most successful fishermen in the 1960s, Tomé supplemented his income with produce from a small farm in one of the nearby agricultural estates. His farm plot, bought in 1964, included over 300 coconut seedlings, which he anticipated would start yielding in seven years. It also provided a variety of fruits and vegetables, mostly used to feed his growing family.

By 1973, Tomé's family had expanded to five sons and one daughter (exactly as in his own sibling set), and Tomé's success was even more obvious. He had been one of the first captain-owners to accept a motorization loan from the cooperative. His example spurred other villagers to join and to begin motorized fishing. Once Tomé determined that he could make more money by marketing his own fish than by delivering them to the cooperative, he became the first Arembepeiro to withdraw. He was soon followed by his younger brother Dinho, who, however, remained angry at Tomé for undermining the cooperative.

As Tomé was phasing out his involvement in the cooperative, he also bought a *barco* (large boat) at about the same time as did two nonfishing owners. Tomé launched the pattern of "ice fishing" that had come to dominate Arembepe's fishing industry by 1980. His tendency had always been to seek new banks and travel to more distant spots than other captains. The bigger boat allowed him to explore fishing zones even farther north. The (paid) captains of the two other *barcos* followed Tomé to offshore Sauipe and Subaúma, as the new pattern was established.

By July 1973, Tomé had become an entrepreneur *extraordinaire*. He had bought a van to market his fish in Itapoan, raising his per-kilogram profit by half. He let his two youngest brothers use his small motorboat (a modified sailboat) to fish and to set his trammel nets—widely used for lobstering in

1973. Another of Tomé's innovative investments was in his children's education. The oldest boy was already studying outside.

As a result of intelligence, innovation, income, and plans for education, it seemed likely that Tomé, raised in poverty, might see at least some of his children rise to the middle class. During a long conversation in August 1973, on a Sunday, when Tomé could find time to talk with me, I determined that his annual earnings surpassed my own (unspectacular) salary then as an associate professor at the University of Michigan. Tomé's rise, from an annual income worth $1,000 in 1964 to over $14,000 in 1973, had been dramatic.

During that interview, Tomé discussed his motivations and aspirations eloquently and poignantly. His main goal was success for himself and his family. He wanted his children to escape the poverty he remembered from his childhood. His father, with whom Tomé, the oldest son, began fishing at the age of fourteen, was never more than an ordinary fisherman. Tomé's parents eventually separated, the father moving in with their *comadre*. (This was a nonsexual arrangement. There is a strong taboo against sexual relations between co-parents.) The mother lived alone, eventually becoming an alcoholic beggar. Tomé and his four brothers and one sister had grown up, he said, in one of a poor village's most destitute homes. Determined to create a different fate, Tomé had set off for Rio in 1954 at the age of twenty-one. On a brief visit home, he had married a woman of his own age in civil and religious ceremonies. During his lonely years in Rio, he sent money to his wife, his mother, and his brothers. One important goal in 1973 was to build a good brick house for his mother, who had never owned more than a wattle-and-daub shack. Responding to the demand for rental housing, Tomé had also nearly finished expanding his own home; there would be two houses—the new one to rent in the rear, the old one in front for his family.

On my earlier visits to Arembepe, Tomé and I had talked of his experiences in Rio de Janeiro. He had considered the years of loneliness and strangeness worthwhile, since his earnings eventually financed his house and boat. In 1973 he was pleased that his oldest son had begun formal study; he also seemed happy with his brothers' success. Two of them owned boats and trammel nets, and the other two had use of Tomé's old but still seaworthy vessel. His brothers were all strong, worked hard, and helped each other, he told me. "I don't much care what other people think of me because I have my brothers and sons to count on."

From what I saw in 1973 I wouldn't have been surprised to find on my next visit that Tomé and his brothers owned most of Arembepe. My biggest shock in 1980 was to discover Tomé's actual fate. Looking out the seaview window of Claudia's Restaurant on the first day of my return, I recognized (by name) Tomé's large boat, beached alongside a half-dozen others. The restaurant owner told me that it and two of the other large beached boats belonged to Tomé. "Aha!" I thought. "I predicted right. Tomé owns an entire fleet."

Assuming he was out fishing that day in a newer vessel, I dismissed Tomé from my mind until two evenings later, when I met him on the beach, returning from a day's fishing in Valter's boat (Valter, Dora's brother, is the common-law husband of Tomé's sister). I greeted Tomé and asked about his own boats, which, he told me, needed repairs. Only later did I learn that Tomé had sold the most dilapidated of the three boats; another had been beached for nine months, while the third had stopped fishing in early April, 1980. Why, I wondered, hadn't Tomé repaired at least one of his boats, and why was he working as an ordinary fisherman? The more I learned about the gap between owners' and fishermen's earnings in Arembepe's new economy, the more intrigued I became with Tomé's situation.

From as far back as 1962 I remembered Tomé's house in the northern rectangle as one of Arembepe's nicest. Even then it had been made of brick and cement, with a tile roof and decorative Portuguese tiles adorning the front facade. Tomé had even added a spacious kitchen and a toilet, one of a half-dozen in Arembepe then. From 1973 I recalled the tour he had proudly given me of his new rental house behind his own. "You'll be able to rent it," he assured me, "the next time you come to Arembepe."

I was shocked to learn in 1980 that Tomé no longer lived in his old house. I later discovered that he had sold it to a summer person to repay debts and meet boat expenses. His family had moved to the smaller rental house behind. A few doors up, facing the northern rectangle, was the house Tomé had built for his mother. Unfortunately, her stay there had been brief. Again to satisfy debtors, Tomé had made a long-term rental agreement with people from Salvador, giving them year-round use of the house until mid-1981.

As I was learning about Tomé's economic decline, I was also hearing about Arembepe's new elite—nonfishing owners of large boats. Prominent among them was Tomé's brother Dinho, who now owned five active boats. Dinho was widely considered to be the richest man in town—the role I had imagined for Tomé. Tomé's other brothers were also doing well. One owned a boat; another owned one boat plus half of another; the youngest brother was still a teenager. All told, Tomé and his brothers owned nine and one half of the twenty-seven boats (active and inactive) registered in Arembepe's fleet. If my predictions about the family had been right, why had I erred about Tomé?

The story unraveled slowly. Fernando, who believed that a Salvador bank had seized Tomé's home, said that Tomé's situation was worsening. Fernando blamed Tomé for his plight: "He doesn't fix his boats because he doesn't have the means, and the reason for that is that he overextended himself. He took too many loans from banks and couldn't pay them back."

Whereas Fernando saw Tomé's plight as self-inflicted, Alberto spoke of Tomé's bad luck, contrasting the uncertainty of fishing with salaried employment on the land. "Even the most successful captain can fail if he has a run of bad luck." Although Alberto was thinking of motor failures and loss of ice, bait, provisions, and time at sea, he still considered the main reason for Tomé's fall to be that "his luck had left him." Tomé himself dwelt on the overwhelming demands he faced as a fishing owner. He described the difficulty of balancing crew loyalty and productive fishing, and the on-land demands of industrial technology and fish marketing. "I simply never got any rest."

I found the missing link in Tomé's story during my visit to the hippie Aldeia. The hippie João told me that he rented his house from Sonia, a hippie who lived in Arembepe with a fisherman, Tomé. Did I know him?

As we walked back to Arembepe, I pestered Alberto, never

prone to idle gossip, for details. I learned that Tomé was not living in the northern rectangle with his wife and children, as Fernando had told me, but in rental quarters in Street Down There, with Sonia, the *ippa*. They had lived together for two years. She had been pregnant with his child but had miscarried. Sonia was a reformed alcoholic who had almost died from illness caused by drinking. She still looked sick and needed expensive medicines, which she could afford, said one man, because she was rich.

Sonia later told us, almost boastfully, that she came from a wealthy Paulista family. Her mother disapproved of her hippie life style and had come to Arembepe to try to break up her living arrangement with Tomé. Sonia had inherited money from a grandparent, but her mother had cut off her access to those funds when Sonia became a hippie. Still, Sonia did get money from her parents from time to time. She also collected rent from two hippies. Sonia had told many villagers about her wealth, and she complained to us that she had problems adjusting to Tomé's life style. For example, she found it hard to walk and take buses in the city as he did. "I'm accustomed to cabs." Tomé had been offended by Sonia's mother, who scolded her daughter for living with "a mere fisherman." Yet a similar disdain showed up in Sonia's own statements about Arembepeiros.

Some villagers linked Tomé's economic decline to his association with Sonia, but others told me that his troubles had preceded their union. His problems had mounted during the past year, when Tomé, unable to afford repairs, had withdrawn both of his boats from fishing. He was waiting to hear about his application for a loan from a government-sponsored rural-credit program. He had requested $6,700 to buy new Japanese-made motors for both his boats. The motors cost $2,700 each; he would use the remainder to repay outstanding debts. Tomé had kept his loan request below the maximum amount for which signature loans were available (about $8,000). He didn't want to risk either of his two remaining houses, worth about $11,000 and $13,000, respectively, or either of his boats, which he valued at $4,200 and $5,800. Tomé pointed out to me that despite his current problems, he still owned property worth more than 2 million cruzeiros ($33,300)—not bad for someone who had earned a mere $1,000 a year, plus food from fishing and farming, in 1964.

What would he do, I asked Tomé, if he were denied the loan? He supposed he would sell one of the boats. Both Alberto, with whom I discussed Tomé's plight, and I thought this a better idea than taking on another debt, given the constraints on the captain-owner's time. Tomé, however, although approaching fifty and complaining about insufficient rest, still regarded himself as a vigorous man. He was the oldest member of the village soccer team. He mentioned a time when his motor had failed offshore. "I tried to get one of the younger men to swim to shore for help, but no one would. Finally, I put on a life preserver and swam to shore myself in forty-five minutes." When Sonia expressed concern about his taking the rural-credit loan, Tomé proclaimed "I fear nothing." In the old Arembepe, men of Tomé's age were planning retirement from the captain's role. Tomé, by contrast, believed that he could still fulfill the demands of the captain-fisherman's role, while owning two boats and marketing their fish.

He had not yet made a realistic plan, given the new economy, to rid himself of debt and to limit demands on his time. To me, the simplest solution was to sell one boat and use the money to buy a motor for the other one. Tomé could then work in it as captain-owner until he repaid his debts. Eventually, of course, Tomé would have to retire from fishing, as his brother Dinho had done. Then he might be able to employ an immigrant captain. At first Alberto said there was no way for Tomé to reverse his luck, but when I suggested selling one boat, Alberto agreed that it was a possible solution. Tomé himself was keeping this option in mind in case he didn't get the loan.

Tomé's reaction to the outside world contrasted sharply with Fernando's. Tomé "had no fear" of using external resources. He had easily repaid the small bank loan (about $1,700) he had taken for his first big boat. He had just obtained this loan when we talked in 1973. A bank official, impressed with Tomé and his collateral, had also encouraged him to apply for financing of a van to transport his fish. Tomé's downfall was linked to excessive borrowing between 1973 and 1980. He *had* overextended himself, as Fernando thought. He had also had some "bad luck," including exploitation of this lower-class, poorly educated man by unscrupulous outsiders. As Sonia remarked, "Arembepeiros don't read contracts."

Tomé's credit rating had plunged after an experience with dishonest loan-agency officials, who had pocketed his payments, then contended that he had defaulted on his loan. The men were eventually caught, since they were doing the same thing to several other rural people, and Tomé believed that the matter had been set right. He hoped he would get his loan despite this incident. Locally, however, Tomé now had a reputation as one who reneges on his debts, and storekeepers denied him credit.

Nor did his brothers help. I asked Tomé and several other people about this. Tomé was especially bitter about Dinho, who, he said, still resented him for his early withdrawal from the cooperative. Tomé insisted that he had done his duty as eldest brother for all his siblings. Before coming home from Rio, he had arranged a good job in fishing there for Dinho. "It was better than the one I had." When Dinho and a younger brother had seen a sailboat they liked in a village north of Arembepe, Tomé had accompanied them there to look it over. When they found the price more than they could afford, he had written a check for the difference. "Dinho could afford to help me. He has just one child, and plenty of money." He expected less of his three youngest brothers, since one had a large family and the other two were still getting established. Tomé recounted that Dinho, acting through an intermediary, had even tried to buy one of his boats, for far less than its worth, adding insult to injury.

What did others think of Tomé's claim? Shouldn't brothers help each other out? Alberto suggested that since none of Tomé's four brothers was willing to help him, the fault must lie with Tomé. Dora even questioned Tomé's contention that he had helped his brothers when they were younger. At first I found these responses surprising, since, from previous visits, I knew for a fact that Tomé had helped his brothers.

I finally figured out that something more was going on in villagers' heads—a reaction, based on local traditions, to a perceived threat to the social system. Tomé, who had always deviated positively, excelling as an entrepreneur, was now deviating negatively. His common-law union with a hippie was testing the limits of villagers' tolerance. Although rarely used in 1980, the *rapariga* label was applied to Sonia. Pointing to Sonia's house I asked a woman to tell me who lived there.

"Sonia, a hippie."

"What kind of work does she do?" I asked.

"I don't see her doing anything, except living off other women's men."

Another woman, who had herself once been classified as a *rapariga* because of a similar involvement with a legally married fisherman, still lambasted Tomé and Sonia: "Tomé's wife can't help being sad he is living with Sonia. Sonia rules in that house. Tomé stays home except when he's fishing, and he doesn't fish like he used to, because he's inside doing all the work that Sonia should be doing, like washing the dishes and other housework. Tomé only wants his 'little Sonia,'" she mimicked. "She calls him 'my little Tomé,' and then yells at him not to spit on the floor. I don't see what he sees in his wife or Sonia. His wife isn't right in the head, and besides she's ugly, just like Sonia is. It looks like Tomé could have found a better woman. Neither of those two is worth much."

Given the surplus of males generally and hippie males in particular, in 1980, villagers viewed Sonia's behavior as particularly selfish. "Always bragging about being rich, she doesn't need Tomé like his family does." In local public opinion, Tomé was wrong to abandon his wife and family, particularly for a member of a fringe social category. Tomé's father had left his mother, but not for a sexual liaison. Tomé's behavior was considered much worse.

Expectably, Tomé had a different view. He portrayed his wife as washed out, listless, mentally and physically sick. His description might have been that of a middle-aged man in the United States, complaining that his marriage lacked excitement, that his wife was no longer vital, attractive, or experimental. "She'd never let me sit on the floor like this." (In Sonia's 'hippie pad' we sat on a mattress covered with bright cloth; we leaned against the wall on throw pillows.) "My wife would tell me that being on the floor gives you a cold. Here I have peace. At home, I never got any rest."

Tomé was particularly resentful about abuses by his wife's two brothers—both mentally ill. "They'd come and drink all my whiskey." Although Tomé showed no signs of incipient alcoholism, he, like Fernando, drank more than in the past. He told me that he enjoyed beer and whiskey, but had trouble affording even the former nowadays. Tomé said that he had been especially bothered by fights and yelling involving his wife and brothers-in-law. "When I got home from several days in a cramped boat on a cold sea, I just wanted to rest. I didn't want people yelling all the time and drinking up my whiskey."

Tomé's hopes for his children's future were fading. His oldest son, in whose education Tomé had invested a fortune, wasn't a good student. He had failed the vestibular exam and was looking for work. The next son had mental problems, "which the doctor called a family thing, from his mother's side," Tomé remembered bitterly.

The recurrent "I need some rest" was Tomé's summary of an overdose of social obligations that went along with success. Leading to his plight, Arembepe's traditional leveling mechanisms had combined with the time demands of the new economy and Tomé's own overreliance on external resources. "Nowadays I usually stay inside when I'm not working, because every time I walk in the streets someone asks me for money. People still expect me to buy them beer, when they should be buying for me. When a hippie in the Aldeia asked me for money the other day, I told him that he should be making loans to me now." Tomé resented villagers' continued expectations of generosity, their failure to recognize his lack of funds, and their lack of concern and help with his current problems.

Tomé sought refuge from marriage, family, in-laws, covillagers, and unbearable responsibility in a common-law relationship, where enduring obligations were absent. Furthermore, in choosing a hippie consort, he made one of the most total and dramatic breaks possible. (When I first heard about Tomé and Sonia, I remarked to my American coworkers that my surprise would hardly have been greater had I learned that Tomé had gone to Paris to study structuralism.) Tomé sought escape with someone on the fringes of local society, an *ippa* who had lived in Arembepe long enough to qualify as a permanent resident. Sonia's reputation would have been better had she not chosen a married man. Their union thus pushed both Sonia and Tomé further toward the social fringes.

No doubt Sonia chose Tomé because he was strong, intelligent, fairly well off, and ambitious. In choosing Sonia, Tomé picked not the strangest hippie but someone enough like himself for a comfortable association. Tomé had middle-class aspirations, and Sonia belonged to the middle class. Their skin color was similar. She looked younger than his wife, as did he.

For the study of family structure and patterns, it is also significant that Tomé found a woman like his mother. Sonia had been an alcoholic, like his mother, who, as an extremely poor woman and a twin, had also been somewhat socially isolated. Several times during our conversation he identified with patterns in his parental family, comparing, for example, his children with his siblings (five older boys and a girl), and his own marital breakup with his parents' separation. He also told us, with irony, that Sonia's father had recently left his wife for a younger woman; he made the analogy with himself explicit.

Tomé's relationship with Sonia also illustrates his willingness to experiment with the outside world. By living with a middle-class hippie from southern urban Brazil, Tomé was innovating again, forging a link with a different social world. It seemed, however, that he had made a bad choice this time, as he had done when he contracted too many debts. Sonia's comments that villagers didn't read contracts and that she feared Tomé's accepting a large rural-credit loan showed her awareness of the dangers that Arembepeiros faced in dealing with the outside world. To make the best of external resources, Tomé could have used the help of a knowledgeable, sympathetic, trustworthy outsider. This was not Sonia. When we asked her why she didn't advise Tomé about the implications of the contracts he signed, she said that she stayed away from his business affairs. "Tomé is always very sure of what he wants to do; it's hard to change his mind once he makes a decision."

Sonia seemed to have a poor grasp both of Tomé's business affairs and of his place in local society. What Tomé needed was someone with better knowledge than Sonia had of how things worked in the outside world. Paradoxically, the very thing that made a member of the middle class available as Tomé's mistress (her wish to remove herself from her background and outside connections) also made her a poor choice to be his mediator with external institutions. Tomé needed someone to help him manage his external affairs, not someone who had withdrawn from Brazilian national culture. More bluntly, Arembepeiros needed outsiders to teach them how to use knives and forks, not how to enjoy bean sprouts and macrobiotic foods.

In August 1980, Tomé was biding his time, waiting to hear about a loan that might lead either to the restoration of his preeminence or the liquidation of his estate. Failing the loan, he would have to make the hard decision to sell one boat to permit his economic survival through the other. In telling me of the meager rewards of ordinary fishing, compared to boat ownership, Tomé clung to his accustomed captain-owner's perspective. This wasn't unrealistic; there were still ways for him to right himself.

Tomé and Sonia planned to move to new rental quarters once his boats were fishing again. Their current apartment was too small for a freezer—necessary if he was going to market his fish. They had been trying to find something for less than $125 per month. He might even move back into the house registered in his and his mother's name, once his rental agreement with the city people expired.

Tomé's story, through August 1980, illustrates how Arembepe's past haunted its present and its near future. The leveling mechanisms discussed in Chapters 3 and 4 were still there. Mired in the social obligations that accompanied success, Tomé sought escape in deviance. Through behavior perceived as antisocial, he cut himself off from the kin-based support that might otherwise have been offered. In the final analysis, good *was* limited—not just in people's minds but in reality— in Tomé's victimization by outsiders and in his lack of education, power, and other middle-class advantages. Poverty was the most durable legacy of the old Arembepe. And poverty, now fully contextualized within the national class structure, was a generations-old malady that neither a double dose of achievement motivation nor a liaison with a middle-class dropout could do much to cure.

Better Then?[1]

"It was better then, wasn't it, Conrado?" remarked a native woman my age, the new principal of the local junior high school, about my early times in Arembepe. For her family things had been better. In 1962 her father had run the town's main store, co-owned a productive sailboat, and extended credit to almost everyone in Arembepe. Over the years his business had fallen off, as villagers bought groceries in Salvador, Itapoan, or from the supermarket bus that came once a week. A dozen bars, restaurants, and small stores also offered competition.

By 1980 differences in Arembepeiros' perspectives on change were obvious. Some, like Alberto, had only good things to say about the new Arembepe. For most villagers, however, novelty no longer excited and tantalized as it had on my previous visit. In 1973 it had seemed as though Arembepeiros were so fascinated by new people, new technology, and new opportunities that they had little time for us—familiar, unexciting outsiders. In 1980, by contrast, many villagers spoke of the old days nostalgically. Several people made a point of telling us that they remembered the automobile rides we had given them during the 1960s. A fishing captain mentioned that he would be forever grateful to field team leader Marvin Harris for driving his wife to a Salvador hospital. Villagers would never forget that a baby girl had been born in the field team vehicle in 1963, as assistant field leader Shepard Forman rushed the mother to the hospital. Aunt Dalia's son remembered I had once given him a ride from Portão to Arembepe, as I did for Dinho, now Arembepe's biggest capitalist, the day he returned from two years of commercial fishing in Rio de Janeiro.

"You don't forget Arembepe," said a villager to Betty. "You and Conrado always come back." Many villagers seemed genuinely moved by our 1980 return. I think they saw us as a kind of complex symbol of the confrontation that has been the subject of this book. We were not just a simple reminder of the preasphalt, prehippie, pretourist, prefactory past. We simultaneously symbolized tradition and change, past and present. Middle-class and alien, we had been unknowing scouts in a coming invasion; but we had been early and special enough to be captured and assimilated by the hosts, and because of this we had been fused into their deeper social history. To be sure, in 1980 we were still outsiders, but long-familiar ones who had witnessed and been part of Arembepe as it used to be.

After my pleasant 1980 stay, I was particularly sorry to

leave. I had arranged to work with Alberto the Saturday afternoon before my Sunday departure, clearing up some points and asking final questions. When I entered his house, expecting to sit on his balcony and talk as we had often done, I was annoyed to find a crew of boisterous weekend drinkers in the place I had planned for us. Alberto, my son Nicholas, and I got in my rental car and I drove us far south, beyond the last summer house and the neighborhood where I lived in 1973.

We sat and talked on the beach, constantly forced back as the rising tide threatened the field notes I was holding in my lap. After a late August squall the sea was still strong, and yellower than I had ever seen it. There was a powerful scent of rotten eggs in the air. Currents churned by the storm were bringing factory wastes closer to shore than usual. How long, I wondered, could Arembepe's tourist appeal and its fishing industry last? Would pollution eventually destroy this place

Conrad Kottak does fieldwork in Street Down There in 1980. This time villagers seemed genuinely moved by our return. We had become a kind of representation of the confrontation that has been the subject of this book, simultaneously symbolizing tradition and change, past and present. (Courtesy Jerald T. Milanich)

that held such importance in my life? What would Arembepe be like on my next visit? Would the boat owners stay as rich? Would Dora build her dream house? Could Tomé strike back? These were among the questions I pondered as, filtered through Tibrás fumes, the rays of the setting sun shone on the sulfuric sea, turning waters once aqua to the color of blood.

So ended the first edition of *Assault on Paradise*.

12 *The Global Village*

My visits to Arembepe increased after the 1980 field trip, which served as the basis of Chapters 7 through 11 (and which completed the first edition of this book). A team research project I planned and directed took us (Betty, me, and our children, Juliet and Nicholas) back to Arembepe annually between 1982 and 1987. (We also visited several other Brazilian towns, where other team researchers were doing field work—see below.) This new project built on my growing interest in the impact of the mass media, especially television, on local culture and social change. (This research and its findings are more fully described in my book *Prime-Time Society: An Anthropological Analysis of Television and Culture* [1990]).

My observations in the United States and Brazil had convinced me that television is one of the most powerful information disseminators, opinion molders, and socializing agents in today's world. TV instantaneously transmits images and information within and across national boundaries. The media help propel a globally spreading culture of consumption, spurring participation in the cash economy (Hujanen, 1976). TV has become a major socializing agent competing with family, school, peers, community, and church (Comstock, 1978). The media play a major role in focusing attention on national-level issues and events (Hirsch, 1979).

A Link to Nation and World

Television has extended Brazilians' horizons beyond home and community, forming a bridge between family and nation. Operating on a daily basis, the TV set has become the main mechanism by which alien images, and people who are not relatives, friends, or neighbors enter the home. It introduces otherwise unfamiliar settings and types of people. Country people glimpse urban life; city dwellers meet rural folk. Given massive illiteracy and lingering rural isolation, Brazilian television is a key mediator. For millions it is the sole source, rather than one among many, of exposure to global information and social interactions involving strangers.

Arembepe's first TV had been a battery-powered set purchased in 1973 by a local woman named Luminata (appropriately, "the illuminated one"), who lived in the central square. During my 1973 stay, I had noticed, but didn't pay much attention to, the people who gathered each night at her window, trying to interpret the flickering and fuzzy black-and-white images that now poured into Luminata's living room. Television only affected Arembepe significantly after electrification (1977), when many villagers bought their own sets

Most Arembepeiros now have TV sets. A few even have home telephones. Television introduces otherwise unfamiliar settings and types of people, like this title character from the 1991 telenovela, Salomé. (Conrad P. Kottak)

Downtown Arembepe, 1991. Most of the central square (St. Francis Square), now cobblestoned, is off-limits to cars. A children's play area has been added, along with benches and coconut trees. (Conrad P. Kottak)

and through them became much more informed about external events and systems. I first noticed the role of television in bringing external information into Arembepe in 1980. I could view this information explosion against the backdrop of the 1960s, when local men had interrogated me endlessly about the animals to be found in North America. Back then, Arembepeiros had been starved for information about the outside world. Limited media access, educational deficiencies, illiteracy, poverty, and poor transportation had all contributed to their isolation.

Now, Arembepeiros, like millions of other Brazilians formerly marginalized by isolation and illiteracy, join in a single national communication system. Through TV, they have regular access to external information, to urban, national, and international culture. Villagers of the 1980s repeatedly told

Betty and Nick (1991) stroll south down a paved street leading into Coconut Square (the northern rectangle). Arembepe is fully electrified, with regular bus service. (Conrad P. Kottak)

me that TV brings in knowledge. As one young man put it, "You sit here in this little place and learn about the whole world because you have television." Richard Pace reached similar conclusions in Gurupá, where TV ownership spread rapidly after the town's satellite dish arrived:

> Before the spread of television, conversation often focused on local events, local gossip, soccer, or an occasional diffuse comment on regional or national politics. A foreign anthropologist was often asked vague questions such as—what kind of jungle grows in the United States, are all Americans rich, and what are cowboys like? With the spread of television, however, conversation took on a more cosmopolitan, more diverse nature. Events in North America, Europe, and the Middle East were discussed in detail. National politics were scrutinized (it was the year [1985] that the military regime gave power back to a civilian government). I found myself discussing the goals of the American space program, the ideology of President Reagan, poverty in the United States, international terrorism, and the geophysical causes of earthquakes. (Pace, n.d.)

By the mid-1980s, as a direct result of television, Arembepeiros had also become much more world-wise. In a brief survey we did in 1984 Arembepeiros identified Michael Jackson's photo as readily as the Pope's, and more easily than Ronald Reagan's, or than photos of the major Brazilian presidential candidates then. However, the more detailed research we did later showed that although international stars like Jackson, Madonna, and Julio Iglésias are well known in Brazil, Brazilian TV actually does more to spread national than international culture.

Cultural Differences: TV and Reading

Television is the foremost mass medium in North America as in Brazil, but it is one among many familiar media that have

Adeli's restaurant is still successful (see her 1980 photo, p. 225). Now she has a color TV and advertises "Brazilian Food" in English. (Conrad P. Kottak)

been available for decades. Compared with Brazil, a much longer and greater exposure to print media and radio has mediated television's impact in the United States. Brazil has never been very reading-oriented; it actually outlawed printing presses until the nineteenth century.

The contrast in cultural traditions about reading is evident in everyday settings. For example, it's easy to identify foreigners (particularly North Americans) on Brazilian beaches. They're the ones with books. Brazilians sometimes take newspapers, rarely books, to the beach, where they go to socialize. The scarcity of reading lamps in Brazilian hotel rooms and homes also illustrates the cultural difference in reading habits. Brazilians see books and print as part of the public world of school, formal education, work, and the rules and records of the bureaucratic state, and they view reading as antisocial. Printed matter thus stands apart from the more intimate world of home and family (see DaMatta, 1987). By contrast, radio and TV, which can more easily be shared, are welcome guests in Brazilian homes.

Brazilians don't regard television or radio, both of which can be used socially (see below), as being as antisocial as print is. Although radio was available in Brazilian cities and county seats by the 1950s, its arrival in remote rural villages is more recent. Small transistor radios had become a fad in Arembepe by the early 1960s, and by 1965 the portable radio was a common status symbol. Men with cash bought these in Salvador or Rio (if they had fished there commercially). Showing their radios off, and so that others might listen (that is, using radio socially), men like Tomé carried their "information boxes" around the village. They tuned in soccer games, music, and news—including reports from the Voice of America in Portuguese.

Arembepeiros had little exposure to print. The literacy rate was low; the schoolteacher had just a fourth-grade education. Although almost no one read for pleasure, people did enjoy the picture magazines that were occasionally brought back from the city, and few villagers liked to read pamphlet versions of regional ballads.

Given Brazil's print media history and attitudes about reading, most Brazilians were truly media-disadvantaged when TV reached them. Compared with other media, television's

Florisea Tavares, one of Arembepe's new group of well-educated local teachers. She is standing in front of her house in Caraúnas, near the school where she teaches. (Conrad P. Kottak)

infiltration of the home has been much more exclusive in Brazil than in the United States. For most Brazilians TV has become the primary, often exclusive, conduit to regional, national, and international information. Especially for nonelites, the TV set is the main gate to the global village.

Studying TV

The information explosion I observed in Arembepe was one reason I decided to study television's impact on Brazilians. Brazil also has special significance for understanding the influence of the mass media because it has *the world's most watched commercial television network* (Globo), which shows mainly its own productions. The most popular are Globo's national news and "soaps," or *telenovelas* (more simply, *novelas*). These serials are broadcast nationally six nights per week, drawing 40 to 95 percent audience shares, in three time slots. Known as the *novelas* of six, seven, and eight, they actually air at 6:10, 6:55, and 8:25. The seven and eight o'clock *novelas*, separated by local and national news, get the biggest audiences.

Unlike American soaps, *telenovelas* air six (not five) times a week and at night. Another difference is that *novelas* end, whereas American soaps can go on for years. The typical *novela* has 150 to 180 chapters and lasts six or seven months. Like the novels of Charles Dickens, written in (monthly) installments and originally published (as pamphlets) to fit a set length,[1] *telenovelas* use the serial form to examine a series of conflicts and problems, usually featuring status reversals—especially upward mobility. Most *novelas* have an urban setting—usually Rio or São Paulo.

Although Brazil has three other (much less popular) networks (all commercial), Globo blankets the air as no network has ever done in North America. It consistently attracts a spectacular nightly audience of 60 to 80 million people. Globo also exports its productions to more than 100 countries, spanning Latin America, Europe, Asia, and Africa.

The TV research project I planned and directed (1983–1987) included field work at four (eventually seven) sites in different parts of Brazil. Besides Arembepe, the three other main sites were Gurupá (in the Amazon state of Pará), Ibirama (Santa Catarina state, southern Brazil), and Cunha (São Paulo state, southcentral Brazil). Like Arembepe, those three towns[2] had all been studied previously, at least twenty years earlier, before TV. Our strategy was to compare people and places with various degrees of exposure to television, which had reached our field sites at different times.

We used a uniform set of procedures to gather data at each site. Besides ethnography we also used two printed questionnaires (more accurately, interview schedules, because the interviewers rather than the respondents wrote down the answers). We developed those schedules in Rio de Janeiro in early 1984 and pretested them in a pilot study in Arembepe that July. After we had refined, formatted, and printed the schedules, intensive interviewing began in May 1985.

Before this, from late 1984 or early 1985, field workers

Alberto Costa, Richard Pace, and Rosane Prado had been working to build rapport and networks while living in Ibirama, Gurupá, and Cunha, respectively. The final field work, in the fourth main site, Arembepe, took place from June through October 1985. This research was done by a four-person team: Betty and I, Iraní Escolano, and Penny Magee.

Once data were collected, we could assess relationships between length and degree of TV exposure and many other variables.[3] We were able to find and interview[4]—particularly in Gurupá and the rural estates near Arembepe—many people with almost no exposure to TV. One reason we chose Gurupá was that, when our research began, it lacked a satellite dish. It had only a dozen sets, which relied on expensive antennas to receive very poor signals from the state capital, Belém. We focused on television's influence on knowledge, attitudes, perceptions, emotions, and images of the world, and in promoting social change and economic development.

Warming Up to the World System

It's hard for most of us to perceive the full range of TV's social impact, because we so rarely meet anyone who hasn't been raised in the daily presence of television. Here ethnography in another culture can contribute significantly:

> In using portraits of other cultural patterns to reflect self-criti-
> cally on our own ways, anthropology disrupts common sense
> and makes us reexamine our taken-for-granted assumptions.
> (Marcus and Fisher, 1986, p. 1)

Most North Americans will never have a chance to observe, through before-after comparison of individual cases, the dramatic role that TV can play in (1) stimulating curiosity and a thirst for knowledge and (2) increasing skills in social navigation and communication with outsiders. In Brazil regular viewers of TV have more general knowledge and can recognize and interpret more information from outside. By training villagers in national norms, TV makes it easier for them to deal with the outsiders they meet. To illustrate these effects, I introduce Nadia, a woman who lives in Arembepe.

In July 1984, during a trial run (pilot test) of the interview schedule we planned to use at each site, I interviewed my next door neighbor, Nadia, a media-deprived person in her mid-twenties. Nadia was barely literate and had spent a lifetime without TV. She did have a radio, on which she listened mostly to music. Nadia had moved to Arembepe with her husband, a caretaker for a summer home, in 1981. They came from a remote Bahian village, much more isolated from urban life than Arembepe is.

Although Nadia had been in Arembepe for three years, she lived in substantial isolation from local society. She dared visit just one of her neighbors. She even let her husband do the shopping. Nadia found strangers, including most Arembepeiros, threatening. She and her husband didn't let their three young sons play in the street, even during the day, because they were afraid of problems with neighbors.

Although Nadia had trouble talking to strangers, she agreed to answer my questions. But as I interviewed her, I felt guiltier and guiltier for "inflicting" my questions. Nadia responded reluctantly, tears occasionally streaking her face. She said she had no friends and that she missed her mother, the most important person in her life.

Nadia longed for a home of her own. She would build one (and feed her kids better) if she won the lottery. She knew little about Rio or São Paulo and found it hard to imagine life there. My impression was that Nadia was a terrible informant, unaccustomed to and uninterested in talking to strangers. The interview was like pulling teeth, an unpleasant experience for me and probably a terrifying one for her.

No doubt some of Nadia's behavior reflected her individual personality, gender, and class position. A member of the lower working class, she had little contact with elites, especially men. Her experience provided no clue about why I would want to talk to her for more than a minute—particularly to elicit her opinions. Whenever I met her that year, Nadia displayed the obsequious, eye-averting, voice-lowering, limp-handed demeanor often adopted by poor rural Bahians—especially women—when they deal with their perceived social superiors. For Nadia that meant almost everyone she met.

Still, there's also reason to conclude that some of Nadia's behavior reflected her lack of media exposure. In July 1985, a year after the disastrous interview, I returned to Arembepe to do formal interviewing. Meanwhile Nadia's family had acquired a black-and-white TV set, which they watched constantly. I soon noticed a change in Nadia's demeanor. She was no longer quite the shy, quiet person she had been in 1984. She now visited her neighbors, chatted with Betty, looked me in the eye when we talked, sang as she worked, and made a few jokes. She proved an average respondent when I interviewed her again.

These changes were obvious to Betty and me, but for Nadia and the people who saw her every day, she had changed gradually, and without any obvious relation to television. Although Nadia could say that she was "happier" in 1985 and that she felt more at home, she couldn't conclude that "television had changed her life." But it had.

My research in Brazil has convinced me that such changes in demeanor and social behavior as took place in Nadia are effects of televiewing. Television familiarizes provincial folk with urban and national norms. It makes them less reluctant and less uncertain in dealing with strangers, including people from higher social classes. Many North Americans make the erroneous "common-sense" assumption that TV isolates people. Cross-cultural evidence says otherwise. Far from cutting Nadia off from society, TV enhanced her social skills.

As further illustration of TV's effects, consider my encounter with Olga, one of the first people I interviewed in Arembepe in summer 1985. Olga was a fifty-five-year-old woman I had known in the 1960s, who expressed delight to see me again. Unlike Nadia, she was eager to talk to me and answer my questions. But to my surprise after such a warm welcome, she was as difficult an informant as Nadia had been the year before.

Olga lived with her daughter and grandchild in downtown Arembepe. She had never owned a set and rarely watched TV in her neighbors' homes, but she was an avid participant in candomblé and other local festivities. Olga reminded me of many older unmarried women (then classified as raparigas) whom I had known during the 1960s. Her exuberance stood out against the more demure behavior of married women.

As I interviewed Olga, she showed none of Nadia's shyness. But she failed to understand certain questions most villagers (particularly those exposed to television) answered easily.

What did she think of a homosexual relationship?

"Just fine," said Olga, obviously never having heard the term, though probably familiar with cases of homosexual behavior.

Did she agree that "a friend of a friend is also a friend?"

"That's right. Friends are good."

"What's most important—what you learn in the streets, what you learn from your family, or what you learn in school?"

"Yes," responded Olga, "what you learn at school is important."

"Is it more important than what you learn in the streets?"

"Yes, what you learn in the streets is very important."

"Is it more important than what you learn in your family?"

"Oh yes, what you learn in your family is very important."

"What's the most important one of them all?"

"They're important, all right. That's right."

From this and similar early interviews, our field team soon became sensitive to "Olga-type informants." This is what we called people who were so unfamiliar with the kind of information processing our survey called for that they had trouble with opinion questions and with answers that came "naturally" to most villagers. The Olga types were usually people with little TV exposure.

Another interesting, but very different, case was Paulo, a fairly wealthy but illiterate fisherman who loved to watch his giant color set and listen to his stereo. Paulo still found time to manage and occasionally captain his fishing boat, and to support three wives and two families. (He was Arembepe's best-known polygynist.) He got most of his information about the outside world from TV. He was a news addict, much better informed about political issues than most villagers were. (Paulo was probably also better informed about "current events" than most middle-class Americans are.) An eager participant in external systems, Paulo worried he might not be able to vote in the coming elections because he had never learned to read and write.

Another TV addict, but literate and better educated, was Jaime, our Tibrás worker friend and former water boy discussed in Chapter 8. Jaime said he often bought books (including an encyclopedia set he proudly showed me) to learn more about stories he'd seen reported on television. As Jaime illustrates, our findings contradict the "commonsense" assumption that televiewing hurts reading. We found just the reverse: televiewing correlated with greater use of print media—especially in the three communities that had received TV most recently—Cunha, Arembepe, and Gurupá.[5]

Televiewing both expresses and hones a more general information hunger. TV hooks villagers on information and stimulates curiosity, so that many people read more. Given literacy and access to print, heavy televiewers in Brazil are also the people who are most likely to devour books, magazines, and newspapers.

Márcio wants to be a professional soccer player and has attended a training camp in Salvador. He is also an excellent student. In rural Brazil televiewing spurs greater use of books, as in Márcio's home. (There's even a pamphlet on ecólogia *on the lower shelf.)* (Conrad P. Kottak)

Images, Attitudes, and Aspirations

With its mainly urban content, Brazilian TV brings the city to the country and the metropolis to smaller cities and towns. Life in such overpopulated, polluted, crime-ridden megacities as Rio and São Paulo is very different from life in villages, towns, and small cities. Globo's *novelas* bring images of urban glamour and sophistication. The camera caresses the natural and architectural attractions of Rio and São Paulo, ignoring their more sordid aspects. By contrast, news programs, which are also popular, offer more negative images of the city, especially about crime.

Because TV transmits contradictory images, the impact of viewing on images of urban life was unclear in our study.[6] For example, viewing patterns told us little about answers to our question "Would you like your children to live in a big city?"[7] Rural Brazilians, especially Arembepeiros, did view Rio (the setting of most *novelas*) more positively than they viewed São Paulo.

Commercial TV—in the United States, Brazil, and elsewhere—dotes on people who can afford to live, or aspire to, glamorous lives. Rich TV families encourage the culture of consumption by illustrating it. Characters must be able to afford the products that sponsor the show. TV brings product information directly to rural people, and new consumer patterns show up in hair styles, diet, and clothing.

Advertising can be direct (commercials) or indirect (with products introduced as part of entertainment program content). *Novelas* spur buying by having characters chat about products. For example, two young men discuss their hopes of eventually buying a home and a car, and to have meat on the table ("like rich people do"). Two women extol a new corn-popper. Outdoor locales feature a sponsor bank, in front of which characters stop to talk, with the bank logo easily visible.

One of our questions designed to elicit information on the culture of consumption was "If you won the lottery, what would you do with the money?" Most villagers said they'd put it in a savings account. We also asked people if and when they had opened a savings account, because TV constantly advertised that option. No one in Arembepe had a savings account in the mid-1960s, but many did twenty years later. Televiewing level was an excellent predictor of having a savings account.[8] (Better roads and bus service also increased access to banks and made participation in a consumer economy much easier.)

The decision to open a savings account wasn't just TV-conditioned behavior. It was also a rational response to an attractive use of extra cash. A savings account offered both interest and "monetary correction" (additional guaranteed monthly interest equaling the national inflation rate). The savings account was popular because it was a risk-free investment. The existence of millions of savings accounts with monetary correction (and, therefore, TV's impact on economic behavior) has helped fuel the inflation for which Brazil is famous.

TV hones the wish to be upwardly mobile. *Subir na vida,* to rise in life, is a common *novela* expression. Most *novelas* are *Cinderella* stories in which a girl or boy from a lower-status (sometimes rural) family marries someone from a richer (usually urban) family. The interclass friendships and romances of Brazilian TV link members of classes A (upper), B (middle), and sometimes C (upper working).[9] Rarely is there a romance between a working-class character and someone from the upper or upper middle class. Even rarer in entertainment programming are members of class D (lower working, unemployed poor), with their impoverished, untelegenic life styles. Even the fantasy world of the *novela* recognizes that such people have almost no chance to "rise in life" by marrying into the elites.

One of our clearest research findings[10] was that Brazilian TV cultivates "liberal" views about social issues, especially about sex and gender roles. Heavier viewers were strikingly more liberal—less traditional in their opinions on such matters as whether women "belong at home," should work when their husbands earn well, should work when pregnant, go to bars, leave a husband they no longer love, pursue men they like, and about whether men should cook and wash clothes, and whether parents should talk to their kids about sex. All these questions elicit TV-biased answers, in that Brazilian TV draws on an urban-modern reality in which sex-gender roles really are less traditional than in communities like Arembepe.

Are we dealing with effects, or just correlations? That is, does Brazilian TV make people more liberal, or do already liberal people, seeking reinforcement for their views, simply watch more TV? Do they look to television and its urban-elite world for moral options that are missing or suppressed in their own, more traditional, towns?

I've concluded that liberalization is both a correlation and an effect of watching TV. We found a strong *correlation* between liberal social views and *current* viewing hours. Liberal small-town Brazilians watched more TV than more traditional villagers did, probably to validate personal views that the local setting suppressed. However, confirming that TV exposure, over time, also affected such attitudes, we found an even stronger correlation between years of home viewing and liberal social views.

Heavy viewers seem predisposed to liberal views. Over time, *telenovela* content, entering homes each day, reinforces those views. TV-biased and TV-reinforced attitudes spread as villagers take courage from the daily validation of their unorthodox (local) views in (national) programming. More and more townsfolk encounter nontraditional views and come to see them as normal.

Despite the rise of more liberal sex-gender views, local women still do all the laundry. Here they socialize as they wash clothes in the lagoon on Arembepe's northern edge. (Conrad P. Kottak)

Festivals, Local Culture, and the World System

We also found that TV increases the popularity of mass celebrations of national and international scale. These include Christmas and Carnival, the Brazilian equivalent of Mardi Gras. However, the perceived importance of the main *local* festival declined strikingly among people with longer exposure to television. Thus, in Gurupá, the most recently exposed site, 55 percent of our respondents said a traditional local celebration was most important to them. This fell to 21 percent in Arembepe. At our longest-exposed sites, no local ceremony retained much significance. There was a similar drop in the importance of minor saints' days, but the importance of Christmas and New Year's rose with length of community TV exposure.[11]

Although TV has helped spread Carnival beyond its traditional centers (e.g., Rio de Janeiro), local reactions to TV images of Carnival aren't simple or uniform responses to external stimuli. Instead of direct adoption of Carnival, or rote imitation of it, local people respond in various ways. Their reactions include processes called "stimulus diffusion" and "reactive opposition." Towns are modifying their traditional *local* festivities, sometimes to fit (stimulus diffusion), sometimes to avoid (reactive opposition) Carnival images.

Stimulus diffusion is more common than direct borrowing through simple imitation. That is, local groups don't work hard on Carnival per se, but they add Carnival elements and themes to their local ceremonies. Some of these have grown in scale, in imitation of Carnival celebrations shown on national television.

Local reactions also can be negative, even hostile, as in Arembepe, where Carnival was never very important. This is probably because of its calendrical closeness to the main local festival, which honors Saint Francis and takes place in February. Nowadays, not only do many Arembepeiros reject Carnival, they are also growing hostile to their main local festivity. Villagers resent the fact that Saint Francis has become "an outsiders' event." It draws thousands of tourists each February. Commercial interests and outsiders have appropriated Saint Francis.

In reaction, many Arembepeiros now say they like and participate more in the June festivals honoring Saint John, Saint Peter, and Saint Anthony. Compared with Saint Francis these were minor affairs in the 1960s. Villagers celebrate them now with a new vigor and enthusiasm, as they react to outsiders and their celebrations, real and televised.

For another traditional event, external attention has generated a more favorable local reaction. TV coverage has spurred greater participation in a traditional annual performance, the *Chegança*. This is a fishermen's dance-play that reenacts the Portuguese discovery of Brazil. For the first time in 1985, Arembepeiros went to a suburb of Salvador to perform the *Chegança* for TV cameras. This was part of a program featuring traditional performances from many Bahian towns. Here one sees television's potential role in allowing local groups to express themselves and in publicizing subcultures.

These are some of many ways in which TV has affected local life in Arembepe (and elsewhere in rural Brazil). I should emphasize that TV impact isn't a matter of simple, automatic, responses to irresistible, omnipotent stimuli. Viewers shouldn't be seen as passive victims of a media assault. They are not the "couch potatoes" who populate contemporary North American conversations. Instead, they are human beings who use this new source of ideas and information in ways that make sense to them. They watch to validate beliefs, develop fantasies, or find answers to questions that the local setting may discourage or condemn. People use TV to relieve frustrations, build or enhance images of self, plan performances, chart social courses, and formulate daring life plans. Sometimes the interaction between viewer and set leads to unrealistic plans, false hopes, disappointment, and frustration. However, the process of TV impact is not one in which an all-powerful Big Brother zaps a defenseless zombie.

Merely Players

My ongoing research in Arembepe continues to provide new information on forces of social change. Now that the most recent findings have been discussed, there are stories to continue, destinies to be resolved.

Our main research in Arembepe for the TV project took

This fisherman, Aurino Alves (Zuca), shown here with his younger daughter, has a major role in the new, televised, Chegança *(fishermen's dance play).* (Conrad P. Kottak)

place in the summers of 1984 and 1985. We worked in small teams each time, as we had in the 1960s. Brazilian anthropology graduate students Alberto Costa and Rosane Prado joined us in 1984—to pilot test the interview schedules we had spent several weeks developing in Rio. Prado was preparing for fieldwork in Cunha, São Paulo state. Costa would work in Ibirama, Santa Catarina. In 1985, to do the formal interviewing in Arembepe, two new researchers joined Betty and me. Iraní Escolano, a Brazilian, was a graduate student in survey methods at Hunter College of the City University of New York. Pennie Magee, an anthropology graduate student at the University of Florida, had previously spent many years in Brazil.

These were the new players. What of our old friends?

Alberto helped out and visited us as usual from 1982 through 1985, but he was increasingly debilitated by lung cancer, which caused his death in 1987. Dora died suddenly in early 1985—struck down by a hit-and-run drunk driver. Once our TV research was complete, and with our two best friends gone, our visits to Arembepe became briefer. Saddened by the deaths of Dora and Alberto, we were not so eager to stay.

Alberto had been one of the few villagers who smoked cigarettes in the 1960s, and his smoking increased in the 1970s. He had given up the habit (as I had) by 1980, but I noticed his hacking cough that year and in 1982. Alberto eventually consulted doctors in Salvador and had an operation for lung cancer in a hospital there in 1983. In July 1984 he seemed to have made a good recovery, but he was coughing more in 1985 and showed me his latest chest x-rays, which I couldn't decipher. He was much weaker in 1986, and his family realized he didn't have long to live. Carolina planned to move—after his death—to her house in Volta do Robalo, where her daughter Maria José and her "husband" Ivan had lived since 1985.

In February 1987, at my desk in Ann Arbor, I got a call from Iraní Escolano. She was in Arembepe briefly, checking some information for the TV project. Iraní was phoning me from the local hotel to tell me that Alberto had died last night. She'd visited him the day before and wanted me to know especially that he had spoken of our friendship just before his death.

Back for a short visit in August 1987, I found that Alberto's family had sold his house in Street Down There. Carolina had moved in with Maria José, Ivan, and her grandchildren in Volta do Robalo. Ivan and Maria José ran a bar at the front of the house, like the one Carolina and Alberto had run in Arembepe.

We had years to prepare for Alberto's death, but Dora's was a shock. We saw Dora often in July and August 1984, when we were doing pilot work for the TV project. I remember testing our interview schedule on her. When I asked how someone "rose in life" (to assess her familiarity with common *telenovela* jargon), Dora, in typical jest, climbed onto a chair in her living room.

I vividly remember saying goodbye to Dora that year. Betty, the kids, and I were getting in our rental car, happily assured of funding to return a year later. "Until next year," we promised, with characteristic North American confidence. (Money made things certain.) "Till next year," Dora replied. "God willing," she added—"God willing."

That encounter was not to be. No more would Dora's grand exuberance grace our lives. In spring 1985 I received my first-ever letter from Alberto and deciphered the cryptic message in his crude handwriting: "I'm sorry to tell you that Dora passed away." How she died, he didn't say.

We learned the details from Dora's sister, Fernando's wife, when we returned to Arembepe in July. A hit-and-run driver, a city man and weekend drinker, had struck and instantly killed Dora as she walked home one Sunday evening from downtown Arembepe, where she worked in the bar run by her *comadre* (comother). Dora now lived in Volta do Robalo, where she had managed to build her dream house on a good lot. Dora was hit as she waited for her six-year-old daughter to urinate by the side of the road. She died instantly.

Dora had financed her new home with our help and through her bar job and tips provided by weekend and summer revellers. Ironically, that same weekend drinking pattern—expressed in the drunken inattentiveness of her killer (never brought to trial)—also caused Dora's death.

Alberto and Dora had benefited from the new economy, but both became victims of "progress." Arembepe's traditional pipes and chewing tobacco wouldn't have caused Alberto's lung cancer, and drunk driving had been a minor threat in the old Arembepe.

Tomé and Fernando were luckier. Happily negating my prediction in Chapter 11, Tomé's liaison with Sonia helped him after all. Sonia's father decided to retire to Arembepe with his young mistress and to use Tomé as his personal Individual Retirement Account. Sonia's dad bought his aging but still vigorous "son-in-law" a lavish new fishing boat, which Tomé operated out of Salvador. Fishing profits supported an improved life style for Tomé and Sonia in downtown Arembepe, while the old man enjoyed his dalliance and the sea breeze beneath the coconut palms of the Hippie Aldeia.

Fernando's situation changed the least. He maintained the

Dora built her dream house on this street, one of four in Volta do Robalo.
(Conrad P. Kottak)

life style moderation I had observed in 1980. Fernando still fished occasionally, but mostly he rented his small boat to others, including summer people and village men who took tourists out to fish. Fernando and his wife also benefited from their large family. Several of their children were grown; some were well educated. One son worked at Tibrás, and another was about to get a job there. Remarkably, a third son was a college student.

A Vida Continua

Because my research took my family to Arembepe in 1973, 1980, and annually from 1982 to 1987, Arembepe has also been important in the lives of my children, Juliet (born in 1968) and Nicholas (1971). Juliet remembers her fifth birthday, an occasion we used to invite village children, their parents, and our old friends to our summer house, just before we left Arembepe in August 1973. Juliet also recalls her friendship with Alberto's youngest daughter, Wanda, who surprised her by getting pregnant at the age of fifteen.

Irene Tavares, homemaker, in her dining room. (Conrad P. Kottak)

We spent so much time with Alberto that Nick grew very close to him. Alberto sometimes took charge of Nick while I was out interviewing other people. The teacher had found a new pupil. Alberto followed the pattern established with Niles Eldredge and me in the 1960s. He wanted to teach Nick about fishing.

Alberto was impressed with Nick's athletic abilities, especially his running. One day he bet Nick he couldn't run to Caraúnas (about a mile away, by the road), count the houses there, and be back in an hour. As Alberto and I talked on his porch in Street Down There, Nick accomplished his mission— to Alberto's surprise and praise. (Caraúnas had well over 100 houses.)

It isn't surprising that Nick focused on Alberto when he was asked to write a personal essay on "the circumstances of your upbringing or experiences that have influenced your life" when he applied to Columbia College in 1988. Nick has allowed me to reproduce part of that essay here.

Remembrance of Alberto (by Nicholas Charles Kottak)

Adding up the many times I have been to Brazil, I have spent a significant portion of my life in that country, both in Rio de Janeiro, where my mother (a native Brazilian) has an enormous family, and in Arembepe, a village on the northeastern coast. Until February 1987 that small fishing community was the home of a very special man by the name of Alberto. In 1964 Alberto, a fisherman, became an informant and friend of my father, Conrad Kottak, who was doing his doctoral research in cultural anthropology at Columbia. My father's research continued after his dissertation, and as a result I have spent many months in Arembepe, over several years (1973, 1980, 1982, 1983, 1984, 1985, and 1987). At age two I became well known to villagers as the light-skinned, blond-haired son of Conrado and Betty (the nickname of my mother). Alberto, however, was the villager who took greatest interest in me. It was the beginning of a unique father-son relationship.

Alberto's wife, Carolina, had given birth to thirteen children, all but three of whom had died at early ages, because of their poverty and malnutrition and inadequate local health care. Their three surviving children were all daughters, and this is why, I believe, Alberto became so attached to me. I was to be the son he never had.

I recall one time when Alberto and I were walking down the recently completed paved road. As a car approached from behind, I felt his maimed hand grab my arm tightly and pull me further from the road. He seemed frightened, perhaps because he had seen so many young ones die. When I was two Alberto liked to take me to the beach, where he would capture one of the tiny white crabs and then set it loose in front of me. I would run after the crab shouting "siri, siri." Siri, "little crab," was one of the first words I ever learned, and Alberto taught me many more that summer and later on. He always made me say each word several times to make sure I had the correct pronunciation. When I was older he told me stories of his fishing experiences, including the time he blew three fingers off his hand in the process of using dynamite sticks to fish in the harbor. He told me the best places to catch various kinds of aquatic life. He was constantly trying to teach me new things.

The time he demonstrated the greatest affection for me was on my thirteenth birthday, when he brought me a huge lobster to be cooked for dinner. He claimed to have caught it on the reef, as he used to do, occasionally with me tagging along, but I knew this to be false because the reef had few lobsters left and Alberto, after an operation for lung cancer, was no longer nimble enough to hunt on the reef. Although he never admitted it, I knew that he had, in fact, bought this expensive present out of his barely ample income.

In February 1987 I learned that Alberto had died of cancer, which had debilitated him for the last few years. It was with sadness that I paid my last visit to his wife, daughter, and grandchildren the following summer. *"A vida continua"* (Life continues), his daughter commented, and I realized that she was right. Alberto is a memory I share with my father that has, in effect, drawn us extremely close to one another, and this will be so for the rest of our lives. The fact that I was able to grow so close to this intelligent and attentive Brazilian fisherman is one of my most memorable experiences, and that is why I chose it as subject matter for this essay.

Epilogue, 1991

After 1987, we didn't get back to Arembepe until June 1991,[1] when Betty, Nick, and I returned for a new research project, on the emergence of ecological awareness in Brazil.[2] Nick at nineteen was now an anthropology major at Columbia College, like me when I first did fieldwork in Arembepe in 1962. He came along to do some ethnography and to pilot test the interview schedule (questionnaire) to be used in the new research. My daughter, Juliet, was in Switzerland, a medical student doing a summer internship at the World Health Organization.

Like the TV research, this new project has a team of Brazilian and American researchers. Again we are doing comparable field studies in different areas of Brazil. Last time we chose towns exposed to TV for different lengths of time. This time our sites face different kinds and degrees of environmental threats, such as water and air pollution, radioactivity, and deforestation. We are studying the nature, extent, and causes of environmental awareness and possible remedial action. We believe that local people will not act to preserve the environment if they perceive no risks to it. (Furthermore, even when there is risk perception, this does not guarantee environmental organization and action.)

Ecological awareness is burgeoning in Brazil, but it is strongest in the southcentral part of the country, especially in the cities. Increased media coverage of environmental issues reaches places like Arembepe, where, however, ecological risk perception remains rudimentary—despite two decades of air and water pollution from Tibrás. Another immediate threat is regional water pollution from the Pólo petrochemical complex in Arembepe's municipal seat. Since 1965 Camaçari has grown tenfold and has become a petrochemical inferno.

Toxic wastes now permeate the region's streams, rivers, and coastal waters.

Arembepeiros and others in the municipality of Camaçari are truly at risk from industrial pollution. Several times, reporters from Salvador have covered the threats to ocean, rivers, and lagoons. Villagers watch those reports on TV, but local concern about the environment hasn't grown in tandem with the risks.

Arembepeiros don't automatically absorb or accept lessons from the world system—even potentially beneficial ones about ecology. We saw in Chapter 12 how local resistance affects the spread of festivals like Carnival. For reasons embedded in a local culture or economy, people also may resist the ecological values that the world system now offers as an alternative to its longstanding model of economic development. Often, environmentalism comes into conflict with locally perceived needs for employment. Our interviews showed that most Arembepeiros considered Tibrás advantageous for their town—even when they recognized the ecological problems it has caused.

Concern about the environment is necessary if there is to be remedial action, but ecological consciousness is underdeveloped in the Brazilian lower class. Most Arembepeiros, for example, think of "ecology," a word they hear on TV, as relating to the Amazon, international conferences, Indian chiefs, and rock stars, rather than to local problems like air and water pollution.

I trace my recognition of Arembepe's low level of environmental risk perception to a long walk on the beach in 1985. Just north of the village, I began to pass dead sea gulls every few yards—hundreds of birds in all. I watched the birds glide feebly to the beach, where they set down and soon died. Stunned and curious, I wondered about an oil spill or mercury poisoning. Villagers, however, paid little attention. When I sought explanations, people said simply, "the birds are sick."

Ecological awareness among Brazilians (especially among educated people in the cities) started growing in the mid-1980s. One reason for this growth was the return of public debate with democracy—*abertura*, the Brazilian *glasnost*, after two decades of military rule. Since then, increased media coverage of ecological threats has raised risk perception. Especially significant was an accident involving radioactivity. This took place in the city of Goiânia, Goias state, central Brazil, in September 1987. A diagnostic machine from an abandoned clinic was found by scavengers and sold to scrap metal dealers, who opened it. It contained a capsule of cesium 137 powder, which they also opened. The friends and family of the junk dealer handled the phosphorescent powder. Viewing the radioactive cesium as magical and possibly curative, they rubbed it on their bodies. All this came to light on September 28, 1987, as exposed people (more than 100, eventually) started showing signs of radiation sickness.

Other nationally publicized ecorisks followed Goiânia. Most Brazilians have heard about the burning of the Amazon rain forest and the effects of road building, gold panning (using toxic mercury), and other intrusions of the world system on native groups and their lands. The media have also reported risks posed by oil spills, riverine mercury, industrial pollution and poor waste disposal, and the murder of the environmentally minded labor leader Chico Mendes.

Brazil encapsulates a series of issues now being considered by scientists, governments, environmentalists, and the public. In this context, our new research focuses on local perceptions and actions related to ecological risks. We seek answers to several questions: How aware are ordinary Brazilians of environmental hazards? Can and will they respond to them? Why do some people ignore real and evident risks, while other people allow very slight risks to inspire inordinate fears? How is risk perception related to actions that might reduce threats to the environment and to health?

During our two-week 1991 stay in Arembepe, we did the ground work for a later (1992) systematic investigation of local risk perception in relation to the environment. We needed to pilot test the interview schedule being developed for Arembepe and other communities. This questionnaire explores people's ideas about nature, progress, economic development, risks, and the environment.

With Nick doing most of the pilot testing of the questionnaire, we managed to complete fifteen formal interviews (1 to 2 hours each). We also had informal talks with local people about many issues, including ecology and pollution, and we caught up on the news since our last visit. The news can be reported here, but our conclusions about ecological awareness must await completion of the new research project.

Continuity in Change

We arrived in Arembepe in 1991 on a not so sunny day in June. I remembered our first day in 1980 (Chapter 7), which launched a very successful field trip, culminating in the first edition of this book. Now, revising the book, I wanted to retrace my steps. So we went to Claudia's restaurant just as we had done in 1980. The dining room was full, but we found a place to sit in the bar area outside, in front of the old harbor. The roof protected us from the rain. Next to Claudia's bar, just south, was the area where boats are beached.

Amy, Claudia's daughter and the owner of the restaurant-bar, helped us catch up on local news. As in 1980 the first name she mentioned was that of Tomé, resurgent in the mid-1980s, who had fallen again. In 1989 Tomé's large boat, on which he

Two members of the next generation—Nick Kottak interviews Francisco Nascimento. (Conrad P. Kottak)

had fished for up to ten days at a time, had been wrecked close to Arembepe as he tried to return to harbor. Now it lay on the beach near Claudia's bar—falling apart. The sight reminded me of iconoclast Laurentino's failed boats, chopped up for firewood in the 1960s. The traditional leveling mechanisms seemed still to operate. People who isolated themselves from local society couldn't go on profiting from it.

Days later, we found Sonia, Tomé's wife, the former *ippa*, weeping outside their home in the northern rectangle. It was Sunday evening and raining. Sonia stood there in a shawl awaiting her husband's return from an unexpectedly long day at sea. Tomé had left home at 3 A.M. for the second day in a row. We knew he hadn't planned to stay out long, since he'd invited us for a midday meal. He hadn't bothered to eat breakfast.

The previous afternoon Betty and I had visited Sonia and Tomé, who was exhausted and sleepy after a long day's fishing. He invited us back for Sunday lunch, to try the lobsters that were now his specialty.

Sonia passed by our house early Sunday afternoon to say

Nick and Betty visit in the northern rectangle (Coconut Square). (Conrad P. Kottak)

Tomé wasn't back yet, but she expected him soon. We changed our plans, arranging to have dinner with them instead of lunch.

Tomé was out alone in his small, old-style, motorless sailboat. He now did net fishing, mainly for lobster. Again he was innovating—this time by returning to a less world-system-dependent reliance on wind power and rowing.

The day before he had told me about the wreck of his big boat and his lack of funds to repair it. This followed the coincident failure of the bank where he had a line of credit. Tomé chose to captain his own small boat rather than work as an ordinary fisherman for someone else, like his brother Dinho, who still owned three large vessels. Tomé said he was tired of days at sea and the responsibilities of fishing, owning, and employing. But he still thought like an owner. He complained as he had in 1980 about the owner's predicament— constantly loaning money to crew members, spending profits on expensive boat repairs, and the risky local harbor (because of it he'd often operated his big boat out of Salvador).

Now free of his old responsibilities, Tomé drew an adequate income from his lobster catch ("and I don't have to share it with anyone"). Instead of buying a motor for his small boat, Tomé had invested in a good freezer, to store his lobsters for sale to summer people. He did hope to motorize soon. A motor would make his work quicker, less arduous, and more secure—since he fished alone, and sailing was hard work.

Tomé seemed happy enough with his situation, but others made fun of him. "There goes 'Captain' Tomé," remarked one young man as we watched Tomé struggle with his sail just beyond the reef. "Poor miserable man. He used to have a boat so fine it had a color TV. Now he doesn't even have a motor. No one wants to fish with him, because he's so miserable."

Most villagers considered Tomé's solitary fishing "crazy." "Out there alone he could fall in the water and drown. He could get tangled up in his net and drown. He could get stung by a ray, pass out, and drown," enumerated Fernando— always a good commentator on danger.

Sonia, it seemed to me, had good reason to be worried. On that rainy day in June, with Tomé alone in a small craft on a rough sea, fears were reasonable.

Being a case study in *Assault on Paradise,* commented Betty, hardly seemed to bring good luck.

Sonia wanted someone to go out and look for Tomé. We walked a few doors down to Fernando's house. He was concerned about Tomé, but it was night, the sea was rough, and Fernando had no boat of his own. I asked about Tomé's brothers and son, all of whom owned boats. Sonia said she had talked to his brothers, but everyone was drunk. Even the local municipal delegate, succumbing to the weekend drinking syndrome, was drunk.

"Let's go see his brother," Betty suggested. "Maybe Dinho will have some ideas." Sonia got in our car, and we drove down to Dinho's house in the main square. It was closed and dark. "Come there with me, Conrado," said Sonia. "Dinho's wife likes to yell; she'll tell me off if you're not there." We pounded on the door several times before the woman came. "Dinho's asleep, and I'm not going to disturb him. It's too dark to look anyway. Tomorrow's time enough to look if Tomé's not back by then. He knows how to handle a boat. I'll

Francisco dos Santos enjoys finding his photo from the 1960s (p. 84) in the first edition of Assault on Paradise. *(Conrad P. Kottak)*

bet the winds were contrary and he decided to land in Jauá."

"Let's call Jauá," I proposed. I knew that one of Alberto's brothers lived there and probably had a phone. Sonia ran over to Alberto's mother's house to get the number and called from the hotel. She talked to a man in Jauá who "knows Tomé and his boat, sees them every day when Tomé sets his nets." He hadn't seen him that day.

Having heard nothing to reduce her anxiety, Sonia went off to urge Tomé's son to go out in search of his father. We went off to call the ever-vigilant town patron, Jorge Camões, to see if there was now some sort of coast guard that might intervene. (We discovered, to our surprise, that Arembepe did have a local coast guard representative.)

As we spoke with Jorge, the good word came. Tomé was back. What had kept him? Untangling his nets, which had become hopelessly entangled in the storm. And the winds had been contrary. But Tomé hadn't gone to Jauá; he had been mooring in Arembepe while Dinho's wife was yelling at Sonia on her doorstep.

That night we learned, more vividly than ever, the dangers of fishing alone without a motor.

What impressed me the most as I took part in the unfolding story was social isolation. Sonia, an amiable person with many friends among outsiders and summer people, still stands apart from native Arembepeiros. She has even employed a maid—which is just not done by a fisherman's wife. Tomé, through a series of choices and actions, also preferred outsiders to the local social system. So local society responded as it always did to iconoclasts—even the best of them.

*   *   *

As I noted in Chapter 6, by 1973 the stage had been set for the main changes evident in Arembepe in the 1980s—and in 1991. Ongoing change continues to be in scale—change of degree rather than of kind.

Thus, the government increasingly intrudes on local life. Villagers think the municipal government brings mostly benefits, including a new and larger medical post, staffed by six physicians and a social worker. Arembepe now has garbage collection, municipal cleanup, and postal service. Thanks mostly to municipal efforts, the town looks better than ever. Both the central square (now named Saint Francis Square for the patron saint whose chapel is there) and the northern rectangle (now Coconut Square) have been paved. Attractive tables and shelters with thatch roofs give the main square a park-like flavor.

Local opinions of the federal government—traditionally negative—were more so. People blamed the government (especially President Fernando Collor de Mello) for the cost of living and the latest economic "crisis"—a recession. Inflation had temporarily slowed to 8 percent per month, but there seemed to be more unemployment. A few villagers noted the irony that Arembepe had both more jobs and more joblessness than in the past. (Jorge Camões, scion of the landlord family, was still the benevolent patron, helping villagers find jobs in a recession.)

The complaints about inflation, unemployment, and government corruption hadn't changed much since the mid-1980s. Indeed, these problems have plagued Brazil for decades. Thus Charles Wagley (1960), describing social change in Brazil from the 1930s through the 1950s, signaled political scandals, inflation, and a sense of crisis as characteristic features of an industrializing and urbanizing nation.

Our new interview schedule, like the one we used for the TV project, asked people to name Brazil's—and then Arem-

In northern Arembepe, a garbage truck rumbles past some summer houses. (Conrad P. Kottak)

bepe's—three main problems. There was little change in the local and national problems mentioned from 1985 to 1991. Despite the media's ecoblitz, people mentioned corruption, inflation, unemployment, and crime much more often than deforestation or pollution. (Note the irony: Crime is a nonexistent local problem; pollution is a real one.)

Arembepeiros said they felt Brazil's latest economic "crisis" (recession), but they were positive about local life. When we asked if life in Arembepe is better than it used to be, almost everyone said yes. When we asked people if they'd like to live in a big city, almost everyone said no. When we asked if local life was better or worse than life in a big city, everyone preferred Arembepe.

Arembepe had grown noticeably. The local building boom continued despite the national recession. Volta do Robalo, with its four long streets—new houses fronting on both sides—had as many houses as Arembepe proper. One clear new development was the social segmentation of Arembepe into two communities. Arembepe proper was increasingly a town of outsiders and transients; most native Arembepeiros now preferred Volta do Robalo. Caraúnas, still squalid and occasionally flooded, kept its noncohesive mix of summer people, native villagers, and more marginal immigrants. It showed no sign of Volta's evident community spirit.

For the sons and daughters of Arembepe, Volta had become the neighborhood of choice. No doubt this expressed native resistance to the perceived appropriation of the community by outsiders. We saw several signs of Volta's community identity. In a newly built church the German priest based in Abrantes gave regular masses. (He held mass in Arembepe on a different day.) The people of Volta had even chosen their own patron saint, Conceição (Our Lady of Conception). They were planning an annual festival in her honor, as an alternative to Arembepe's now alienated Saint Francis celebration.

Ivan, Alberto's able, hard-working "son-in-law" had, in the words of Dora's son Chico, become a "chief" in Volta do Robalo. Ivan and Maria José ran a prosperous bar-restaurant (Carolina's house was in back) and were wealthy enough to afford an automobile. Ivan mobilized his neighbors for local events, including Volta's festive 1991 Saint John's observance.

The celebration of Saint John's eve and day (June 23–24),

which we had first witnessed in 1962, had grown dramatically. Villagers still offered their guests canjica (mushy corn pudding), boiled peanuts, roasted corn on the cob, and *cachaça*-based liqueurs. People still danced in the streets, but the traditional bonfires were now set in front of almost every home. The people of Arembepe (including an influx of summer people) celebrated in the main village, while the people of Volta do Robalo held a rival festival.

The trend of increasing occupational diversity also continued. More native sons now worked at Tibrás than as fishermen—though a recent wave of factory layoffs had heightened the perception of unemployment as a problem. As the building boom continued, so did jobs in construction.

The issue of industrial pollution remained unresolved. The municipality had at last taken notice of the pollution of rivers and the ocean by the Pólo petrochemical complex in Camaçari. Under construction just a few kilometers north of Arembepe was a tubing system leading into the Atlantic from Pólo's liquid wastes treatment facility. (That treatment cen-

Francisco Nascimento, a school guard and part-time mason, is proud of the tomb he built for his mother. Tombs and tombstones are another new feature in Arembepe. (Conrad P. Kottak)

ter, called CETREL, is located between Camaçari and the coast a few kilometers northwest of Arembepe.) CETREL now dumps its treated liquid wastes into a tributary of the Jacuipe River. The new tubing will convey those wastes 4.5 kilometers out to sea.

Some villagers feared that toxic wastes would wash down to Arembepe, since the prevailing marine currents run south. Others considered 4.5 kilometers too far out for the wastes to wash back. Municipal officials contended that the new system would be much safer than the current dumping into the Jacuipe River, which enters the Atlantic less than 10 kilometers north of Arembepe. Pólo petrochemical pollution does reach Arembepe now; its red foam scum was visible many days in 1991, as it had been in the mid-1980s.

The pollution spawned by Pólo Petrochemical and CETREL's river dumping has grown as a risk as the Tibrás threat to Arembepe has receded. Tibrás smokestacks still pollute the air, but the prevailing winds carry the smoke inland, south-

Progress or a new ecological threat? This tubing will convey treated petro-chemical wastes 4.5 kilometers out to sea, just a few kilometers north of Arembepe. (Conrad P. Kottak)

west of Arembepe. Sturdy tubing now takes Tibrás's sulfuric residues 6 kilometers out to sea, south of Arembepe. With the ocean currents running south, Tibrás threatens Jauá more than Arembepe.

In my 1980 epilogue I wondered whether pollution would eventually destroy Arembepe's tourist appeal, its fishing industry, and its environment. I don't yet have an answer.

Arembepe is still beautiful, and tourists and summer people keep on coming. Villagers continue to seek jobs in Tibrás and to fish in polluted waters. Many—perhaps most—local people perceive no threats to fish or to human health. A few fishermen (including Tomé) have noticed changes in bottom composition (sulfuric mud now covers rocky bottoms near the Tibrás tubes) and in the kinds of fish being caught. Some fishers have seen burned and deformed fish; others mention declining catches.

Local ecological awareness *is* growing. IBAMA, the federal environmental agency, now employs two local agents. One weighs the fish catches. The other monitors predatory fish-

Ester and Jaime Coelho Pinto, members of Arembepe's traditional land-owning family, stand near their summer home. (Conrad P. Kottak)

ing—e.g., out-of-season lobstering and dynamite fishing. A protected nesting area for sea turtles has been established near the "Hippie Aldeia," which itself has been declared a "protected area," which no cars may enter.

The Next Generation

Coming back, we see things we can't know, won't discover unless we keep on coming back. In a process of change we may detect continuity and persistence. As things change, stasis (that which remains unchanged) becomes more obvious. Enduring and recurrent patterns and relationships are revealed as anthropologists study a setting across the generations. People and patterns live on in new generations. Ties established among anthropologists, informants, and friends continue and are renewed.

Fernando and Tomé, both nearing sixty, greeted us with great warmth, but it was mostly a new generation that guided us in 1991. The children of our old friends were now adults with progeny of their own. The most welcome was Dora's granddaughter, two years old, the first child of Dora's oldest son, Chico. The little girl shares Dora's name and some of her exuberance.

I was touched by the way the new generation took us in hand. Chico, Dora's son, Red, Fernando's son, and Maria José, Alberto's daughter, helped us as their parents had. Red, an environmentally conscious Tibrás worker, helped Nick find members of various social categories to interview for our pilot study. Assuming Dora's traditional role as facilitator, Chico helped us schedule several interviews. When we first told him what we planned to do, Chico remarked, with a humor like his mother's, "I'll be the tour guide for your survey." (This comment[3] illustrated local familiarity with the polling routinely done by TV researchers in Brazil.)

Maria José, who is well educated, having studied to be a school teacher, will assume part of her father's role. I've asked her to be my local assistant in 1992, to help do the formal interviewing I plan for the ecology project.

Summer 1992 will mark the thirtieth anniversary of our first trip to Arembepe. Developments in transportation and com-

I sit near Ozete, a member of the next generation, who runs a successful bar and restaurant. (Conrad P. Kottak)

munication continue to make it easier for anthropologists to keep in touch with "the field." I now suspect that I'll keep on going back—and finding new research challenges in Arembepe—for the rest of my life. I can even imagine my grandchildren renewing relationships with the descendants of Alberto, Dora, and Fernando. Alberto and Dora would be happy to know that new generations may continue the collaboration that underlies this longitudinal study.

Appendixes

Appendix 1. Ranking of Household Budgets, Arembepe, 1964

Rank	Occupations in Household°	Total Annual Budget (in 1,000 cruzeiros)†
118	Female earner	58
117	Ordinary fisherman	72
116	Female earner	73
115	Female earner	86
114	Female earner	87
113	Female earner	98
112	Female earner	108
111	2 female earners	161
110	Agricultural worker, 2 female earners	166
109	Fisherman, female earner	169
108	Female earner	180
107	Captain, female earner	184
106	Fisherman, female earner	195
105	Retired fisherman, supported	197
104	Mason, 3 female earners	218
103	Female earner, supported	219
102	Mason, midwife	221
101	Female earner	221
100	Fisherman	234
99	2 fishermen	236
98	Supported	239
97	Female earner	252
96	Captain, fisherman, female earner	254
95	Dragnet owner	268
94	Fisherman	278
93	Fisherman, female earner	282
92	Barber-businessman, 2 female earners	286
91	Fisherman	295
90	Fisherman, female earner	300
89	Captain—half-owner, fisherman, occasional fisherman	309
88	Captain—half-owner, stevedore, 2 female earners	312
87	Fisherman	316
86	Captain—half-owner, fisherman	317
85	Fisherman, female earner	322
84	Fisherman-owner, 3 female earners	333

Rank	Occupations in Household°	Total Annual Budget (in 1,000 cruzeiros)†
83	Captain—half-owner, female earner	335
82	Captain—half-owner	336
81	2 fishermen	342
80	Fisherman, female earner	343
79	Fisherman, agriculturalist	348
78	Fisherman, female earner	359
77	Captain—half-owner	362
76	2 fishermen, caulker	372
75	2 fishermen, 2 female earners	373
74	Fisherman	374
73	Barber, store worker	375
72	2 female earners, landowner	377
71	Fisherman, female earner	394
70	Storekeeper, female earner, cattle owner	404
69	Fisherman, female earner	405
68	Fisherman, 2 female earners	418
67	3 female earners, supported	418
66	Fisherman, female earner	418
65	Storekeeper	420
64	Captain, female earner	420
63	Fisherman	421
62	Fisherman, female earner	423
61	Fisherman	430
60	Fisherman—occasional captain	431
59	Fisherman, agricultural worker	435
58	Storekeeper	435
57	Fisherman, female earner	440
56	Mason, 2 fishermen, 2 female earners	441
55	Fisherman	446
54	Captain—half-owner, 3 female earners	452
53	Fisherman	453
52	Fisherman, 2 occasional fishermen, female earner	457
51	Captain—half-owner, fisherman	461
50	Fisherman, female earner	462
49	Captain—half-owner-agriculturalist, female earner	465
48	2 fishermen	470
47	2 fishermen, caulker, female earner	478

(Cont.)

Rank	Occupations in Household*	Total Annual Budget (in 1,000 cruzeiros)†
46	2 fishermen, schoolteacher, mason	484
45	Fish marketer—farmer, female earner	489
44	Captain	495
43	Fisherman, storekeeper	496
42	3 fishermen, mason	498
41	Fisherman—coconut picker	502
40	Captain-owner, nonfishing boat owner—carpenter—coconut marketer—fish marketer	503
39	Captain—half-owner	503
38	Captain—owner	503
37	Captain—half-owner, agriculturalist	515
36	3 fishermen, occasional fisherman	520
35	Captain, 2 female earners	529
34	2 fishermen	533
33	Fish marketer—landowner, supported	544
32	Fisherman, female earner	547
31	Captain—half-owner—agriculturalist	553
30	Fisherman—half-owner—coconut marketer	555
29	Captain—half-owner	560
28	Fisherman—sometimes captain, fisherman	562
27	Captain—half-owner, fisherman-half-owner	564
26	2 fishermen, carpenter	570
25	3 fishermen	573
24	Fisherman	577
23	Farmer-businessman	580
22	Fish marketer—nonfishing boat owner	582
21	Storekeeper	597
20	Fisherman, 2 female earners, supported	603
19	Captain—half-owner	605
18	Petrobrás worker	606
17	Fisherman	608
16	Storekeeper—farmer	640
15	Fish marketer, boat owner, female earner	650
14	Fisherman—half-owner—barber	664
13	Captain, storekeeper, cowboy, fisherman	665
12	Captain—half-owner—cowboy—farmer	673

(Cont.)

Rank	Occupations in Household°	Total Annual Budget (in 1,000 cruzeiros)†
11	Petrobrás worker—boat owner	680
10	2 Petrobrás workers, carpenter, fisherman	697
9	Captain—half-owner—farmer	708
8	Boat carpenter—boat owner	713
7	Fisherman—half-owner, farmer, storekeeper	783
6	Port captain, fisherman	792
5	Fisherman, businessman—land owner—fish marketer	846
4	Captain, fish marketer, landowner	884
3	Storekeeper, boat owner, landowner	1049
2	Storekeeper, boat owner, landowner	1125
1	Storekeeper, boat owner—landowner— farmer—marketer of coconuts, fish, and cereals	1201
	Mean budget	435
	Median budget	439

°Occupations joined by dashes indicate a single individual with plural occupations. Occupations separated by commas indicate different individuals living in the same household.
†Figures are for August 1964. 1,500 (old) cruzeiros = $1.

Appendix 2. *Primary Occupations of Arembepe Males in 1964, 1973, and 1980, by Percentage*

Type of Occupation	1964 N = 173*	1973 N = 231*	1980 N = 230†
Fishing-related	74.0	53.2	40.4
Building, lotting	5.2	14.7	16.1
Odd jobber	2.8	2.6	3.0
Business, food, bar	11.0	8.7	13.5
Hippie work	0.0	2.6	2.6
Factory employment	1.7	11.3	17.0
Municipal, external work	1.7	3.9	4.3
Local service	1.2	1.7	2.6
Agriculture	2.3	1.3	0.0
Total	99.9	100.0	99.9

°*Based on complete census, by household, of adult males' occupations.*
†*The 1980 percentages are based on averages of data from two samples obtained that year: (1) an occupational survey of the 61 inhabited houses in southern Arembepe; and (2) information on the current occupations of 157 men from the 1973 sample who are still alive, employed, and living in Arembepe.*

Appendix 3. Fish Marketing by Ten Crews through Arembepe's Fishermen's Cooperative during 1972

Month	Kilograms Sold	Price Received per kg. (new cruzeiros)*	Percentage of Monthly Average Caught This Month
1	3,550	2.2	77
2	8,750	2.6	190
3	3,575	2.8	78
4	5,600	2.7	121
5	6,575	2.5	142
6	4,375	2.6	95
7	5,725	3.2	124
8	3,550	3.1	77
9	2,600	3.5	56
10	2,700	3.5	59
11	2,400	3.3	52
12	5,950	3.3	129
Total	55,350		
Monthly Average	4,600	2.9	

*2.2 new cruzeiros = 2,200 old cruzeiros. In July 1973, 6.1 new cruzeiros = $1.

Appendix 4. 1980 Occupations of Men Who Had Fished in 1973*

	Number	% of Active Men	% of All 1973 Fishermen
Active			
Fishing-related	51	71.8	48.6
Building, lotting	2	2.8	1.9
Odd jobber	1	1.4	1.0
Business, food, bar	8	11.3	7.6
Factory employment	7	9.9	6.7
External, municipal work	1	1.4	1.0
Local service	1	1.4	1.0
Agriculture	0	0.0	0.0
Subtotal	71	100.0	67.6
Inactive			
Pensioned, disabled	14		13.3
Sick, alcoholic	5		4.8
Moved away	3		2.9
Dead	12		11.4
Total	105		100.2

**Based on household census, Arembepe and Caraúnas.*

Appendix 5. Types of Marital Union in Arembepe and Caraúnas in 1980, According to Main Occupations, Compared with Arembepe in 1964 and Caraúnas in 1973

	Common-law		Formal		
	No.	%	No.	%	Total No.
Arembepe and Caraúnas 1980					
Ordinary fishermen	39	76.5	12	23.5	51
Captains	11	57.9	8	42.1	19
Tibrás workers*	18	60.0	12	40.0	30
Nonfishing boat owners	7	46.7	8	53.3	15
Total	75	65.2	40	34.8[†]	115
Arembepe 1964					
Wealthier half	22	37.9	36	62.1	58
Poorer half	36	69.2	16	30.8	52
Total	58	52.7	52	47.3[‡]	110
Caraúnas 1973					
All residents	33	91.7	3	8.3	36

*Because Tibrás workers were younger in 1980 than the average captain, their percentage of formal marriage can be expected eventually to surpass that of captains.

†Correlation coefficient (θ) for association of wealth and formal marriage in 1980 was .25. Average wealth increases from ordinary fishermen to captains to Tibrás workers to boat owners.

‡Correlation coefficient (θ) for association between wealth and formal marriage in 1964 was .31.

Appendix 6. Male and Female Employment in Arembepe by Percentage, 1973 and 1980

	1973*			1980†		
	Male	*Female*	*Total*	*Male*	*Female*	*Total*
Fishing-related	53.2	0.0	41.6	37.1	0.0	26.5
Building, lotting	14.7	1.5	11.8	20.5	0.0	14.7
Odd jobber	2.6	49.2	12.8	4.1	51.7	17.6
Business, food, bar	8.7	24.6	12.2	16.4	31.0	20.6
Hippie work	2.6	3.1	2.7	8.2	10.3	8.8
Factory employment	11.3	0.0	8.8	8.2	0.0	5.9
Municipal, external work	3.9	6.2	4.4	2.7	6.9	3.9
Local service	1.7	4.6	2.4	2.7	0.0	2.0
Agriculture	1.3	10.8	3.4	0.0	0.0	0.0
Total	100.0	100.0	100.1	99.9	99.9	100.0
Sample size	231	65	296	73	29	102

*Based on occupational census of all households in Arembepe and Caraúnas.
†Includes only surveyed area in southern Arembepe; for fuller sample of adult male employment in 1980, see Appendix 2.

Chapter Notes

Chapter 1

[1]Arembepe is too well known to be disguised by giving it another name. However, names of villagers and certain details about them have been changed to protect their privacy.

Chapter 3

[1]The exchange rate of old cruzeiros per U.S. dollar increased from 475 in 1962 to 620 in 1963, 1,500 in 1964, and 1,800 in 1965. [It rose to 6,500 (6.5 new cruzeiros) in 1973 and had reached 60,000 (60) by 1980.]

[2]Correlation coefficients (Pearson's r: All variables were treated as interval variables in assessing the association between coconut-tree ownership and light skin color, and between boat ownership and light skin color) were .124 and − .044, respectively. Neither coefficient was statistically significant.

Chapter 4

[1]As noted previously, even technologically advanced open-sea fishing remains a form of foraging—the appropriation of natural or wild, rather than domesticated, resources. Even the most sophisticated fisheries do little to increase the resources of the sea. Fish farming can proceed in restricted areas of water, e.g., ponds and rice paddies, but is virtually impossible on the open sea. Fishermen, of course, can attempt to increase catches by avoiding overfished areas until fish have returned and reproduced. And electronic instruments such as radar, radio telephone, direction finders, and echosounders may help to locate fish. However, these devices, which of course were not used in Arembepe, are just better ways to conserve or track game.

[2]The surest way to catch more fish is to do more fishing. Here we find one of the main differences between open-sea fishing and other forms of foraging. In most hunting-gathering societies, the primary

danger in intensifying production is that strategic resources—particularly game—may be threatened if people take too much of what nature has to offer. For this reason hunter-gatherers have been characterized by Marshall Sahlins (1972) as the original leisured or "affluent" society. A reduced workload helps to conserve game and vegetation by keeping use of the environment below its actual capacity to support its human population. With rudimentary technology, marine fishing offers a contrast. Given the vastness of their marine environment, fishermen such as those of Arembepe *could* intensify production without endangering the species they depended on. Among fishing peoples not living in modern nations—such as the native populations of the North Pacific coast of North America—the potlatch (a system of competitive feasting) stimulated production, as people stepped up production of fish and other resources that were consumed and given away in monumental feasts (see Harris, 1974). In Arembepe, as in other modern-day fishing villages, increases in production could instead be funneled into an outside market. Indeed, because fish are so perishable, if there is to be increased production, it must always be accompanied by appropriate opportunities for distribution.

Chapter 5

[1]Shepard Forman (1975, pp. 112–115; originally in Forman and Riegelhaupt, 1970) has identified five stages in the development of the regional marketing system in northeastern Brazil. By 1965 Arembepe was moving from Stage 3 to Stage 4. In Stage 3 several middlemen go to producers (fishermen) to buy for resale in the marketplace or to wholesalers. In Stage 4 wholesalers begin to bypass the middlemen, going directly to rural producers. An aspect of the transition noted by Forman is that sale for credit (paid in cash only after resale) is replaced by sale to wholesalers for cash. Although this shift from credit to cash sales had occurred in Arembepe by 1965, Forman's observation that when producers receive immediate cash they often sell for less did not apply to Arembepe, where the price of fish had continued to rise. The increasing value of Arembepe's fish reflected progressively easier access to Salvador and the shortage of food to feed the capital's growing population (Forman, 1975, pp. 88–89). Arembepe's subsequent evolution toward Forman's Stage 5, in which wholesalers deal directly with large-scale producers at a central delivery point, was an aspect of change in Arembepe after 1965 that is examined later in this chapter.

Arembepeiros in 1965 had not replaced their arrangement of selling to particular agents with sale on a first-come, first-served basis. Forman (1975) found such a change to be usual when wholesalers bought directly from producers. No doubt this was because of fish's perishability. Producers had to be sure that someone would take their fish to market, even if this meant selling for less (which it didn't in Arembepe).

Unlike fish marketing, Arembepeiros had no regular sales agreements with the buyers of their coconuts, the second major export, which local middlemen took to market in Salvador. The price that villagers got for their coconuts, which were sold in Salvador for later resale, varied with supply and demand. Arembepeiros had to compete on an open market with other rural Bahians. In 1965 Arembepeiros were drawing a total annual income of about $6,000 from the fruits of 16,000 coconut trees owned by seventy-seven villagers. Coconut marketing was in the second stage of Forman's model. That is, rural people sold to middlemen locally or in distribution fairs, i.e., the markets in Salvador just mentioned.

[2]Through education and by offering benefits of patronage, Jorge and a few others were exceptions and received special respect, if not the outright deference that native Arembepeiros knew so little about giving.

Chapter 6

[1]In 1973, annual marketed catches averaged 5,500 kilograms at 3.4 cruzeiros per kilogram, or about $3,050.

Chapter 7

[1]Characterization of Arembepe as "the land of dreams" is taken from hippie wall graffiti noted by Maxine Margolis.

[2]I censused 313 people in 130 houses in the sampled area of southern Arembepe. This gives an average of 5.1 inhabitants in the (61) inhabited houses, and 2.4 on average for the 130. Multiplying 2.4 by 617, the number of homes in the government census of Arembepe in 1980, gives 1,481 people, not far off the official count of 1,561.

Chapter 8

[1]Historian E. Bradford Burns (1980, pp. 534–535) notes that the poor were experiencing something similar throughout Brazil. The working class had to work harder just to maintain a precarious living standard. The work-time cost of a monthly subsistence ration (same amount of same supplies) increased from 87 hours in 1965 to 187 hours in 1976.

[2]Since some members had withdrawn before repaying their debts, SUDEPE apparently cut its losses by dipping into the cooperative's

remaining general funds, including payments due to fishermen for the previous month's catches. No legal action was ever taken in connection with the cooperative's collapse.

[3]After 1976 SUDEPE employed F., a fairly well educated Arembepeiro, to note the weights of all fish brought to shore in the village. Whenever fish were unloaded, he visited the fish stores to record weights. I am grateful to Maria Gomes Pereira, a marine biologist employed by SUDEPE in Salvador, for making available to me unpublished data on fishing productivity in Arembepe and Bahia generally. Her figures for Arembepe, which show total annual marketed catches to have been 140,000, 125,000, and 130,000 kilograms in 1977, 1978, and 1979, respectively, are based on F.'s notes, which he delivered monthly to SUDEPE headquarters in Salvador. SUDEPE has hired similar recorders in all Bahian fishing communities. F.'s own estimates of Arembepe's productivity were higher. He thought that the fleet produced between 15,000 and 20,000 kilograms per month, which would give an annual production of between 180,000 and 240,000 kilograms. Assuming fifteen to twenty vessels active for twelve months, the average annual production per boat would then be 12,000 kilograms. To arrive at a (lower) estimate of proceeds from Arembepe's fishing industry, I have averaged three years of SUDEPE figures, arriving at 132,000 kilograms annually. This is about 9,000 per boat, assuming that fifteen boats fished regularly during the year. This is a big jump over the 1972 figures given in Appendix 3.

[4]Only four boats of the nineteen active in Arembepe in 1980 had close kin connections among crew members, including captain. Significantly, in three of these, the captain was also the boat owner. Profit taking was less mercenary in these boats than in the others. For example, the owner and true captain of one boat gave his aging uncle the captain's (double) share, maintaining the fiction that the old man still held that position. Of the fifteen other active boats, ten with nonfishing owners, two crews included only distant kin (beyond first cousins). The other thirteen crews lacked *any kin ties at all*. This is another measure of the extent to which most crews had become purely economic units.

[5]The total number of fishermen (counting captains) had also shrunk, from 128 in 1964 to 90 in 1980, supplying five-man crews for most of the nineteen active boats.

[6]In 1973, 113 men fished out of Arembepe. 105 lived in Arembepe and Caraúnas. The others came from nearby settlements, including agricultural estates to the west.

[7]In sharp contrast to the past, when fishermen had no retirement benefits and needed to rely on kin and investments, about 13 per-

cent of the 1973 fishermen were receiving government pensions by 1980. Equivalent to $40 monthly, these benefits were a welcome supplement, particularly since obligations decreased with age. Fishermen could still draw on the informal fund of kin-based social security built up before retirement.

Twelve (19 percent) of the 1973 fishermen had died, moved away, or become alcoholics or pensionless invalids. Of the seventy-one still active men, fifty-one (72 percent) still fished, seven had entered business, and eight worked for Tibrás. The other five had turned to other occupations.

The contrast with the past was clear. Among still employed men, more job shifting had occurred between 1973 and 1980 than between 1964 and 1973. Given deaths and retirement, less than half the 105 men who had fished in 1973 still did so in 1980.

[8]Fishermen got to sell fewer fish in 1980 than in 1965, although their individual productivity had increased from 850 kilograms per year in 1965 to 1,450 in 1980. Ninety fishermen in 1980 outproduced 127 in 1964. They caught about 130,000 kilograms annually, versus 108,000 kilograms when thirty-one boats fished offshore Arembepe.

Chapter 9

[1]I thank Nelson Pinheiro, the Director of Statistical Services in Camaçari, for sending me the results of the 1980 census.

[2]The correlation coefficient (θ) for the association of wealth and formal marriage in Arembepe in 1964 was .31. This computation is based on the figures given in Appendix 5. Other figures in that appendix show that the correlation was weaker in 1980.

[3]However, 54 percent of the population between the ages of ten and forty-nine were female, intensifying the scarcity of husbands.

Chapter 11

[1]This section was the epilogue of the first edition.

Chapter 12

[1]*David Copperfield*, for example, was written in nineteen monthly installments, each thirty-two pages long, between May 1849 and November 1850.

[2]The Department of Social Anthropology of the National Museum, a division of the Federal University of Rio de Janeiro, cooperated in this project by offering Conrad Kottak an institutional affiliation and providing field researchers Rosane Prado and Alberto Costa. Professor Roberto DaMatta, then of the National Museum, now of the University of Notre Dame, graciously acted as our Brazilian liaison.

[3]For many of our statistical analyses we used a technique called "multiple regression." This measures the separate effects (and the combined effects) of several "potential *predictors*" on a *dependent variable*. For example, to predict "risk of heart attack" (the dependent variable), potential predictors include sex, age, family history, weight, blood pressure, serum cholesterol, exercise, and cigarette smoking. Each one makes a separate contribution, and some have more impact than others. However, someone with many "risk factors" (particularly the most significant ones) has a greater risk of heart attack than someone with few predictors.

For our TV impact study we used a standard set of nine predictor variables and examined their effects on many dependent variables. Our nine predictors were: gender, age, skin color, class, education, income, religiosity, length of home TV exposure, and current televiewing level. Note that our research design allowed us to examine the predictive value of two TV variables: current viewing level and length of home exposure. We could do this because our sample included people with television in their homes for different lengths of time. American research, by contrast, must rely on current viewing level as the main potential predictor of TV impact. This is because there is little variation in length of home exposure, except for variation related to age. Most Americans aged 40 and below have never known a world without TV.

Sometimes, age is used as an indirect measure of TV's cumulative effects in the United States. The assumption is that TV will have influenced older people (up to a point, around age forty) for a longer time than younger people and thus will have had a cumulatively greater effect. However, with this approach it is difficult to distinguish the effects of length of TV exposure from the effects of other aspects of aging. By contrast, our Brazilian research sample included people of the same age who had been exposed to TV for different lengths of time. This allowed us to separate years of home TV exposure from aging per se. It also permitted us to compare the impact of *current* viewing habits with *cumulative effects* associated with length of home exposure. We assessed the effects of these predictors on many dependent variables (e.g., opinions, attitudes, buying patterns).

[4]We used a set of uniform quantitative and qualitative procedures to collect data at each site. We used two printed interview schedules, for more than 1,800 structured interviews, ranging over hundreds of variables. One schedule was for households ($n = 847$) and another, for individuals ($n = 1032$).

[5]There was a strong statistical correlation between number of books in the home and daily TV hours. Televiewing was also strongly

correlated with literacy (personal literacy, literacy of household head, number of books in home, and allied measures) throughout our sample—among both lower- and higher-income people.

In the overall sample, current TV viewing hours was the second of only two predictors (after education, which had a much greater effect) of our "reading index" (based on whether the respondent regularly reads books plus magazines plus newspapers).

[6]Some of the questions we asked were: How do you imagine life in Rio? São Paulo? The state capital? Would you like to visit each of them? Would you like to live in any of those places? In which of the three would you most/least like to live? Would you want your children to live in those cities?

[7](Darker) skin color, gender (being male), and (younger) age were associated with yes responses.

[8]Current viewing hours was the second of seven predictors of a yes response to "Do you have a savings account?"

[9]IBOPE (the Brazilian Statistical Public Opinion Research Institute) has established a useful social-class scale to evaluate audience buying power. Its categories are A (upper class), B1 (upper middle), B2 (middle middle), B3 (lower middle), C (upper working), and D (lower working and people without significant income). The basis of the scale is the proportion and amount of household income remaining after certain basic expenditures. These "necessities" encompass food, utilities (including telephone), school expenses, clothing, transportation, personal hygiene items, medical care, and domestic help. Note that IBOPE uses Brazilian cultural standards to define middle-class existence. For instance, most middle-class Brazilians consider "domestic help" (a maid or cook) a necessity. (The American equivalent might be the washing machine.)

IBOPE adds the amounts expended on all these items and deducts the total from gross income. What remains is divided by total earnings to give a percentage of gross income (i.e., disposable income) available for consumer's goods. IBOPE uses this percentage to assign people to social classes. The organization also pays attention to actual gross income. IBOPE recognizes that some very poor people manage to reduce their expenses on basics in various ways, yet still lack enough money to spend on the items hawked on television.

[10]In order the predictors of a high score on our "liberal social attitudes" index were: years of education, years of home TV exposure, gender (female), daily viewing hours, religiosity (negatively correlated), and household income.

[11]Length of home TV exposure was the key statistical predictor of a low ranking of local celebrations. Also as predicted, we confirmed

statistically that long home exposure did increase the importance attributed to Carnival.

Epilogue, 1991

[1]My 1991 field trip to Arembepe was facilitated by a grant to the University of Michigan from NASA (National Aeronautics and Space Administration), through CIESIN (Consortium for International Earth Science Information Network).

[2]Pilot work for this research began in 1989, with funding from three agencies: the Michigan Memorial Phoenix Project (Project #714—The Social Context and Impact of Nuclear Energy in Brazil) and two Brazilian agencies—ANPOCS and Faperj.

[3]He used the word IBOPE, the acronym for the Brazilian Statistical Public Opinion Research Institute, Brazil's foremost survey and polling organization. IBOPE has come to mean survey or rating (of a TV program).

References Cited

Barry, H., M. K. Bacon, and I. L. Child
  1959   "Relation of Child Training to Subsistence Economy." *American Anthropologist* 61:51–63.
Becker, Howard S.
  1963   *Outsiders*. New York: Free Press.
Brown, Diana
  1979   "Umbanda and Class Relations in Brazil." In *Brazil: Anthropological Perspectives*, ed. Maxine L. Margolis and William E. Carter. New York: Columbia University Press, pp. 270–304.
Burns, E. Bradford
  1980   *A History of Brazil*, 2nd ed. New York: Columbia University Press.
Chagnon, Napoleon
  1977   *Yanomamo: The Fierce People*, 2nd ed. New York: Holt, Rinehart and Winston.
Comitas, Lambros
  1962   "Fishermen and Cooperation in Rural Jamaica." Ph.D. dissertation, Columbia University. Ann Arbor, Michigan: Xerox University Microfilm.
Comstock, George, Steven Chaffee, Natan Katzman, Maxwell McCombs, and Donald Roberts
  1978   *Television and Human Behavior*. New York: Columbia University Press.
DaMatta, Roberto
  1987   *A Casa e a Rua*, 2nd ed. Rio de Janeiro: Guanabara.
Dickens, Charles
  1962   (orig. 1850) *David Copperfield*. New York: Signet Classics, New American Library.
Economist, The (London)
  1979   "Oh! Brazil: A Survey." August 4, 1979.
Eldredge, Niles
  1963   "Some Technological Aspects of the Fishing Industry of a Town on the Northeast Coast of Brazil." New York: Columbia-Cornell-Harvard-Illinois Summer Field Studies Program in Anthropology. (Program Files, Columbia University.)
Farrell, Ronald A., and Victoria Lynn Swigert, eds.
  1975   *Social Deviance*. Philadelphia: Lippincott.
Forman, Shepard
  1967   "Cognition and the Catch: The Location of Fishing Spots in a Brazilian Coastal Village." *Ethnology* 6:417–426.
  1970   *The Raft Fishermen: Tradition and Change in the Brazilian Peasant Economy*. Bloomington: Indiana University Press.
  1975   *The Brazilian Peasantry*. New York: Columbia University Press.
Forman, Shepard, and Joyce Riegelhaupt

1970   "Market Place and Marketing System: Toward a Theory of Peasant Eco-
        nomic Integration." *Comparative Studies in Society and History*
        12(2):188–212.
Foster, George M.
1965   "Peasant Society and the Image of Limited Good." *American Anthropolo-
        gist* 67:293–315.
Freeman, Linton
1965   *Elementary Applied Statistics for Students in the Behavioral Sciences.*
        New York: Wiley.
Fried, Morton
1960   "On the Evolution of Social Stratification and the State." In *Culture in
        History*, ed. S. Diamond. New York: Columbia University Press, pp. 713–
        731.
Gross, Daniel R.
1973   "Factionalism and Local Level Politics in Rural Brazil." *Journal of Anthro-
        pological Research* 29:123–144.
Gross, Rose Lee
1964   "Local Politics and Administration: Camaçari, Bahia, Brazil." New York:
        Columbia-Cornell-Harvard-Illinois Summer Field Studies Program in An-
        thropology. (Program Files, Columbia University.)
Harding, Susan
1975   "Women and Words in a Spanish Village." In *Toward an Anthropology of
        Women*, ed. Rayna Reiter. New York: Monthly Review Press, pp. 283–
        308.
Harris, Marvin
1974   *Cows, Pigs, Wars, and Witches.* New York: Random House.
Harris, Marvin, and Conrad Kottak
1963   "The Structural Significance of Brazilian Racial Categories." *Sociologia*
        25:203–209.
Hausmann, F., and J. Haar
1978   *Education in Brazil.* Hamden, Conn.: Archon.
Havinghurst, Robert, and J. Roberto Moreira
1965   *Society and Education in Brazil.* Pittsburgh: University of Pittsburgh
        Press.
Hewlett, Sylvia Ann
1980   *The Cruel Dilemmas of Development: Twentieth-Century Brazil.* New
        York: Basic Books.
Hirsch, Paul M.
1979   "The Role of Television and Popular Culture in Contemporary Society."
        In Horace Newcomb, ed. *Television: The Critical View.* New York: Ox-
        ford University Press, pp. 249–279.
Hujanen, T.
1976   *Immigrant Broadcasting and Migration Control in Western Europe.* Tam-
        pere, Finland: Institute of Journalism and Mass Communication, Univer-
        sity of Tampere.
Johnson, Allen
1971   *Sharecroppers of the Sertão: Economics and Dependence on a Brazilian
        Plantation*, Stanford, Calif.: Stanford University Press.
Kottak, Conrad Phillip
1966   "The Structure of Equality in a Brazilian Fishing Community." Ph.D.
        dissertation, Columbia University. Ann Arbor: Xerox University Mi-
        crofilms.
1967a   "Kinship and Class in Brazil." *Ethnology* 6:427–443.
1967b   "Race Relations in a Bahian Fishing Village." *Luso-Brazilian Review*
        4:35–52.

1980   *The Past in the Present: History, Ecology, and Cultural Variation in High-land Madagascar*. Ann Arbor: University of Michigan Press.
1990   *Prime-Time Society: An Anthropological Analysis of Television and Culture*. Belmont, Calif.: Wadsworth.
Kottak, Isabel Wagley
1977   "A Village Prostitute in Northeastern Brazil." *Michigan Discussions in Anthropology* 2:245–252.
Labov, William
1972   *Sociolinguistic Patterns*. Philadelphia: University of Pennsylvania Press.
Lemert, Edwin M.
1951   *Social Pathology: A Systematic Approach to the Theory of Sociopathic Behavior*. New York: McGraw-Hill.
Lévi-Strauss, Claude
1967   *Structural Anthropology*. New York: Basic Books.
Malinowski, Bronislaw
1961   (orig. 1922) *Argonauts of the Western Pacific*. New York: Dutton.
Marcus, George E. and Michael M. J. Fisher
1986   *Anthropology as Cultural Critique. An Experimental Moment in the Human Sciences*. Chicago: The University of Chicago Press.
Marshall, Mac
1979   *Weekend Warriors: Alcohol in a Micronesian Culture*. Palo Alto, Calif.: Mayfield.
Mintz, Sidney, and Eric R. Wolf
1950   "An Analysis of Ritual Co-parenthood *(Compadrazgo)*." *Southwestern Journal of Anthropology* 6:341–368.
Pace, Richard B.
n.d.   Television in Itá. Unpublished paper. To appear in Conrad Phillip Kottak, ed. *Television's Social Impact in Brazil*—in preparation.
Redfield, Robert
1948   *The Folk Culture of Yucatan*. Chicago: University of Chicago Press.
1960   *Peasant Society and Culture and the Little Community*. Chicago: University of Chicago Press.
Reiter, Rayna
1975   "Men and Women in the South of France: Public and Private Domains." In *Toward an Anthropology of Women*, ed. Rayna Reiter. New York: Monthly Review Press, pp. 252–282.
Robock, Stefan H.
1975   *Brazil: A Study in Development Progress*. Lexington, Mass.: Heath.
Sahlins, Marshall D.
1972   *Stone Age Economics:* Chicago: Aldine.
Tolkien, J. R. R.
1965   *The Lord of the Rings*. Part III: *The Return of the King*. New York: Ballantine.
Wagley, Charles W.
1960   "The Brazilian Revolution: Social Change since 1930." In *Social Change in Latin America Today*, ed. Richard Adams. New York: Harpers, pp. 177–230.
1963   *Introduction to Brazil*. New York: Columbia University Press.
Wagley, Charles W., ed.
1952   *Race and Class in Rural Brazil*. Paris: UNESCO.
Weber, Max
1958   (orig. 1920) *The Protestant Ethic and the Spirit of Capitalism*. New York: Scribner's.
Wolf, Eric R.
1955   "Types of Latin American Peasantry." *American Anthropologist* 57:452.

Index